THE FRUGAL SHOPPER

Insurance	Lawyers
Automobiles	Utilities
Contractors	Food
Credit	Doctors
Banking	Housing

And Other Topics

Ralph Nader & Wesley J. Smith

Acknowledgments
    The following people assisted in the preparation of this book: Amy Allina, Bill Day, Jennifer Gifford, Karen Horton, Jennifer Kassan, Holley Knaus, Eleanor Lewis, Dan Newman, Beverly Orr, Bryan Penas, John Richard, Lois Riley, Ann Wei, Robert Weissman and Eric Weltman.

Published by:

Center for Study of Responsive Law
P.O. Box 19367
Washington, DC 20036   Price $10.00

ISBN # 0-936758-30-9
Printed in the United States of America.

 Printed on 50% Recycled Stock With 10% Post-Consumer Waste

Contents

WINNING THE CONSUMER GAME

Typical game show theme music fills the air. The studio audience bursts into enthusiastic applause. The television studio lights brighten. Television monitors reveal a close-up of the stage where brightly colored strobe lights flash on the game show set. Suddenly, the "on air" sign lights red. The audience applauds.

Announcer: It's time to play The Consumer Game, where average consumers play to save money in the products and services they buy! Now, here's the host of The Consumer Game, Maxamillian Moneysaver.

The audience begins to cheer even more wildly. Many yell "woof, woof, woof, woof!" A dapper, handsome man with graying blow dried hair and a twinkle in his eye runs onto the stage. He bows deeply and walks over to the game show set. Two people are waiting for him sitting next to each other on a podium. Both appear slightly nervous.

Max: And now, let's meet our contestants on today's version of The Consumer Game.

He walks over to a woman seated on the left.

Max: First to our champion, back for her fourth straight appearance. For those who may be tuning in for the first time, what is your name and what do you do?
Penny: Hello again, Max. My name is Penny Smart. I'm a homemaker with two children and I own my own pet store.

The audience applauds.

Max: Very good. And now, let's meet our challenger. What is your name and what do you do?
Cliff: Hi Max. I'm Cliff Clueless and I work for Conglomerate Inc., a major international corporation where I work in the widget purchasing division.
Max: Wow. That must involve a lot of money.
Cliff: Yes, I deal in millions of dollars, yen, marks and francs, every week.
Max: Than you should make a formidable challenger to our champion. Welcome to the game, Cliff.

Max walks to the center podium.

Max: Before we start round one, let's go over the rules of The Consumer Game. You each will be presented with real life consumer experiences sent in to us by members of our vast television audience. You will be given several options in choosing how the smart consumer will respond. Based on your answer, you will either save money, time or heartache, or you will hear the BAAAAA sound, which will mean that you have picked the choice that allows you to be sheared like a sheep. The contestant who has saved the most time, money or heartache will be our champion and will be eligible for our lightening round.

But before we begin our first round, let's hear a word from our sponsor, Hardsell Insurance Company, filling all your personal insurance needs. Remember, with Hardsell Insurance, you're in the bag!

There is a commercial presented by Hardsell Insurance, where the company mascot, "Pinky", an adorable cartoon pig that sings an adorable little jingle as he erases a downcast couple's crashed car, burned house, and hospital bed with a huge pink eraser. Their problems erased, a wholesome looking couple leap to their feet, hug the pig saying, "Thank you Pinky!" and dance arm in arm into the sunset. The pig looks into the camera and smiles adorably. "Remember, you're in the bag with Hardsell!"

The commercial fades and is replaced by a close-up on Max's white, capped toothed smile.

Max: Welcome back to The Consumer Game. Now, our first question to our champion, Penny Smart. Here is an envelope containing your credit card statement. What is the first thing you should do?
Stick it in a drawer until it is due?
Check the billing statements with your receipts to make sure it is accurate?
Pay the bill and throw the bill away so that your desk remains nice and neat?
Pay the minimum amount due?

The Consumer Game "think jingle" plays while the contestant thinks over her answer.

Penny: I check the billing statement to see if there are any errors.
Max: Correct! Let's look at your statement to see how much you saved. (An enlarged picture of Penny's credit statement appears in the background.) Look! The Shi-Shi Restaurant you took your aunt to for her birthday charged you twice for the same meal! If you had not reviewed your bill, you would have paid $125 you didn't owe! Congratulations, Penny you just won $125!!!

(The audience roars its approval.)

Max: Now our challenger, Cliff Clueless. Are you ready to play The Consumer Game, Cliff?
Cliff: I'm ready!
Max: You have just been sued for divorce and you need a lawyer. Do you:
Hire your Uncle Joe, a competent lawyer who specializes in "drunk driving" cases?
Call the local bar association for the name of a divorce lawyer?

Choose a lawyer because you saw her advertising on television?

Take your time, interview several lawyers and find the best one at the best price?

Cliff: I know! I know! I hire my Uncle Joe. He'll give me a good price and I trust him!

The loser sound effect of a sheep is heard. BAAAAA!

Max: No, I'm sorry. You've been sheared like a sheep, Cliff. Your uncle knew a lot about drunk driving law but almost nothing about divorce law. You not only lost your house but had to pay too much alimony as well. The total cost to you - $25,000, not including your attorneys fees!

And now a word from our sponsor.

Of course, there is no television game show called The Consumer Game. But there is real life, and in real life, you play the consumer game every time you purchase a product or service.

The way you go about this task can have a very profound impact on your family's health, safety and financial well-being. If you allow yourself to be swept away by clever corporate advertising, for example, you could very well spend far more than you needed to for the product or service. Moreover, you may purchase hazardous or shoddy products you really do not want or need.

The hypothetical insurance sponsor for The Consumer Game was an example of just such empty corporate advertising. It had a cute cartoon pig and a clever slogan but nowhere in the commercial was there any statement about whether "Hardsell Insurance" offered good prices, good services or a quality insurance product. Think about some real-life advertisement you see every day on television and you will see similar empty commercials, designed to do one thing: get you to remember the name of the product or company. And if there is one thing that should not be the sole basis for a purchase, it is mere name recognition created by clever and manipulative advertising.

This book is designed as an all-purpose reference book which will assist you to develop your own consuming game plan and help you make smart and cost effective purchases. It is our hope that the information contained between these covers will give you the tools to save money, find better quality, protect your safety and, very importantly, improve your ability to work with other consumers to exercise organized consumer-power throughout the marketplace.

Some of what we tell you may seem like hard work but it isn't. Once you get the hang of effective shopping, it will become second nature to you. You will become a presence that merchants, producers and repairers of products and providers of services will have to treat fairly and with respect. Moreover, you will learn how to stand up for yourself on those occasions when you do not receive true value, that is, a quality product or service for a fair price.

So, read and increase your consumer power. Who knows? Maybe someday there will be a television game show called The Consumer Game. But you don't have to wait until that time comes. Apply the tools of effective shopping and you will be a joyous winner today so as not to be an anguished loser tomorrow.

R.N.
W.J.S

Part One

JUST SAY, "CHARGE IT!"

THE WORLD OF CREDIT CARDS

P resident Calvin Coolidge once said, "The business of America is business." And he was right. In the 1920's business was most of what this country was all about and for the most part, it still is.

But business, like the old gray mare, just ain't what it used to be. In "Silent Cal's" day, most business for the average consumer was conducted under the rules of a game known as "cash and carry." The rules of cash and carry were simple: the merchant said, "You give me the cash and I'll let you carry the merchandise." No muss, no fuss, no monthly credit card bills charging loan shark rates of interest. And the nation prospered: until it hit the wall of the Great Depression.

After World War II, the pace of life in the United States picked up. The depression was history! We were a world power! We had the strongest economy the world had ever seen! And, while the business of America remained business, the nature of the business conducted began to change. Not so slowly but ever so surely, we fell into the grips of what has become known as the "consumer economy."

Sociologists and historians can fill in the details of why, how and when, but somewhere along the line Americans found a new national pastime: shopping, led by bellicose calls to spending, such as "When in doubt, shop," "When the going gets tough, the tough go shopping," "Shop until you drop" and "Born to shop." And the cash registers of America could be heard ringing throughout the land.

There was only one problem with this new found prosperity. Few people could afford to feed their shopping habits, and thus keep the good times rolling, by paying cash. Not only did they not have the money, but buying all that merchandise with cash was a painful reminder of just how much money they were really spending. Something had to be done.

And it was. A new entity was created, an almost mythical thing made of plastic known as THE CREDIT CARD. And with its advent, the rules of the shopping game became far more complicated and impactful on people's lives, and the words "minimum payments" took on a whole new meaning. In fact, total consumer debt in the United States, (the natural result of using credit) now stands at over 700 BILLION DOLLARS.

We invite you now to join us in looking at the world of credit in general and credit cards in specific. The journey may be painful, it may bring up old wounds, it may enrage, but hopefully, it will educate you, empower you and allow you to save money on one of the most important areas of your consumer activities.

Chapter One

THE NUTS AND BOLTS OF CREDIT

There is a song from the musical *Cabaret* that says, "Money makes the world go around, the world go around, the world go around. Money makes the world go around, it makes the world go around." Well, no more. Now, credit makes the world go around. This being so, credit is a vital issue in your life as a consumer.

At first glimpse, credit may seem simple. But it really isn't. There are issues within issues, when dealing with the subject of credit: issues which you need to understand to be an effective shopper, issues which can save or cost you a lot of money. In order to deal effectively with these issues, you need to have knowledge power, and the first step in achieving "knowledgeicity" (as Woody Allen might say) is to understand how the system works. That's what the balance of this chapter will be all about.

Credit, like any substantial facet of life, has a jargon and a culture all its own. In order to fully understand what the powers that be in the world of credit are telling you in your business dealings with them, you need to understand the meaning of the words and phrases they use. Here is a credit user's handy guide to the language of credit.

THE TYPES OF CREDIT

Credit usually comes in two basic types:

OPEN ENDED

As the name implies, an **open ended** credit agreement is just that, open ended. In other words, you have not agreed to borrow a specific, preset amount and you have a wide range of latitude in the manner in which you can pay back the money you have borrowed. The typical open ended credit arrangement is the credit card, be it bank card or retail card. (See below.) Open ended credit is also known as **revolving credit.**

CLOSED ENDED

At the other end of the credit spectrum is the **closed ended** credit transaction. In a closed ended credit agreement, you borrow a specified amount of money and are given a defined repayment schedule. Typical of closed ended credit transactions are car loans (See Part Three) and mortgages.

Closed ended transactions are generally used for larger loans.

ANNUAL PERCENTAGE RATE AND FINANCE CHARGE

According to the federal **Truth In Lending Act,** you have the right to know how much a loan is going to cost you. In that regard, there are two things to look out for, the **annual percentage rate** (i.e. the percentage of interest you will be charged) and more importantly, the **finance charge** (the actual dollars you will pay out of pocket for the loan). Obviously, the lower the finance charge and the annual percentage rate **(APR),** the lower the cost of the loan to you.

MONTHLY PAYMENTS

If you borrow money, you will be making partial reimbursements known as **payments.** A closed ended loan usually has fixed monthly payments that remain unchanged throughout the "life of the loan." The amount of these payments will depend on the interest rate charged and the length of time you are given to pay the loan back. Open ended loans, in contrast, require "minimum monthly payments," the size of which will vary from month to month depending on the outstanding balance of the loan and the interest charges that apply.

BALLOON PAYMENTS

Sometimes **balloon payments** are built into closed ended loans, which can cause problems. A balloon payment is a large lump sum amount due at the end of a loan. Often, loans with balloon payments at the end allow the lender to pay interest-only monthly payments with the **principal** (the total amount of money borrowed) due at the end of the loan period. There are, of course, variations on this theme. Balloon payments can be very dangerous to consumers since the relatively low monthly interest payments will induce them to take out the loan, only to find out at the end of the loan that they do not have sufficient funds to pay off the loan.

SECURITY

Often, a closed ended loan will require that you give title to a piece of property to the lender as a **security.** For example, when you take out a home mortgage, real property is used to "secure" the loan. When you take out a car loan with a bank, they will control the "pink slip" (proof of ownership) until the loan has been paid in full.

ADJUSTABLE RATE LOANS

Some closed ended loans have interest rates which fluctuate depending on some economic index, such as the prime rate index or the consumer price index. These adjustable rates are often called **variable interest rate** loans. Variable rate loans are often easier to get because they usually start with a lower interest rate than **fixed interest rate** loans. However, there is a down side to this. You do not know what the loan will actually cost you when you sign up because unless you are psychic, you will not know how much interest you will be paying in the future.

> **CONSUMER ALERT: IF YOU DECIDE TO TAKE OUT A VARIABLE INTEREST RATE LOAN, BE SURE THERE IS A MAXIMUM INTEREST RATE THAT CAN BE CHARGED TO PROTECT YOU AGAINST AN OUT OF CONTROL INFLATIONARY PERIOD SUCH AS OCCURRED IN THE 1970S.**

THE WORLD OF CREDIT CARDS

Most of the credit consumers use on a daily basis are open ended loans known as **credit cards**. A credit card, in reality, is simply an easy and convenient tool for borrowing money. You are issued your "plastic" and when you wish to purchase a product or service, you present it to a merchant who takes the plastic in lieu of money as payment for the merchandise, meal, travel or whatever you are "charging." The merchant then sends a bill to the credit card company for the amount you have charged, which, in turn, pays the merchant, less a fee based on a percentage of the total transaction. (That is why we believe merchants should allow a small discount for cash.) The credit card company then adds the total amount you charged to your ledger and sends you a monthly bill detailing your credit transactions, known in the trade as a **monthly statement**.

THE TYPES OF CREDIT CARDS

Credit cards come in three basic forms:

The Bank Card

The term "bank card" is a little misleading in that institutions other than banks can issue these kinds of cards. The bank card is usually a "Visa" card, or a "MasterCard" card. Bank cards are usually accepted in restaurants, most merchant shops and stores, by airlines and virtually any business which accepts credit cards, including, it has been reported, illegal bordellos.

The Retail Credit Card

Most retail chains issue credit cards of their own. These cards work similarly to bank cards but can usually only be used in the retail stores of the issuing company. Unlike bank cards, most retail credit cards do not charge a yearly membership fee.

> CONSUMER ALERT: MOST OF YOU HAVE BEEN "ASSAULTED" BY DEPARTMENT STORE EMPLOYEES SEEKING YOUR SIGNA- TURE ON A CREDIT CARD APPLICATION. THEY ARE NOT DOING THIS BECAUSE THEY LIKE YOU BUT BECAUSE THEY KNOW THAT YOU WILL SPEND MORE MONEY IN THEIR STORE IF YOU HAVE THEIR CREDIT CARDS AND ARE MORE LIKELY TO *IMPULSE BUY*.

"Pay as You Go" Cards (aka Travel and Entertainment Cards)

Some companies issue cards that must be paid in full each month. In other words, using the card has the same effect on your pocket book as paying cash since you are not allowed to repay the loan slowly over time. Travel cards don't usually have preset credit limits. The most famous pay as you go card is American Express.

> CONSUMER ALERT: THERE IS A NEW CARD ON THE PERSONAL FINANCE BLOCK WHICH LOOKS LIKE A CREDIT CARD, FEELS LIKE A CREDIT CARD BUT IS NOT A CREDIT CARD. IT IS THE *DEBIT CARD* (AKA THE ATM CARD), WHICH IS A FORM OF CHECKING ACCOUNT IN PLASTIC FORM. THE DEBIT CARD

CAN BE USED IN A GROWING NUMBER OF BUSINESS ESTAB-
LISHMENTS JUST LIKE A CREDIT CARD. BUT INSTEAD OF
BORROWING FROM A CREDIT CARD COMPANY, THE MONEY
TO PAY THE MERCHANT IS DEDUCTED FROM YOUR OWN
BANK ACCOUNT. DEBIT CARDS CAN ALSO BE USED IN AUTO-
MATIC TELLER MACHINES TO WITHDRAW CASH FROM YOUR
BANK ACCOUNTS.

THE CREDIT CARD AGREEMENT

The terms of your credit card rights and obligations are set forth in the **credit agreement** you will have signed in order to have the credit card issued to you. A credit agreement is a *contract* and is thus legally enforceable in a court of law. This being so, it is vital that you understand the terms of this important business agreement you will have entered into so that you will both understand your obligations and your contractual rights. The important terms of any credit agreement will consist of the following:

Your Maximum Credit Limit

This sets the maximum amount of money you will be permitted to borrow.

Interest Rate

You will be charged for the use of your credit card company's money (which was sent to the merchant you charged from). This fee goes under the innocuous name of **interest**. Interest will be based on a fixed pre-set percentage, using one of the following methods:
The adjusted monthly balance Under this method of charging interest, all credits (payments, returns, etc) are credited to your account before charging your account with the monthly interest.
Previous balance method Under this type of billing method, interest is charged on the amount of money owed on the first day of the billing period without deducting for payments or credits on the account during the month.
Average daily balance Under this method of charging interest to your account, the daily balances are added up and than divided by the number of days in the billing period. This simple math equation gives the creditor the average daily balance and interest is charged based on that figure.

Both the amount of interest you will be charged and the method used to compute the interest are important, for they determine the cost of the credit card transaction to you.

Grace Period

The only way to avoid paying interest is to pay the balance in full within the time allowed in the agreement. Typically you have twenty to thirty days or so from the date of the statement, but each card company's agreement is different, so be sure to check your credit agreement, and statement, for each of your credit cards. This time period is often called the **grace period**.

CONSUMER ALERT: THERE ARE TWO TERMS USED TO DE-
SCRIBE THE COST OF CREDIT. THIS CAN BE CONFUSING. ONE
IS *FINANCE CHARGE* AND ONE IS *ANNUAL PERCENTAGE RATE*
(OF INTEREST), ALSO KNOWN AS *APR*. THE DIFFERENCE BE-
TWEEN THE TWO ARE AS FOLLOWS:

FINANCE CHARGES THE FINANCE CHARGE IS THE ACTUAL TOTAL DOLLAR AMOUNT YOU ARE CHARGED FOR USING YOUR CREDIT.

ANNUAL PERCENTAGE RATE THIS IS THE PERCENTAGE OF INTEREST YOU ARE CHARGED PER YEAR. THUS, IF YOU ARE BEING CHARGED 1.5% PER MONTH, THE ANNUAL RATE OF INTEREST IS 18%.

THE AMOUNT OF THE APR DETERMINES HOW MUCH MONEY YOU WILL PAY IN FINANCE CHARGES. OF COURSE, THE HIGHER THE APR, THE MORE MONEY WILL COME OUT OF YOUR POCKET IF YOU DO NOT PAY YOUR BALANCE IN FULL.

Membership Fee

Most bank cards also charge annual **membership fees** which can range from $25 to more than $50 per year. The amount of the fee will be set forth in your agreement.

Minimum Payment

In a revolving credit account, you can pay any amount from the total owed down to a **minimum** payment level established by the credit card issuer.

Late Fees And Other Charges

If you do not pay your bill in a timely manner you will be charged a **late fee**. If you go over your maximum credit limit, you may also be charged a fee, depending on what your credit card agreement says on the subject. For a complete list of the fees your credit card company can charge against you, refer to your credit card agreement.

Billing Cycle

Your account will be billed to you periodically, with details of charges made, interest and fees charged, payments received and other important information. The length of the cycle will be established in your credit card agreement.

Account Statement

Each month you will receive a statement informing you of the charges that have been billed, the payments the company acknowledges receiving and any other credits or charges made during your billing cycle.

Cash Advance Rights

Some credit cards allow you to borrow cash from your credit card in a transaction known as the **cash advance**.

Perquisites

In order to get your business and to get you to use their card, many credit card companies offer you special perquisites or benefits for using their cards, such as extended warranty protection. Some of these can be valuable and it pays you to know what your "perqs" are, if any. The place to look is your credit agreement and/or the written material you will have been sent with your card.

CONSUMER ALERT: MOST CREDIT CARDS ARE *"UNSECURED."* THAT IS, NONE OF YOUR PROPERTY HAS BEEN SET ASIDE TO "SECURE" YOUR REPAYMENT. HOWEVER, SOME CREDIT CARDS AND/OR OPEN LINES OF CREDIT ARE *SECURED* BY EQUITY IN REAL ESTATE OR OTHER PROPERTY (SUCH AS A BANK ACCOUNT). IF YOU CHOOSE TO OPEN SUCH A SECURED LINE OF CREDIT REMEMBER THAT IF YOU FAIL TO PAY YOUR BILL, *YOUR PROPERTY CAN BE FORECLOSED UPON.*

THE CREDIT RATING

As the use of credit became the norm rather than the exception, merchants and credit companies needed to find a way to separate the wheat (good credit risks) from the chaff (bad credit risks). Enhanced by the mighty computer, a solution was found, and thus the **credit bureau** (aka the **credit reporting agency**) was born. The purpose of credit bureaus is to serve as a clearing house for companies who are considering giving you credit, and where they can go to check on your credit history to help them decide whether you are a good credit risk.

Credit bureaus are in the business of obtaining, storing and disseminating information about anybody who uses credit. The system works through a sophisticated method of trading information. Every few months, as regular as a computer's microchip, your credit card companies and other creditors send to one or more credit bureaus information about your credit history with them, i.e. are you paying on time, what your balance is, whether you are in excess of your credit limit, etc..

This information is stored by in the credit bureau's computer and is coughed up by the computer upon request. Usually, the information will be requested when you apply for new credit. At such time, the merchant, credit card company, finance company, bank or other proposed creditor will make a request for information on you from the credit bureau (which they pay for by subscribing to the credit bureau's services). The bureau will, in turn, issue to the creditor a computerized credit report on you, which will be used by the company to decide whether to give your request for credit the "thumbs up" or "thumbs down."

Since much of the decision making concerning your credit worthiness will be based on your credit record, it is vital that you maintain a good credit rating if you plan to use credit as part of your consuming life. We will discuss more about credit reports and show you how to obtain and translate yours in the next chapter.

CONSUMER ALERT: IF YOUR CREDIT REPORT CONTAINS SOME BAD NEWS, IT MAY BE IN THE COMPUTER FOR A VERY LONG TIME. CREDIT REPORTING BUREAUS CAN KEEP INFORMATION ABOUT BANKRUPTCY FOR UP TO TEN YEARS AND INFORMATION INDICATING YOU MAY BE A POOR RISK FOR SEVEN YEARS. SO, BE SURE TO KEEP YOURSELF IN THE BEST CREDIT STANDING THAT YOU CAN. OTHERWISE, YOUR CREDIT PAST MAY COME BACK TO HAUNT YOU.

Well, that about covers the basics, so let's get down to the nitty gritty of credit. We'll start at the beginning, which as the old saying goes, is a very good place to start: applying for credit.

Chapter Two

THE GOLD CARD AT THE END OF THE RAINBOW

APPLYING FOR CREDIT

An unfortunate fact of American life is that it is increasingly difficult to engage in commerce without credit or a credit card. In fact, if you do not have credit, you may find it difficult to cash a check, rent a car or obtain lodging at a hotel!

This being so, you undoubtedly already have credit or, if you don't, sooner or later (probably sooner) you will be applying for it. Unfortunately, too many of us go about this task with little forethought or insight in how to do it so that the credit we obtain is the most economical and convenient. This ends up costing most of us money.

CHOOSING THE RIGHT CREDIT CARD

Unlike men and women, all credit cards are not created equal. Each will have differences which will translate into money spending or money savings for you. REMEMBER, BY CHOOSING THE RIGHT CREDIT CARD, YOU CAN SAVE YOURSELF A SUBSTANTIAL AMOUNT OF MONEY! Here are a few of the things to look out for when applying for a credit card:

THE INTEREST RATE

The lower the interest rate, the less your credit use will cost you, assuming you do not pay the total amount you owe each billing period. When choosing a credit card, *do not select one with a high APR*. Also, *be sure you choose a company that computes interest in a way that saves you money*: The rate of interest charged is important but so is the way that interest is computed. The best method for you is the **adjusted balance method** followed by the **average daily balance method**.

MAKE SURE THE CREDIT CARD ALLOWS A GRACE PERIOD

Many cards allow twenty to thirty days before adding interest. However, some start accruing interest from the moment that the charge is made against your account. The effect of such an interest charging scheme is to deny you a grace period, and even if you pay your bill in full upon receiving your statement, you will have to pay interest.

SELECT A COMPANY WITH A LOW ANNUAL MEMBERSHIP FEE

The lower the fee, the less it costs you to use credit.

> **CONSUMER ALERT: IN ORDER TO GET YOUR BUSINESS, SOME CREDIT CARD COMPANIES OFFER TO WAIVE THE FIRST YEAR'S MEMBERSHIP FEE. THIS IS WELL AND GOOD AND WE APPLAUD SUCH "GENEROSITY." BUT BEFORE YOU JOIN UP FOR THE CRUISE, MAKE SURE YOU KNOW WHAT YOU WILL BE CHARGED IN THE SECOND YEAR.**

CHECK THE AMOUNT OF LATE FEE OR PENALTY

If you are late in making your payment, you will be charged a late fee or penalty. The amount that each card charges differs, so it doesn't hurt to investigate the amount each company charges for late payments.

> **CONSUMER ALERT: ACCORDING TO THE BANKCARD HOLDERS OF AMERICA (SEE BELOW), THE TYPICAL CONSUMER CAN SAVE OVER $100 PER YEAR JUST BY TURNING IN AN OLD EXPENSIVE CREDIT CARD FOR A USER FRIENDLY ONE THAT OFFERS REASONABLE INTEREST AND A LOW OR GRATIS YEARLY FEE.**

> **CONSUMER ALERT: SOMETIMES CREDIT CARD COMPANIES UNILATERALLY CHANGE THE TERMS OF THEIR CREDIT AGREEMENT WITH YOU. IN SUCH CASES, YOU WILL RECEIVE ADVANCE NOTICE OF THE CHANGES, USUALLY WITH YOUR MONTHLY BILL. IF AND WHEN YOU RECEIVE SUCH A NOTICE - READ IT CAREFULLY! IF YOU DO NOT WISH TO ABIDE BY THOSE TERMS, CANCEL YOUR CREDIT CARD. IF YOU DO NOT CANCEL AND USE YOUR CARD AFTER THE DATE THE TERM CHANGES GO INTO EFFECT, YOUR NEW CHARGES WILL BE GOVERNED BY THE NEW AGREEMENT.**

DECIDE WHETHER TO "GO FOR THE GOLD"

There are many credit cards that offer "goodies" in addition to the "privilege" of charging merchandise or services. Often (but not always), these extras come in the form of what is known in the vernacular as a **gold card** or even a **platinum card**.

A gold card offers extra benefits not always available to the users of a "regular" credit card. As we will see, many of these benefits can save you some significant dollars, both directly with discounts and indirectly with purchase protection plans. These "gold card benefits" usually include:

- A higher credit line.
- Extra services or "perquisites."
- Prestige (for what that is worth and we think it is worth zero).

The main benefit of gold cards are the perqs which you can receive by using them when you charge. These often include the following:

Travel Benefits

Many companies offer **discounts** from hotels, airlines and rental cars if the service is purchased with the gold card. Often **emergency services** are also provided in the event you find yourself in some trouble when you are traveling. **Emergency roadside services** are also sometimes offered although these do not pay for the services required as a traditional "auto club" usually does. **Travel accident insurance** pays death and dismemberment benefits in the event of an accident. Many gold cards also offer **lost or damaged baggage insurance** when you use your card to pay for your travel. Other benefits commonly offered include **emergency medical and legal referrals** and **emergency cash** and **card replacement benefits**. Some companies also offer **rental car collision insurance benefits** if you rent a car.

Additional Purchase Protection Services

Another benefit offered by many gold cards is **purchase insurance** protection when you purchase merchandise. Usually, the purchaser receives replacement or repair (depending on the program) benefits if the merchandise breaks, is damaged, lost or stolen, within 90 days of purchase. (KEEP THOSE RECEIPTS!) Many gold cards will also provide **extended warranties** for many items *purchased with the card* which add time to an existing warranty provided by the product's manufacturer.

Credit Card Registration

Some companies offer free **credit card registration services** which will notify all of your credit card companies in the event your cards are lost or stolen. Before you sign up for such a service offered for a fee, be sure to see if any of your other cards offer the registration for free.

Discount Buying Services

Many cards (not all of them gold) offer discount buying programs based on how often you use your card. While these discounts can save you money and can be of benefit, they are not a reason to use your card and incur interest charges you would not otherwise have incurred just to receive the discount.

The down side to gold cards is that *you usually pay for these extras in the form of higher annual fees*. Also, there are often *loopholes* which reduce the actual benefit you may receive. Thus, be sure that the extra expense of a gold card is worth the price.

In these days of economic difficulty and consumer disempowerment, consumers need all of the friends they can get. One such friend of the credit card consumer is the BANKCARD HOLDERS OF AMERICA. The Bankcard Holders of America is a nonprofit organization which helps bankcard holders become informed consumers.

The organization is not funded by any foundation, the credit card industry or the government. Its finances are totally generated by membership dues which as of the date of this writing are $18 per year and $30 for two years.

Among the benefits members receive are a bi-monthly newsletter, designed to inform members about credit and personal finance issues, educational pamphlets which inform about specific credit - related topics and valuable lists to help consumers shop for a credit card. Currently the lists offered are the No Annual Fee List, *which tells you which banks offer credit cards without charging a fee (which can save you a lot of money over the years) a* Fair Deal List, *which reveals the cards offering low interest rates (which can save you even more money) and the* Secured Card List, *which contains banks that issue cards to consumers with no credit or a poor credit history if they are willing to put up a security, usually in the form of a savings account.*

The Bankcard Holders provides credit card consumers a valuable service. They can be reached at 460 Spring Park Place, Suite 1000, Herndon, VA 22070, or call them at (703) 481-1110.

IF YOU GET "TURNED DOWN"

Just because you apply for a credit card or are sent an application in the mail does not mean that you will be accepted. Clearly, the company is at risk when they lend you money in the form of credit card purchases and so they "should" be careful (too often they are not, giving credit to people who already have too much debt). In this increasingly difficult and debt ridden economy, you can expect credit to be more difficult to obtain.

YOUR RIGHTS IF YOU ARE TURNED DOWN

If you are turned down for credit, *you have the right to know why*. After all, fair is fair. Thus, under the **Federal Credit Reporting Act (FCRA)** and the **Equal Credit Opportunity Act (ECOA)**, you have the right to know the *specific reasons* why you were rejected. The reasons for rejection are usually one or more of the following:

REASON FOR REJECTION	SOLUTION
Your credit application was incomplete.	Go back and review the credit application and supply any information you may have omitted. NOTE: There may be a privacy issue here. You should decide for yourself whether the credit is worth the invasion of your personal privacy.
Insufficient number of credit references provided.	Go back over the application and fill in any references you may have missed.
Unable to verify credit references.	Review your application to make sure that you gave accurate information.
Temporary or irregular employment.	Try again when you have been at the same job for a longer time or try a different company.
Income is insufficient for amount of credit requested.	Reapply asking for a lower credit limit or try another company.

Excessive obligations.	Pay down on existing debt and reapply.
Length of residence.	Wait six months and try again.
No credit file or credit experience.	Establish credit elsewhere and reapply.
Delinquent past or present credit obligations.	Obtain a copy of your credit report and correct any mistakes.
Bankruptcy, garnishments, repossessions, judgments, etc.	Obtain copy of credit report and/or contact company to correct any mistakes that may have appeared in the report.

CONSUMER ALERT: CREDIT IS BIG BUSINESS IN THE UNITED STATES. IT IS SO LARGE IN FACT THAT:
 •150 MILLION PEOPLE IN THE UNITED STATES HAVE CREDIT RECORDS.
 • UNITED STATES CREDIT BUREAUS ISSUE AROUND *450 MILLION* CREDIT REPORTS EACH YEAR.
(SOURCE: ASSOCIATED CREDIT BUREAUS, INC.)

CONSUMER ALERT: THERE IS A LOT OF FRAUD AND/OR LESS THAN ETHICAL MARKETING GOING ON WHEN IT COMES TO CREDIT CARDS. MANY "MARKETING SERVICES" ARE OFFERING 900 TELEPHONE NUMBERS WHICH WILL ALLOW YOU TO MAKE APPLICATIONS FOR A SECURED LINE OF CREDIT FOR A FEE. YOU CAN DO THAT AT YOUR LOCAL BANK WITHOUT PAYING ANYBODY. OTHERS OFFER LISTS OF LOW INTEREST CREDIT CARDS FOR FEES WHICH RANGE UP TO $200 (ACCORDING TO THE N.Y. TIMES, 2/9/91.) THIS SAME INFORMATION IS AVAILABLE FROM THE BANKCARD HOLDERS OF AMERICA FOR A NOMINAL FEE.

HOW TO CORRECT MISTAKES IN YOUR CREDIT RECORD

If you were denied credit because of adverse information in your credit report, you have the absolute right under federal law to know the name and address of the credit reporting company which issued the report. YOU ALSO HAVE THE ABSOLUTE RIGHT TO REQUEST A *FREE COPY* OF YOUR REPORT from that agency if you make the request in writing within 30 days of your turn-down. Make sure you take advantage of these rights. They are the first step in dealing with a credit denial.

CORRECTING MISTAKES IN A CREDIT REPORT

So, you find that you have been denied credit because of a mistake or misinterpretation of your credit report. What do you do? You speak up, that's what you do, only you let your pen, word processor or typewriter do your talking for you.

The following is a sample letter of a written request to correct mistakes on your credit report.

CREDIT REPORTS "R" US
50 DUN 'EM SQUARE
DESTITUTION GULCH, PA 11111

RE: CREDIT REPORT DATED JAN 12, 1991

TO WHOM IT MAY CONCERN:

ON JANUARY 12, 1991, YOU ISSUED A CREDIT REPORT ON ME TO AJAX CREDIT CARD COMPANY. I HAVE ENCLOSED A COPY OF THAT REPORT FOR YOUR PERUSAL.

THIS CREDIT REPORT CONTAINS ERRONEOUS INFORMATION. SPECIFICALLY, THE FOLLOWING MISTAKES APPEAR:

1) I HAVE NEVER BORROWED MONEY FROM USURY CREDIT CORPORATION. THEREFORE, I CANNOT HAVE FAILED TO MAKE PAYMENTS TO THEM.

2) I WAS LATE IN PAYING ON MY ACCOUNT TO NEW JERSEY BANK MASTERCARD IN THE FALL OF 1989. THE REASON I WAS LATE WITH PAYMENTS IS THAT MY HOUSE WAS DESTROYED IN A FIRE AND THERE WAS A PERIOD OF TIME WHEN ALL OF MY BUSINESS AFFAIRS WERE IN A STATE OF CONFUSION. I DID MAKE UP ALL LATE PAYMENTS AND IN FACT, HAVE PAID THAT BILL ENTIRELY. WOULD YOU PLEASE REFLECT THE CAUSE FOR MY LATE PAYMENTS ON ALL FUTURE CREDIT REPORTS.

ONCE YOU HAVE INVESTIGATED AND VERIFIED THE ABOVE WILL YOU PLEASE NOTIFY ALL PARTIES WHO HAVE REQUESTED MY CREDIT REPORT FROM YOU IN THE LAST TWO YEARS AND SEND ME WRITTEN PROOF THAT YOU HAVE DONE SO.

VERY TRULY YOURS,

MARY ACTIVE - CONSUMER

When you send a letter of complaint such as the one above, remember the following:
•By putting the credit reporting company on notice that there are errors in your report, you compel them to conduct an investigation in order to determine the truth of your credit record. If their records are inaccurate, they are compelled by law to correct them.

•By explaining any problems with your report, you allow any companies from whom you are requesting credit to see your side of the story. Without an explanation, all they will see is the bad news.

•You have the right by law to have your corrected credit report sent to all credit companies who have requested a credit report on you in the last six months and all prospective employers who have requested a report within the last two years.

CONSUMER ALERT: MANY PEOPLE INCORRECTLY ASSUME THAT CREDIT BUREAUS MAKE THE DECISION ON WHETHER OR NOT A CONSUMER SHOULD BE ISSUED CREDIT. THIS IS NOT TRUE. *THE BUREAUS ONLY ISSUE REPORTS.* THE CREDIT COMPANIES MAKE THE BUSINESS DECISION WHETHER TO ISSUE CREDIT BASED ON CRITERIA THEY CHOOSE FOR THEMSELVES.

The way the credit reporting system actually works and the manner in which it is supposed to work can be two different things. Many consumers feel abused by a system that does not fulfill its promises. If you believe you have been the victim of credit abuse, complain to one or all of the following:

•The credit reporting agency that you believe has acted improperly;

•The chairman of the board or authorized officer of the company who you believe has acted improperly. For example. if the credit problem is with a bank credit card, contact the bank in question. If the problem is with a retail store card, contact the officers of the retail company.

•The appropriate federal agencies.

The Federal Trade Commission
Division of Credit Practices
Washington, DC 20580
(202) 326-3233 or check phone book for local number
(Department store credit cards, consumer finance companies, travel companies, travel and entertainment cards, credit bureaus.)

Federal Reserve Board
Division of Consumer and Community Affairs
20th and C Streets
Washington, DC 20551
(202) 452-3946 or check phone book for local number
(State banks that belong to the Federal Reserve system.)

Federal Deposit Insurance Corporation
Office of Consumer Affairs
550 17th Street, NW (F130)
Washington, DC 20429
1 (800) 424-5488 or check phone book for local number
(State chartered banks.)

Comptroller of the Currency
Compliance Management Department
Department of the Treasury
490 L'Enfant Plaza, SW
Washington, DC 20219
(202) 874-4820 or check phone book for local number

(All National banks, i.e. those with the word National in their title or the initials N.A.)

Office of Thrift Supervision
Consumer Affairs
1700 G Street, NW
Washington, DC 20552
1 (800) 842-6929 or check phone book for local number

(Savings and Loan Associations and Savings Banks)

•The appropriate state agencies: many state agencies have jurisdiction over certain credit transactions. Contact your State Attorney General's office or the State Department of Banking.

As you can see, the regulation of credit problems is a real maze. If in doubt, you can call one of the federal information centers which can refer you to the proper agency to help you with problems regarding credit or other issues.

CONSUMER ALERT: THERE ARE BUSINESSES, OFTEN CALLED "CREDIT REPAIR CLINICS" THAT PROMISE TO CLEAN UP CREDIT PROBLEMS FOR CONSUMERS - FOR A FEE, SOMETIMES A VERY HEFTY FEE. BEWARE OF THESE BUSINESSES! THERE ARE NO MAGIC PILLS OR FORMULAS TO CORRECT PROBLEMS AND THESE AGENCIES CAN DO NOTHING THAT YOU CANNOT DO FOR YOURSELF.

ESTABLISHING OR REESTABLISHING CREDIT

Obtaining credit can be a "Catch 22" situation: you can't get credit unless you already have it and you can't already have it unless you have been able to get it. If you find yourself in this seemingly intractable trap, consider the following strategies in trying to establish, or reestablish, credit:

Get a Co-signer

If you know someone who will be willing to back your credit use, and that person has a good credit record, the credit card company may be willing to issue you credit based on the promise of your co-signer to pay them if you don't.

Seek Credit With a Low Credit Limit

If you ask for a low credit limit - say $500 or so, you may be able to get a company to take a risk. In this way, you will be able to show your credit worthiness and prove to the credit companies that you are entitled to a greater level of trust.

Apply For Credit From a Company You Have Business Relationships With

If you have a business relationship with a bank or are the member of an organization that offers credit, you may be able to qualify for credit based on easier credit criteria.

Apply For Retail Credit That Uses Merchandise as a Security

If you purchase merchandise, say furniture or a car, many retail outlets will be willing to extend you credit (closed ended), using the merchandise as a security (collateral).

Give the Credit Company a Security

Sometimes you can get a bank company to grant you credit if you place a monetary deposit with them as a security to your payment of your credit bills.

AND BY ALL MEANS, ONCE YOU HAVE RECEIVED CREDIT, BE SURE TO PAY YOUR OBLIGATIONS IN A TIMELY FASHION. IN THAT WAY YOU WILL ESTABLISH OR REESTABLISH YOUR CREDIT WORTHINESS.

Women and Credit

Under the Equal Opportunity Credit Act (EOCA), women have the right to apply for credit without fear of discrimination on the basis of gender or marital status. This means that the only basis for denying credit must be on an objective finding of credit unworthiness and not sex. Practically, this law has the following benefits:

•It gives married women a credit history. Formerly, most credit records of married couples joint accounts were kept in the name of the husband only. This meant that married women who divorced, were widowed and/or who sought credit in their own names were often denied on the basis of no credit history. Under the EOCA, credit grantors must now report credit history of joint accounts in both spouses' names, giving married women a credit history.

•If your marital status changes, that fact alone cannot be the basis for revoking credit privileges. However, the creditor can compel you to fill out a new application if credit had been issued on the basis of your former husband's income.

•If you are applying for credit in your own name, you usually cannot be asked about your marital status. The exceptions to this rule are as follows: if you live in a "community property state" (such as California), if your husband will be using your account or if he will be partially or fully responsible for payments on the account.

•Your statistical likelihood of having children in the future cannot be used in determining your credit worthiness. Nor can the credit grantor ask you personal questions such as whether you use birth control or your future plans regarding family size. (Of course, you can be asked about existing children since dependents affect your ability to pay.)

•You need not have your husband's signature on a credit application. If you are applying for credit in your own name, you do not need your husband's consent or signature. If, however, you intend to use property you and he own as a security, his signature probably will be required.

•*If a co-signer is needed to obtain credit, the creditor cannot compel you to use your husband for that purpose. If you need a co-signer, you can choose anyone that will meet the credit worthiness standards of the credit grantor.*

If you believe you have been denied credit on the basis of gender, complain - first to the credit company and then to the appropriate government agencies.

Now that you have successfully applied for credit, let's move on to the proper use of credit and a course in credit self defense.

Chapter Three

USE IT - DON'T ABUSE IT
A GUIDE TO RESPONSIBLE
CREDIT CONSUMING

W hile tens of millions of consumers do not use credit in any form, the overwhelming majority of Americans depend on credit as part of their everyday consuming lives. That being the case, it is vital that all consumers learn to use credit in a manner that is both economic and protective of their interests as consumers both in the area of credit and within the market economy as a whole.

YOUR CREDIT CARD STATEMENT

Your credit card statement is a vital link in your consumer self defense arsenal. That's because in part, it tells you exactly which goods and services were purchased with credit during the previous billing period, which payments were received by the credit company and which credits, if any, were credited to your account.

KEEP YOUR RECEIPTS
Since many consumers make many charges a month, often using several different credit cards, it is very important that you keep all receipts so that you do not forget which purchases you have made.

REVIEW YOUR MONTHLY STATEMENT
When your bill arrives, you should carefully check it against the receipts you have in your possession to make sure that your bill is accurate. FAILURE TO CHECK YOUR BILL CAN COST YOU MONEY, BECAUSE YOU WILL END UP PAYING FOR UNDIS-COVERED MISTAKES.
When you check your statement, look out for the following billing errors:

Charges For Items You Did Not Purchase
Whether due to mistakes or someone getting your credit card number and using it in a fraudulent manner, you may be billed for merchandise and/or services that you did not purchase.

Double Billing
Sometimes a charge for one credit card purchase will appear twice on your monthly statement or on two consecutive monthly statements.

Charges You Do Not Understand

On occasion, you may find a bill on your monthly statement that you cannot decipher. This frequently happens when you make phone charges. Remember, when in doubt, inquire. The money you save may be your own.

Charges For Merchandise You Returned

Make sure that you are properly credited for returns you have made which were to be credited to your charge account.

Mathematical or Typographical Mistakes

People often think that because computers are such a vital part of credit card billing that errors in arithmetic don't happen. Unfortunately, they do. In fact, Wesley Smith, a co-author of this book, once made a $5,760.00 payment on a credit bill and was credited by the company with a payment of $57.60.

Failure to Mail Your Statement to Your Current Address

If you fulfill your obligation to tell your credit card company in writing that you have changed your address, their failure to send your statement to you counts as a billing error.

CHECK THE QUALITY OF THE MERCHANDISE PURCHASED

If you purchase merchandise with credit, you have an additional weapon at your disposal to make sure that it meets your expectations. Thus, make sure you keep your receipts and credit card statements in the event something goes wrong with your purchase. For example, if the merchandise breaks, is not delivered in a timely fashion or otherwise goes awry, you can protect yourself by complaining to the credit card company whose card was used to make the purchase.

CORRECTING BILLING ERRORS

Federal law has established a simple mechanism for correcting any of the above billing problems which may appear on your statement (or virtually any problem, since if you call something a billing error, it will generally be treated as one). Specifically, the **Federal Fair Credit Billing Act** provides the following method of correcting mistakes:

You Must Notify Your Creditor *in Writing* of the Mistake

When you catch a billing error, your first step is to notify the credit card company. You must do so in writing in order to preserve your rights under the law.

Your letter should contain the following information:
- Your name and address
- Your account number
- The suspected amount of error

We also believe that you should make a copy of the incorrect bill (and any receipts, a copy of a cancelled check, or other writing that supports your position) to include with your letter.

The following is a sample letter complaining about your bill:

JUNE 25, 1992

BLEW IT AGAIN CREDIT CARD COMPANY
4444 MONEY GRUBBING LANE
FLAKEY, WISCONSIN 44444

RE: BILLING ERROR - ACCOUNT NUMBER 1234 -56 -789

TO WHOM IT MAY CONCERN:

THE PURPOSE OF THIS LETTER IS TO INFORM YOU IN WRITING PURSUANT TO THE PROVISIONS OF THE FAIR CREDIT BILLING ACT, THAT I HAVE DISCOVERED A BILLING ERROR IN MY STATEMENT OF JUNE 1, 1992. I HAVE ENCLOSED A COPY OF THAT STATEMENT FOR YOUR CONVENIENCE.

SPECIFICALLY, THE MISTAKES I HAVE DISCOVERED ARE AS FOLLOWS:

1) MY STATEMENT REFLECTS A PURCHASE FROM BOB'S PLUMBING OF $84.33, ON MAY 4, 1992. I DID NOT MAKE ANY PURCHASE AT BOB'S PLUMBING ON THAT DATE.

2) I DID MAKE A RETURN ON MAY 4, 1992 TO BOB'S PLUMBING. I HAVE ENCLOSED A COPY OF THE CHARGE CREDIT RECEIPT FOR YOUR CONVENIENCE. THE AMOUNT OF THE CREDIT WAS $84.33.

CLEARLY, WHAT HAS HAPPENED IS THAT I WAS CHARGED $84.33 WHEN I SHOULD HAVE HAD MY ACCOUNT CREDITED FOR THAT AMOUNT.

I LOOK FORWARD TO HEARING FROM YOU ABOUT THIS MATTER WITHIN THIRTY DAYS AS PROVIDED BY LAW.

THANK YOU FOR YOUR COOPERATION,

JUDITH P. GOODCONSUMER

Here are some other tips regarding your letter of notification of billing error:
•Always keep a copy of your letter (as you should with all business correspondence).
•Mark on your calendar 30 days from the date of your letter to remind yourself to see whether the company has responded.
•Send a copy of your letter to the merchant in question, when appropriate. They may be able to help you resolve the problem.

CONSUMER ALERT: BE SURE YOU HANDLE ANY BILLING ER-RORS PROMPTLY! *YOU ONLY HAVE 60 DAYS* **FROM THE DATE THE COMPANY MAILED OUT THE BILL IN ERROR TO WRITE AND SEEK THAT ERRORS BE CORRECTED. AFTER THAT TIME, YOU DO NOT FALL UNDER THE PROTECTION OF THE FEDERAL LAW.**

CONSUMER ALERT: THE ADDRESS WHERE YOU MUST SEND YOUR NOTIFICATION OF BILLING ERRORS IS FREQUENTLY NOT THE SAME ADDRESS AS THE ADDRESS WHERE YOU SEND YOUR PAYMENTS. *THUS, BE SURE TO LOOK CAREFULLY ON YOUR BILL TO SEE WHERE TO ADDRESS BILLING INQUIRIES.*

CONSUMER ALERT: TO AVOID THE PROBLEM OF HAVING THE CREDIT CARD COMPANY CLAIM THAT THEY NEVER RECEIVED YOUR LETTER, IT IS A GOOD IDEA TO SPEND THE TIME AND SMALL EXPENSE TO HAVE YOUR LETTER SENT "CERTIFIED MAIL, RETURN RECEIPT REQUESTED."

While You Are Waiting For An Answer From the Credit Card Company, You Do Not Have to Pay the Amount in Dispute

A very important right you have as a consumer in the event of billing errors is your right not to pay the amount in dispute, assuming, of course, that you have correctly notified the credit company in writing of the error. You also are not obliged to pay any minimum payments or interest that apply to the disputed billing. In addition, the credit company cannot report you as delinquent to a credit bureau if you do not pay on the amount in dispute. However, YOU *ARE* OBLIGED TO PAY THAT PART OF THE BILL THAT IS NOT IN DISPUTE.

Your Creditor Must Acknowledge Your Letter Within 30 Days

The company has 30 days within which to acknowledge your letter of complaint. (That does not mean the problem has to be resolved within 30 days.)

Your Creditor Has Two Billing Periods or 90 Days (Whichever Comes Sooner) to Resolve the Matter

The credit card company is under a time limit within which they must resolve the dispute. Within 90 days or two billing periods, they must either correct the error in question or inform you in writing why they believe that your position is not correct. *If you were wrong, the company can charge you interest on the amount that was in dispute and charge for past minimum payments on the amount in question.*

If the credit company fails to meet its obligations under the act within the time set by law, it may not be able to collect the full amount. This is true even if it is ultimately shown that you were the party in error.

If You Continue to Disagree and You Refuse to Pay, the Credit Company Can Report You as Delinquent to Credit Bureaus

If you and your credit company are still in dispute, the power in the dispute is mostly on the side of the credit company. In such case, they can report you as delinquent to credit bureaus if you don't pay, they *can* restrict your credit and they *can* institute collection proceedings. However, in such cases, the credit company *must inform the credit bureau that you contend the amount is in dispute* and they must *tell you the name and address of any credit bureau* or reporting agency that they inform about your alleged debt and refusal to pay.

CONSUMERS ALERT: IF YOU AND THE CREDITOR CONTINUE TO DISAGREE ON THE BILL, YOU SHOULD CONTINUE TO FIGHT FOR YOUR RIGHTS. IN SUCH CASES, ASK THAT THEY CONTINUE TO HOLD YOUR INTEREST CHARGES AND MINIMUM PAYMENT CHARGES IN ABEYANCE. HOWEVER, IF THEY WON'T DO THAT FOR YOU, IT IS A GOOD IDEA TO MAKE AT LEAST MINIMUM PAYMENTS SO THAT YOUR CREDIT RECORD ISN'T HURT AND YOU DON'T HAVE TO GO THROUGH THE TROUBLE OF CORRECTING YOUR CREDIT REPORT. IF PUSH COMES TO SHOVE, CONSIDER TAKING THE CREDIT CARD COMPANY TO SMALL CLAIMS COURT. AND NEVER BE AFRAID TO MAIL THEM A LETTER CANCELING YOUR CREDIT CARD.

IF YOU RECEIVE DEFECTIVE SERVICE OR MERCHANDISE

Sometimes, using credit cards to purchase goods or services *actually give you more protection* than paying by check or cash. That's because you have extra leverage if you have not received full value for what you have paid for.

CREDIT CARD WARRANTY PROTECTIONS
As we stated in Chapter Two, many credit cards offer extended warranty and/or defective replacement guarantees for purchases of merchandise made with the credit card. If your card contains this valuable protection, be sure you understand the terms of the extended warranty and then act upon the protective services in time of need.

WITHHOLD PAYMENTS TO THE CREDIT CARD COMPANY
The Fair Credit Billing Act gives consumers important leverage if merchandise or service they have purchased on credit is defective. Under the law, you may withhold paying your credit card company on the faulty item or unsatisfactory service, if you:

Inform the credit card company in writing that the merchandise is defective and that you *do not want them to pay the merchant*. In such cases, the matter will be treated as a billing error (see above).

Can prove you have made a good faith effort to return the goods to the merchant or have otherwise tried in to resolve the matter.
In order for these rights to apply, the goods purchased must have exceeded $50 in value (unless the credit was issued by the merchant selling the goods, i.e. a retail credit card) and the sale must have taken place within 100 miles of your current address.

Because part of the law requires that you have made a good faith effort to resolve the matter directly with the merchant or service provider, *make sure you make your complaints in writing* and keep copies of all correspondence.

> **CONSUMER ALERT: THIS PROVISION IN THE FAIR CREDIT BILLING ACT GIVES CONSUMERS A LOT OF LEVERAGE. THUS, IT MAY BE A GOOD IDEA TO PAY FOR "RISKY" ITEMS, SUCH AS CAR REPAIR BY CREDIT CARD, AND THEN PAY THE BILL IN FULL WHEN YOU RECEIVE YOUR BILL, RATHER THAN PAYING THE BILL IN CASH.**

AVOIDING CREDIT CARD FRAUD

It's bedtime, do you know where your credit cards are? You'd better because if you don't, someone else may be using your lost or stolen credit card, which can cost you money - perhaps a lot of money.

Credit cards are very potent purchasing tools. But in unauthorized or crooked hands, they are also the means by which theft and fraud can be and frequently are, perpetrated.

THE CONSEQUENCES OF UNAUTHORIZED USE

If your credit card is used by someone without your permission, are you liable for the charges? The answer is yes and no. During the time before you report your credit card as lost or stolen, you are liable for up to $50 in charges for each card. After you report the unauthorized use, you are not liable for the charges.

It is a very good idea to keep a list of all of your credit cards and the telephone numbers and addresses designated by each credit card company to report lost or stolen cards. You might also want to sign up for a credit card registration and reporting service through one of your credit cards, it they offer the service at low or no charge.

> **CONSUMER ALERT: IT IS IMPORTANT THAT YOU REPORT ALL LOST AND STOLEN CREDIT CARDS AS SOON AS YOU LEARN THAT YOUR CARDS ARE MISSING. NOT ONLY WILL YOU SAVE UP TO $50 PER CREDIT CARD OUT OF YOUR OWN POCKET BUT YOU MAY SAVE INNOCENT MERCHANTS AND/OR CREDIT CARD COMPANIES FROM LOSING A LOT MORE FROM THE UNAUTHORIZED OR FRAUDULENT USE OF YOUR CREDIT CARDS.**

TIPS FOR AVOIDING FRAUD AND/OR UNAUTHORIZED USE:

Report lost or stolen cards immediately.

Always tear up carbons.

Be sure the totals for your purchase have been written in ink.

Don't allow merchants to write your credit card number on a check.

Don't give your credit card number over the phone unless you are very sure you are dealing with a reputable company or organization.

If you receive a personalized credit card sign up solicitation you do not intend to accept, tear up the application.

If you allow someone to use your card, be sure to state in writing the limits of the permission granted.

CASH ADVANCES

Most credit cards offer you a cash advance privilege when they issue you credit. What does this mean? It means that you can borrow cash from the credit card company by presenting the card at the issuing bank or authorized ATM machine. There are also companies that will give you cash on your credit card, charging you a hefty processing fee in the process.

It is not a good idea to use your credit card to get cash. Why? Because it is expensive. Not only is there high interest to be paid, usually from the moment you borrow the money but there is a **cash advance fee** to be paid too (which can be quite costly, especially if based on a percentage of the advance). This interest charge and cash advance fee acts as a "one, two punch," making a loan from your credit card company an exorbitant proposition, even if you pay the bill when it arrives in the mail. Also, if you get cash from an ATM machine, there may also be a fee for using the computerized teller.

That is not to say that you should never use your cash advance benefit. We realize that there are times when circumstances require you to obtain cash in a hurry. However, do not use it as a matter of habit. You will just be putting too much money in the credit card company's already overflowing coffers.

CONSUMER ALERT: MANY COMPANIES NOW OFFER THEIR CREDIT CARD CUSTOMERS *"CREDIT CHECKS"* WHICH LOOK LIKE BANK CHECKS BUT WHICH ARE ACTUALLY CREDIT VOUCHERS. USING CREDIT CHECKS CAN LEAD TO BAD HAB-ITS, LIKE USING CREDIT TO PAY FOR ITEMS, SUCH AS THE PHONE BILL, THAT ARE USUALLY ONLY PAYABLE BY CASH OR CHECK. MOREOVER, A CREDIT CHECK IS USUALLY MORE EXPENSIVE THAN USING THE CREDIT CARD ISSUED BY THE SAME COMPANY SINCE IT IS TREATED AS A CASH ADVANCE. THUS, IF YOU INTEND TO CHARGE SOMETHING, USE THE PLASTIC AND NOT THE CREDIT CHECK.

CREDIT AND PRIVACY

If privacy is important to you, you may not wish to make extensive use of credit. Thanks to the computer, that invaluable tool of commerce and a tremendous source of manipulative power, the details of much of your life now exist in computers. This includes records of your purchases.

Just think about how much of your life can be traced by following your "credit card trail;" what you purchased and where you purchased it; where you ate; your travel habits. Also on computer will be information you have supplied in applications, such as your social security number, your family size, your address and even your earning capacity and educational level.

According to attorney Howard Strong, in his book *Credit Card Secrets That You Will Surely Profit From*, some credit card companies take information from their customers' charge history and sell it to private concerns. And David Burnham, in his book *The Rise Of The Computer State* (1984, Vintage Books, New York), details some of the abuses of credit bureaus with regard to privacy and the accuracy of their credit reporting.

Chapter Four

HELP, I NEED SOMEBODY

WHAT TO DO IF YOU ARE
IN DEBT TROUBLE

C redit is a lot like the miracle of fire. Use it responsibly and life can be more abundant, more safe and more enjoyable overall. But misuse credit, and like the eruption of Mt. St. Helens, you may unleash a conflagration that can wreck havoc on your pocketbook turning the "healthy forest" of your financial life into a "field of ashes."

WARNING SIGNS THAT YOU ARE
A CREDIT CARD JUNKIE

Credit cards are convenient but they are definitely not economical, unless you pay off your bill in full every month. Even then, you will probably be paying yearly fees for the privilege of using your credit card.

Unfortunately, many of you are probably not in the financial position to pay off your credit cards in full every month. That means you are forced into the position of having to "manage your credit" to keep from getting in over your head. But, you ask, how much is too much? Here are some WARNING SIGNALS that will tell you that you are in too deep.

You Only Pay Minimum Payments Each Month

Minimum payments are seductive. They allow you to charge a great deal of merchandise each month and then only pay a small amount at the end of each billing period. Why it's almost like being able to shop for free!

But there is a very high price to be paid for living life in the minimum payment lane. That cost can be found in interest - lots and lots of interest! Here is an example of what we mean: One creditor reports the following transaction:

Amount owed on credit card:	$4662.30
Minimum payment made:	$ 116.00
Interest charged:	$ 75.67
Reduction in principal:	$ 40.33

Thus, by paying the minimum payment, this debtor is paying almost *twice as much in interest as he or she is reducing the debt principal!*

You've Reached Your Credit Limit on Several Cards

Remember, if you are at your maximum credit card level, you are paying a lot of money (and we do mean a lot), in interest.

Your Bills Are so High You Are Unable to Save Any Money

It is important to save money for a rainy day. If your bills keep you from doing so, your bills are too high.

You Use Your Cash Advance Privileges to Pay Other Credit Card Debt

This means you are in real trouble, piling debt, upon debt, upon debt.

You are Late Making Payments

If you are late making payments because you don't have the money when they become due, you are already in big trouble.

More Than 20% of Your After Tax Money Goes to Pay Installment Debt

If this is true, then you are in danger of falling off a financial cliff.

You Use Credit to Pay For Items You Used to Pay For With Cash

If you are finding that you do not have the cash for everyday expenses but must resort to credit in order to afford them, you are probably in need of taking the "credit cure."

You Charge More Per Month Than You Pay Back

There is only one way to describe this practice: living on borrowed time.

You Apply For More Credit to Maintain Your Standard of Living

If it takes credit to keep up with the Jones's, you may be headed for a big fall and the time has probably come to cut back and live within your actual means.

You Are Being Pursued by Debt Collectors

If the hounds are after you, the time has definitely come to take the credit cure.

REMEMBER, ABUSING CREDIT COSTS YOU MONEY - IN OUTRAGEOUS INTEREST CHARGES AND IN ANNUAL FEES FOR HAVING MORE CREDIT CARDS THAN YOU REALLY NEED

GETTING OFF THE CREDIT MERRY-GO-ROUND

All right, so you fell for the seductive siren song of easy credit and minimum payments and now find yourself over the debt barrel. What do you do? Panic? No. Ignore the bill collectors? Absolutely not. You should take charge! (Pardon our pun.)

WORK OUT YOUR FAMILY BUDGET

Add up all of your income and expenses to see what you need to live on.

CUT BACK ON UNNECESSARY EXPENSES

If your expenses exceed your income, or you realize the time has come to reduce your financial outlay, here are some places to look at for cutbacks:

Eating Out

If you are in "debt city," learn to cook and use the money you save to get back into financial health.

Recreation Expenses

We don't mean to be killjoys but if you are in debt, you simply are going to have to cut back on vacations, hobbies and other "nonessential" expenses such as golf or attending sporting events.

Major Purchases

You may want to keep that old car another year, put up with the stained carpet for awhile longer and live with that old bedroom suite that you were given as a wedding gift.

Charge Accounts

Using credit when you are in too deep is like pouring a bucket of water over the head of a drowning man.

CONTACT ALL YOUR CREDITORS

If you find yourself in the credit soup, don't just ignore the problem and stiff your creditors. Instead, call them and tell them honestly that you find yourself in a financial pickle and offer to work *with* them in trying to meet your obligations. Be prepared to disclose the reasons for your difficulties and treat all unsecured creditors equally - that is, don't pay some a higher proportion of your spendable income than others. And by all means, STOP USING CREDIT DURING YOUR TIME OF RESTRUCTURED REPAYMENTS.

If your creditors agree to work with you and restructure your debt payments, confirm in writing the agreement you have reached with each of them. Here is a sample letter you can use:

NICE GUYS CREDIT COMPANY
2222 DEEPDEBT LANE
UP A CREEK, MICHIGAN 23333

ATTN: MS. EMILY GOODHEART, V.P. IN CHARGE OF COLLECTIONS

RE: ACCOUNT NUMBER 333 - 444 - 444

DEAR MS. GOODHEART:

THE PURPOSE OF THIS LETTER IS TO CONFIRM IN WRITING THE AGREEMENT WE REACHED BY PHONE ON MAY 8, 1992. IT IS MY UNDERSTANDING THAT MY OBLIGATIONS TO PAY ON MY ACCOUNT NUMBER 333 - 444 - 444, HAVE BEEN MODIFIED AS FOLLOWS:

1) MY DEBT OF $3,450 REMAINS UNCHANGED.

2) INTEREST WILL BE SUSPENDED FOR SIX MONTHS. THEREAFTER ,IT WILL AGAIN ACCRUE ON THE UNPAID BALANCE AT THE RATE OF 1.5% PER MONTH.

3) I WILL BE ALLOWED TO PAY $40 PER MONTH ON MY ACCOUNT FOR THE NEXT SIX MONTHS. THEREAFTER, I WILL BE REQUIRED TO PAY $75 PER MONTH ON THE ACCOUNT.

4) I SHALL DESTROY MY CREDIT CARD AND CEASE ALL FURTHER CHARGES ON MY ACCOUNT IMMEDIATELY.

THANK YOU VERY MUCH FOR YOUR COOPERATION IN THIS DIFFICULT TIME I AM EXPERIENCING. I TRULY APPRECIATE IT.

VERY TRULY YOURS

DEBORAH REDINK

Many creditors will be willing to work with you if you show a willingness to work with them. However, if you simply ignore the problem and hope it will go away, you will soon find a process server at your door with a notice that says, Summons - go directly to court, do not pass go and do not collect $200.

> **CONSUMER ALERT: IF YOU ARE BEING PURSUED BY A COLLECTION AGENCY FOR A DEBT YOU DO NOT BELIEVE YOU LEGALLY OWE, BE SURE TO WRITE AND TELL THEM SO. ALSO, DO NOT BE AFRAID TO DEFEND YOURSELF IN COURT IF YOU BELIEVE YOU ARE IN THE RIGHT. REMEMBER, IF YOU HAVE A LEGAL DEFENSE AGAINST THE ORIGINAL CREDITOR, IT STILL APPLIES AGAINST THE COLLECTION AGENCY.**

GET HELP

If you find that even with your best efforts to cut back on your expenses, you are still beginning to slip beneath the waves of debt, or if your creditors seem unwilling to give you a break, the time has probably come to ask for some help. Happily, credit management assistance is available through the good offices of the nonprofit organization **Consumer Credit Counselor Services (CCCS)**.

Your local branch of the CCCS can help you get your financial life under control. The cost of their services are very low and they can help you with the following:

Teach You to Better Manage Your Money

If you have gotten so deeply in debt that you need CCCS, this can be of great help in learning a new way of living.

Help You Set Up a Family Budget

If you have difficulty establishing spending limits, the counselors at CCCS can help you.

Set Up a Debt Management Plan

This is the heart of what CCCS can do for you. The Debt Management Plan is a *structured recovery plan*. Under the program, you pay a monthly deposit to your local CCCS and they do the following:

Contact creditors and ask them to accept less money than they may be entitled to. Many creditors cooperate with CCCS since failure to do so may force the creditor into bankruptcy.

Ask creditors to defer litigation or other collection activities so long as you are on the program. Again, many creditors cooperate, taking a lot of pressure off of you.

Ask creditors to reduce or eliminate interest and penalties. This service can save you a lot of money.

Of course, CCCS cannot guarantee that creditors will cooperate and they cannot stop a creditor from pursuing you in court, nor do they try to improve your credit rating with credit bureaus. Moreover, to remain on the program, you cannot incur any new debt. But by allowing CCCS to help you, you prove to your creditors that you are in good faith in your desire to meet your financial obligations, increasing the likelihood that your creditors will give you the breathing room you need to get back on your financial feet.

The Debt Management Plan typically takes two to three years to complete but at the end of it, you will be out of debt and on the verge of a new and more economically healthy lifestyle.

You can find your nearest office of CCCS in your phone book, from your local Chamber of Commerce or contact:

National Foundation for Consumer Credit
8701 Georgia Avenue, Suite 507
Silver Springs, MD 20910
Or call them toll free at **1 (800) 388 - CCCS.**

CONSUMER ALERT: IF YOU ARE BEING HOUNDED BY COLLECTION AGENCIES AND/OR OTHER DEBT COLLECTORS, *YOU HAVE RIGHTS* GUARANTEED BY THE *FAIR DEBT COLLECTION PRACTICES ACT*. IF YOUR DEBTS ARISE FROM A MORTGAGE, FROM THE PURCHASE OF A CAR, FOR MEDICAL CARE, CREDIT CARDS OR OTHER HOUSEHOLD DEBTS YOU ARE COVERED.

THE FAIR DEBT COLLECTION PRACTICES ACT *PERMITS* COLLECTORS TO CONTACT YOU IN PERSON, BY MAIL, PHONE OR TELEGRAM. HOWEVER, YOU MAY NOT BE CONTACTED AT UNUSUAL TIMES OR PLACES, SUCH AS BEFORE 8:00 A.M. OR AFTER 9:00 P.M., UNLESS YOU AGREE. COLLECTORS CANNOT CONTACT YOU AT WORK IF YOUR EMPLOYER DISAPPROVES.

YOU CAN STOP A COLLECTOR FROM CONTACTING YOU IF YOU WRITE A LETTER TO THE COLLECTION AGENCY OR ATTORNEY INSTRUCTING THEM TO STOP. ONCE THEY HAVE RECEIVED THE LETTER THEY MAY NOT CONTACT YOU EX-

CEPT TO STATE THAT THERE WILL BE NO FURTHER CONTACT OR TO INFORM YOU WHAT ACTION THEY WILL TAKE NEXT (SUCH AS A LAWSUIT). HOWEVER, THEY CANNOT THREATEN TO TAKE ACTION AGAINST YOU THAT THEY ARE NOT REALLY INTENDING TO PURSUE.

WE HAVE DESCRIBED WHAT COLLECTORS CAN DO UNDER THE ACT. MORE IMPORTANT ARE THE KINDS OF UNETHICAL COLLECTION PRACTICES THAT THE ACT PROHIBITS. THESE INCLUDE:

HARASSMENT THIS INCLUDES THREATS OF VIOLENCE OR HARM TO PROPERTY, THE PUBLICATION OF A LIST OF CONSUMERS WHO REFUSE TO PAY THEIR DEBTS (THIS DOES NOT INCLUDE REPORTS TO CREDIT AGENCIES), THE USE OF OBSCENE OR PROFANE LANGUAGE, REPEATED TELEPHONE CALLS WITH THE INTENTION TO VEX OR ANNOY AND ADVERTISING YOUR DEBT.

FALSE STATEMENTS DEBT COLLECTORS MAY NOT LIE OR MAKE FALSE STATEMENTS IN THEIR ATTEMPTS TO COLLECT THEIR DEBT. FOR EXAMPLE, DEBT COLLECTORS MAY NOT:

FALSELY IMPLY THAT THEY ARE AN ATTORNEY OR GOVERNMENT REPRESENTATIVE.

FALSELY IMPLY THAT YOU HAVE COMMITTED A CRIME.

FALSELY REPRESENT THAT THEY OPERATE OR WORK OUT OF A CREDIT BUREAU.

MISREPRESENT THE AMOUNT OF YOUR ALLEGED DEBT.

INDICATE THAT PAPERS SENT TO YOU ARE LEGAL FORMS WHEN THEY ARE NOT (OR VISA VERSA).

TELL YOU THAT YOU WILL BE ARRESTED FOR NOT PAYING YOUR DEBT.

USE ANY FALSE NAME.

UNFAIR PRACTICES DEBT COLLECTORS MAY NOT ENGAGE IN ANY FALSE PRACTICES TO COLLECT YOUR DEBT, INCLUDING BUT NOT LIMITED TO THE FOLLOWING:

COLLECT A GREATER AMOUNT THAN YOU ACTUALLY OWE, UNLESS ALLOWED BY LAW.

DEPOSIT A POST DATED CHECK BEFORE THE DATE ON THE CHECK.

TAKE PROPERTY UNLESS ACCOMPLISHED THROUGH LEGAL MEANS.

CONTACT YOU BY POSTCARD.

PUT ANYTHING ON THE OUTSIDE OF AN ENVELOPE OTHER THAN THE DEBT COLLECTOR'S NAME AND ADDRESS. THEY CAN'T PUT THEIR NAME ON THE ENVELOPE IF IT WILL SHOW THE COMMUNICATION IS ABOUT THE COLLECTION OF A DEBT.

IF THE DEBT COLLECTOR BREAKS THE LAW, YOU CAN SUE THEM. IN ADDITION TO THE FEDERAL LAW, YOUR STATE WILL HAVE LAWS PROTECTING YOU FROM UNFAIR OR UN-ETHICAL COLLECTION PRACTICES. IF YOU HAVE ANY QUES-TIONS, CONTACT YOUR STATE CONSUMER PROTECTION AGENCY OR THE STATE ATTORNEY GENERAL.

FOR MORE INFORMATION ON THE FAIR DEBT COLLECTION PRACTICES ACT, CONTACT YOUR LOCAL OFFICE OF THE FEDERAL TRADE COMMISSION (CHECK YOUR PHONE BOOK UNDER FEDERAL GOVERNMENT) OR CONTACT:
   THE FEDERAL TRADE COMMISSION
   BUREAU OF CONSUMER PROTECTION
   6TH AND PENNSYLVANIA, N.W. 20580
   (202) 326-3238

DECLARE BANKRUPTCY

If push really comes to shove and you believe there is simply no way out of your debt dilemma short of running away to a desert island in the South Pacific, the time may have come to consider **bankruptcy.**

Bankruptcy is a very complicated legal proceeding in Federal court. It is intended to "wipe the slate clean" so that you can "start over again." (It is important to note that all debts are not "dischargeable in bankruptcy." These include tax obligations (of course), child support and alimony and debts based on findings of intentional misconduct, such as fraud. Also, if you have a secured debt, such as a trust deed or mortgage, the security rights of the creditor are generally not affected.)

If you do declare bankruptcy, your credit report will reflect that fact for ten years. This will mean that you will have difficulty getting credit except from some credit companies who may give your credit but will charge you very high rates of interest. However, if you are in so deep there is no hope of ever getting out of debt, your credit report is probably already toast, so you may have little to lose.

BANKRUPTCY IS NOT AN ACTION TO BE TAKEN LIGHTLY. WE URGE YOU TO PURSUE OTHER REMEDIES BEFORE UNDERTAKING THIS COMPLICATED LE-GAL ACTION. AND BY ALL MEANS, *CONSULT A BANKRUPTCY ATTORNEY BEFORE PROCEEDING*, EVEN IF YOU INTEND TO FILE THE PETITION YOUR-SELF.

Chapter Five

CONSUMERS' AGENDA

Over the years, government entities have passed several credit laws which are of significant benefit to consumers, some of which we have already discussed. However, more needs to be done to protect you from credit and collection abuses. Here is our suggested list:

Establish a Method of Correcting Errors Before They Hit the Computer

Errors happen and will always happen in a system designed and operated by human beings. Unfortunately, once these errors hit the computer they become a part of your file for years. For example, one disgruntled credit consumer wrote to Ralph Nader:

> I am a professional, as is my wife, and our combined income is well above the national average. We run a financially responsible household. Yet, twice I have had to spend dozens, even hundreds of hours correcting inaccuracies and misrepresentations in the records maintained on us by [name omitted] credit bureau. In one instance, [name omitted] failed to deliver my [loan] payment coupon book until several weeks after the initial payment was due; the creditor's error but a black flag on my credit report.

We believe this correspondent's point is well taken. Some method should be devised to allow credit mistakes to be corrected before they hit the permanent computer record and not after. The correspondent suggests the following:

> Let the credit bureaus bear the true costs of their business by notifying each individual whenever a "black flag" is registered in their credit report. A rebuttal/response period during which citizens could question inappropriate records would allow innocent victims to maintain the integrity of their record at the point of commission rather than months or years later when loans or mortgages are delayed or rejected.

Another approach could be a requirement under the law compelling credit agencies that report bad information to advise you in writing that they plan to do so in order to give you a chance to clear up the problem at either end before it hits your permanent record.

Compel the Credit Bureaus to Give You One Free Credit Report Each Year

Congressman Richard Lehman (D California), has proposed a law which would compel credit bureaus to issue consumers one free credit report per year (in understandable English, rather than computerese) upon request. We can think of no reason this law should not pass, except industry lobbying, which has been and can be expected to be hot and furious against it.

Take the Social Security Number Out of the Credit System

The Social Security number was never meant to be used as a form of national identification card. Yet, many credit companies seem to believe that is exactly what it is. The time has come to keep big business from using the social security card in a way the government denies to itself. Any ambiguity in the law concerning the privacy of social security numbers should be eliminated by a law which specifically proscribes their use in credit records and reports.

Protection Against Unauthorized Use of Credit Records

When you go to a doctor, your records are considered private and confidential. In the law, this is known as the "patient/physician privilege" and it means that absent your written consent or a court order, nobody can obtain copies of your medical records. The same privilege should apply to your credit records. We urge you to support state and federal legislation that would make it illegal for credit reporting bureaus to release your credit report to any person, business or government entity without your specific written approval or an order of court.

Unify the Credit Regulators Into One Department

One way that government sometimes makes it difficult for consumers to assert their rights as consumers is to spread the regulation of activities all over the map. This has the effect of creating confusion in the consumer's mind as to which agency is the one which can help them.

When it comes to credit, this problem stands out in red lettering. As you saw from our discussion of where to go to complain, there are over five federal agencies that have jurisdiction over the same types of credit problems; the correct agency depending on the type of credit used. This is not only confusing but it is extremely inefficient. The time has come for all credit regulation to be placed in one regulatory agency, whether the credit is a bank card, retail card or mortgage loan.

Prohibit the Use of Credit Cards as Identification When Cashing Checks

Many merchants routinely ask consumers to show them a credit card when they purchase merchandise or services using a check. This makes credit card fraud easy since it puts your account number, and its expiration date along with information on your check about you (name, address, phone number, etc) all in one place.

> CONSUMER ALERT: IN 1991, CALIFORNIA PASSED AN IMPORTANT LAW TO PROTECT THE PRIVACY OF CITIZENS WHO PAY TRANSACTIONS BY CHECK OR CREDIT CARD. HERE IS A SUMMARY. IF PAYMENT IS MADE BY CHECK, THE MERCHANT CANNOT:

1) REQUIRE THE PERSON PAYING BY CHECK TO PROVIDE A CREDIT CARD FOR IDENTIFICATION OR FOR ANY OTHER PURPOSE.

2) REQUIRE THE CHECK WRITER TO AUTHORIZE THE MERCHANT TO CHARGE HIS OR HER CREDIT CARD ACCOUNT IF THE CHECK BOUNCES.

3) RECORD THE NUMBER OF A CREDIT CARD IN CONNECTION WITH ANY PART OF THE TRANSACTION.

4) CONTACT THE CHECK WRITER'S BANK OR OTHER CREDIT CARD ISSUER TO DETERMINE IF THE CHECK HAS OVERDRAFT PROTECTION.

IF PAYMENT IS MADE BY CREDIT CARD, THE MERCHANT CANNOT WRITE OR REQUIRE THE CARD HOLDER TO WRITE ANY OF THE CARD HOLDER'S PERSONAL INFORMATION (SUCH AS THE CARD HOLDER'S ADDRESS OR TELEPHONE NUMBER) ON THE CREDIT CARD TRANSACTION FORM OR OTHERWISE. IT IS ALSO IMPERMISSIBLE TO USE A CREDIT CARD FORM THAT CONTAINS PREPRINTED SPACES DESIGNATED FOR FILLING IN PERSONAL INFORMATION ABOUT THE CARD HOLDER.

IF YOU WOULD LIKE A SUMMARY TO SEND TO YOUR LEGISLATURE, CONTACT THE CALIFORNIA DEPT. OF CONSUMER AFFAIRS AND ASK ABOUT ASSEMBLY BILL NUMBERS 2880 AND 2990. THE ADDRESS IS 1020 N STREET, SACRAMENTO, CA, 95814.

Pass Strict Usury Laws

At one time most states had usury laws which prohibited the charging of excess interest to consumers. Unfortunately, with the power of big business to get its way in legislatures, many states have done away with this important form of consumer protection. As a result, consumers routinely pay levels of interest that at one time would have only been seen by shady characters with names like "Vinny the Venal" and "Louie the Louse" who specialized in broken knee caps to enforce the payment of delinquent debts.

This legal form of loan sharking must come to an end! The way to do it is to pass laws that prohibit any rate of interest that exceeds the prime interest rate by 10 percent. Not only would this save consumers millions of dollars a year, but it would keep many from getting into debt so deeply that they are forced to seek legal protection in bankruptcy.

GIVE YOURSELF A RAISE
SAVING MONEY ON CREDIT

We close our discussion with a nutshell listing of the do's and don'ts that you can take heed of right now that WILL SAVE YOU MONEY in your use of credit.

Only use credit cards that charge a low interest rate.

Try to use credit cards that charge no annual fee.

Limit your "credit card collection" to two bank cards and one entertainment and travel card and one or two retail cards.

Pay your bill in full each month.

If you cannot pay your bill in full, pay more than the minimum payment.

Use one credit card for business purposes only. (It will assist you in keeping accurate records for tax purposes.)

Don't use the cash advance feature of your credit card.

Pay your bills on time to avoid late payment fees.

Don't buy credit card insurance. A new form of consumer ripoff is the credit card insurance plans that are being offered by many companies. Here's how they typically work:
•A monthly fee is charged against your account, based on your account balance. (If you don't pay off the account, there will also be interest charged on this fee.) Typically, this will be based on a fee per $100 owed on the account. For example, if you owe $2000 and the fee is 60¢ per $100, the monthly insurance premium for that month would be $12 (20 x .60 = 12.00). Over a year, you would have paid $144! This is definitely not a good deal!
•In return for this fee, you may have the following benefits:
Life insurance Some of these plans offer a life insurance policy which pays off your credit debt upon your death. This is all well and good, but the premium charged is so excessive that the Bankcard Holders of America and the National Insurance Consumer Organization (NICO) recommend against credit life insurance.
Payments during unemployment or disability Some credit insurance pays the minimum payments on your credit card during times of unemployment or disability, up to a maximum of the total amount owed at the date the disability or unemployment begins. Again, the benefit is nice but probably not worth the price being charged month in and month out.

Consolidate your loans into an account with a low interest rate. Then, avoid further debt.

Correct mistakes on your bill.

Part Two

AT YOUR SERVICE

The service sector of the economy of the United States is rapidly expanding. Doctors, lawyers, real estate and insurance agents, electricians, plumbers and others, all make up this important part of capitalist economies.

Unfortunately, the service sector is a growing source of consumer anger and unrest. We've all heard the anti - lawyer jokes that compare legal eagles to white mice and great white sharks. And doctors, insurance people and other professionals can attest that they feel disliked and misunderstood by a public that frequently views them as being only one notch above politicians. Now that's distrust!

But what is the ultimate source of this lack of faith? To put it simply and bluntly, far too many consumers feel victimized and disrespected by the very professionals they pay to serve them. "Horror stories" abound of incompetence, of abandonment and of outright dishonesty. And, while some of these tales of woe are inaccurate or exaggerated, there are so many disgruntled consumers out there in service land that far too many must be true.

But let's look at this from a realistic point of view. Are "the lawyers" really out to "get" you? No. Many are dedicated professionals who really want to do a good job for their clients. Are all doctors' interests truly limited to the depth of your insurance coverage rather than the health of your body? Of course not. Do all insurance agents see you simply as a source of commissions? Again, no. But there is a definite problem here, caused by a corrupting process that provides too little accountability and by simple misunderstandings between two human beings who don't communicate on the same level.

Whatever the cause of the problems you may experience with those you pay to render you a service, *problem prevention* and *consumer empowerment* are the solutions. You *can* be in charge of your own destiny. You *can* get the quality of service you deserve from the professionals you hire to assist you. And you can save money as you do so.

So join us as we take a whirl through the world of the professionals and other service providers. We'll be looking into legal and medical services, real estate, building contracting, personal banking, auto repair and insurance. And by the end of our little tour, we are sure that you will agree, in the words of FDR, that "all you have to fear is fear itself." (But you'd better hold on to your wallet, just in case.)

Chapter Six

LAWYERLAND

THE WORLD OF ATTORNEYS

T he world of lawyers is a strange and often fascinating place. It is populated with all sorts of different characters. First, of course, there are the lawyers, aka attorneys, aka mouth pieces (by those who hate them), aka every mother's dream for her son or daughter. Lawyers in private practice (these are the ones we will be dealing with) are entrepreneurs, people in the business of selling their legal advice and "lawyering" skills.

Then there are the consumers of legal services, called **clients**. That's you. Consumers obviously don't go to lawyers for their health but to get help in solving a legal problem or taking advantage of a legal opportunity. That is, clients hire lawyers to do for them in the legal system, those activities they would do for themselves if they had the knowledge, expertise, training and time. This should not mean, however, that a client turns over control of his or her legal life to the lawyer or that the lawyer should try to take it from them. Unfortunately, this is often what happens, and it is a major cause of the current disharmony that exists between legal professionals and those they serve.

THE KINDS OF LAWYERS

Most people know that doctors "specialize" in various aspects of health care. However, fewer realize that lawyers also limit their practices to relatively restricted areas of the very broad field of law. This is important for you to know because if you hire a divorce lawyer to represent you in a drunk driving case, your chances of landing in the "hoosegow" may be greatly increased.

CONSUMER ALERT: CHOOSING THE WRONG ATTORNEY FOR YOUR PROBLEM CAN COST YOU A LOT OF MONEY. FIRST, YOU WILL WASTE MONEY ON THE WRONG LAWYER AND THEN WILL HAVE TO INVEST GOOD MONEY AFTER BAD TO PAY ANOTHER ATTORNEY TO CLEAN UP THE DAMAGE.

The following are the principal areas of lawyer activity:

Civil Trial Law

Civil trial lawyers conduct trials in cases ranging from breach of contract to will contests to property disputes. Or, to put it more bluntly, civil trial lawyers are the ones you hire to "sue the bastards" or when you are the "bastard" someone else has decided to sue.

Criminal Law

If you have been accused of a crime or think you may be, you need the services of a lawyer who practices in the field of criminal law. The distinction between criminal trial lawyers and civil trial lawyers is an important one since many of the "rules of the game" are different. And you can't win the game if you don't know the rules.

Domestic Relations Law

Also known as divorce lawyers, these attorneys do more than help parting spouses fight it out (or settle it) at the Divorce Court OK Corral. They also deal with such diverse matters as adoptions and obtaining injunctions to prevent violence and/or harassment. Divorce lawyers are also trial lawyers but most of their work does not involve juries.

Personal Injury Law

"P.I" lawyers, as they like to be called (this being a family publication, we won't tell you what insurance company executives call them), handle the cases of people who are suing over auto accidents, "slip and fall" cases, medical malpractice, and products liability. Their work is highly specialized in that it involves injuries to human bodies as well as issues of law.

Business Law

Business lawyers may rarely see the inside of a court room but will help negotiate the purchase and sale of businesses and the formation of partnerships and forming corporations and otherwise give general legal advice to businesses.

Estate Planning and Probate

These attorneys write wills and trusts and assist with the legal aspects of probating estates. Probate lawyers also represent people who desire to establish conservatorships and guardianships.

Workers Compensation

If you are injured on the job and you want a lawyer, you want one who specializes or emphasizes workers compensation. The necessity of retaining a specialist is vital since most states' workers compensation systems are separate from the general trial courts with rules and regulations all their own.

Tax Law

Tax lawyers assist people with legal problems surrounding their taxes and tax planning. If you get into serious trouble with the I.R.S. or other taxing authority, or want to keep from doing so, a tax lawyer is the kind to call.

Real Estate Law

As the name implies, real estate lawyers help with the legal aspects of owning, buying, selling or leasing real property. They also deal with issues such as zoning and land use questions, etc.

In addition to these lawyers, other attorneys specialize in areas as diverse as immigration law, patents, copyrights, administrative law (hearings before government agencies such as a zoning commission), entertainment law and trademarks. Plus, many of these areas overlap. For example, you can have a trial lawyer who emphasizes trials involving real estate.

> **CONSUMER ALERT: SOME STATES ALLOW LAWYERS TO SPECIALIZE IN THE SAME WAY DOCTORS DO BY ISSUING CERTIFICATES OF SPECIALIZATION TO ATTORNEYS WHO HAVE PASSED THE REQUISITE TRAINING AND HAVE SUFFICIENT EXPERIENCE IN THE FIELD.**

FINDING THE RIGHT LAWYER FOR YOU

Perhaps the most important thing you can do for yourself as a client is to find the right lawyer to handle your legal needs. Failure to do so can lead to many unfortunate and potentially expensive problems:

YOU COULD LOSE YOUR CASE

An unfortunate truth about our system of justice is that justice does not always triumph. One reason for this is that some lawyers are better than others at what they do. This truth is magnified when you try to use a "square" lawyer to fit into a "round" legal hole. Lost cases, botched negotiations, improperly prepared documents cost clients dearly. Thus, it is vital that you pick the right lawyer for your particular legal problem.

YOU COULD WASTE MONEY ON LEGAL FEES

Lawyers cost money - often a lot of money. If you hire the wrong lawyer for the job, not only will you pay for poor quality legal services but will have to spend good money after bad to hire the right lawyer to get your case back on track - if that task can be done at all.

YOUR LIFE CAN ENTER A CRISIS

People don't generally hire lawyers unless there are very significant life and/or financial issues at stake. For example, what could be more important than a divorce where the very future of children may be at stake? Thus, choosing the wrong lawyer for the job may cost you more than money, it could cost you personal well being and a great deal of anguish.

Of course, it is easy to write that you should retain the "right" lawyer to handle your case. But the key question is, "how do you go about it?" Happily, that task is not as daunting as you might think.

FIND LAWYERS WHO PRACTICE IN YOUR AREA OF NEED

As stated above, your first step is to do your best to identify your legal problem and then seek out lawyers who emphasize that field. To find lawyers who practice in your area of need, try the following sources:

Your Friends and Relatives

Lawyers' businesses are based on good will, that is, on referrals from satisfied clients. So, if you have a personal injury problem and you have a friend or relative who also had a personal injury case, ask whether their lawyer was a good one, and if so, ask that lawyer for an appointment.

Lawyers

Just as most doctors know the good apples in the physician barrel from the bad ones, so too do most lawyers know the reputations of other lawyers in the local legal community. So, if you know a lawyer, even one who does not practice in your field of need, ask the attorney for a referral. Chances are they may be able to steer you in the right direction.

> CONSUMER ALERT: SOMETIMES LAWYERS GET REFERRAL FEES, EITHER ABOVE OR BELOW THE TABLE, FOR GIVING REFERRALS. THUS, WHEN YOU ASK A LAWYER FOR A REFERRAL, ASK IF THEY RECEIVE MONEY FOR THE RECOMMENDATION. ALSO, ASK FOR THE SPECIFIC REASONS FOR THE REFERRAL TO MAKE SURE THAT EXPERTISE IS THE BASIS FOR THE RECOMMENDATION AND NOT SOME OTHER FACTOR LIKE A FEE OR A FAMILIAL RELATIONSHIP. (IN NO EVENT SHOULD THE AMOUNT YOU PAY IN A FEE BE INCREASED BECAUSE OF A REFERRAL FEE.)

Bar Associations

Local bar associations often have lawyer referral services as part of their function. Often these referrals will be free or at very low cost and will point you to lawyers who practice in your field of need. If you do decide to seek a referral from a bar association, remember that the names you have been given have not been screened for quality but are only names on a list from lawyers interested in receiving referrals. So, don't hire a lawyer just because a bar association has pointed you in his or her direction.

Legal Directories

There are several legal directories that list lawyers in the nation's communities and also list important information about them, such as educational history, field of expertise and honors which they may have been awarded. As with bar associations, it is important to remember that for the most part, these are merely names on a list and each lawyer should be looked at based on his or her own professional qualities (see below).

Prepaid Legal Services

Prepaid legal services refer members to lawyers who are attorney members of the service. Often, these lawyers will serve the client for a reduced cost or no cost for simple matters such as writing a letter. However, a prepaid service usually restricts its referrals to attorney members, which means that you are not necessarily being referred to the best lawyer for you. Prepaid legal services can be purchased by you or are sometimes offered as a union or job benefit.

If you would like more information about prepaid legal services, contact: American Prepaid Legal Services Institute at (312) 988-5751.

Insurance Companies

If you are sued or otherwise are involved in a legal controversy from which you are protected by insurance, make a claim with your insurance company for them to obtain and pay for a lawyer to represent you.

INTERVIEW THE LAWYERS ON YOUR LIST

You should be sure to take the time to interview several lawyers before choosing the one that you want to represent you. When you do so, look for the following qualities and answers to the following concerns:

The Lawyer's Ability to Communicate With You

One of the difficult things about being a lawyer is that you have to show two faces to the world. To other lawyers, you have to be tough, confident and fearless, since the world of lawsuits and negotiations is a rough and tumble affair. This fact leads many lawyers to have an aggressive (some say, obnoxious) personality. On the other hand, when dealing with their own clients, lawyers need to turn off the "adversary switch" in their heads and turn on the human side of their personalities. Thus, your lawyer should be able to communicate with you in words and manners that you can understand so that you can make intelligent and informed choices about your own case.

The Lawyer's Professional Expertise

By interviewing several lawyers, you will be able to do yourself several favors. One of these is that you will have a better frame of reference to compare and contrast each lawyer's grasp of the issues. *You should always ask the lawyer to detail for you his or her experience in handling cases similar to yours.* In addition, by talking to several lawyers, you also will gain a greater understanding of the pros and cons of your own case and about the laws that govern your legal concerns.

What the Case is Going to Cost You

Just about anytime you have to use a lawyer, it is going to cost you money. The issue of how much a lawyer charges and how the case is to be billed can be very important in choosing the lawyer who will best fit your individual needs. (SEE BELOW) In addition, the cost of the case will have an important bearing on how and whether you decide to proceed.

What the Case Prognosis Is

Any case will have pros and cons associated with it. By interviewing several lawyers, you should get an idea of your chances in the case and should make a special point of learning the potential down sides of your case so that you don't receive some unpleasant surprises down the line.

> **CONSUMER ALERT: MANY LAWYERS GIVE FREE INITIAL CONSULTATIONS. IF A LAWYER WON'T GIVE YOU THAT COURTESY OR A LOW COST CONFERENCE, IMAGINE HOW HE OR SHE WILL ACT ONCE THE RETAINER AGREEMENT HAS BEEN SIGNED.**

Many clients find themselves at a loss as to how to interview their potential lawyers. The following are just a few of the questions to ask:

How long have you been in practice?

In law, as in any professional endeavor, experience counts.

What is your experience in cases like mine?

The concept of experience also includes work in the area of your legal concern.

How many other cases are you handling?

If a lawyer is too busy to do a top notch job he or she will not be much good, even if they do have the expertise to do the job.

Do you continue your legal education?

The law is an ever changing field and any lawyer that does not take significant steps to keep on top of his or her field will soon fall behind the times.

What specific action do you recommend?

Don't let the lawyer get away with talking in generalities. You need specific recommendations in order to be able to make decisions about how you want to proceed.

What will be happening step by step?

Nothing is more frustrating to clients than not knowing what is going on. This question will empower you with the knowledge you need in order to stay on top of your case.

What problems do you anticipate?

As we stated earlier, you need to know the bad news as well as the good in order to make informed decisions about your case.

What do you think the outcome will be?

This is the bottom line question and should always be asked, along with questions about why the lawyer thinks as he or she does.

Once you have done your homework and taken the time to compare and contrast several lawyers (as you would when you purchase a car or a stereo), you should be in the position to make an informed choice about the lawyer who best suits your individual needs.

HOW LAWYERS CHARGE YOU
FOR THEIR SERVICES

As we stated earlier, lawyers are in the business of providing legal services to their clients. This means they charge for what they do. Lawyers call their charges the **"fee."**

THE CONTINGENCY FEE

The **contingency fee** is controversial in that it is under attack from the insurance industry and big business. They claim that contingency fees promote frivolous lawsuits and take too much money out of the client's pockets. (You can prevent that by negotiating a fair agreement for yourself.) We say that these powerful financial interests hate the contingency fee because it gives you reasonable access to justice.

Here's how the contingency fee works:

The lawyer agrees to take a percentage of the case instead of an hourly fee.

Usually, the percentage ranges from 25 to 40 percent, although we have heard of some lawyers asking up to 50 percent! David Schrager, former president of the American Trial Lawyers Association, says that 33 percent is the top rate you should pay for a contingency fee, regardless of the complexity of the case.

The percentage of the case is based on the amount actually collected, not what has been awarded.

Thus, if your lawyer wins a $100,000 judgment in court against your neighbor who cannot pay anything, the lawyer receives no fee.

If you lose the case, your lawyer receives no fee.

That sounds like a risk free proposition to you, right? In fact, it sounds so good, many of you may be asking, "What's the catch?" And indeed, there is a catch. And it's a five letter word, known in the legal game as "**costs**."

A cost is any expense that must be paid to move the lawsuit forward. For example, when a suit is filed in court, there is a filing fee. That is a cost. So are the payments to court reporters who take depositions. Costs can really add up in any litigation, and fast! Worse, if you lose a contingency fee case, you do not have to pay a fee but you STILL MAY BE RESPONSIBLE FOR THE COSTS. In addition, *if you lose in court, you could be ordered to pay the other side's costs.* Be sure you discuss this important subject with your lawyer.

Often, lawyers who handle contingency fee cases will "advance" costs on behalf of their client. This is fine since many clients simply cannot afford to pay for costs as they arise. But remember, an advance is just another way of saying "loan." When your lawyer does pay your costs for you during the course of your contingency fee attorney/client relationship, you will have to pay the money back, usually at the end of the case.

This client obligation to repay advanced costs is the reason why it often appears that "the lawyers" receive more of the proceeds from lawsuits than their clients do. In fact, this is usually not what is happening, as this chart illustrates:

Total Client Proceeds	$100,000
Attorneys Fee %40	40,000
Repayment of Advanced costs	15,000
	———
Proceeds Payable to	
	$45,000
Client.	

In the illustration above, the client actually received $60,000. But, he or she owed the lawyer $15,000 for money which was paid out of the lawyer's pocket for the client's costs.

> **CONSUMER ALERT: OFTEN, IN PERSONAL INJURY CASES, PHYSICIANS AND OTHER HEALTH CARE PROFESSIONALS WILL DEFER THE PAYMENT OF THEIR FEE UNTIL THE END OF THE CASE. IN RETURN, THE CLIENT WILL SIGN A "LIEN" GIVING**

THESE PROFESSIONALS THE RIGHT TO BE PAID FROM ANY SETTLEMENT OR JUDGMENT PROCEEDS BEFORE ANY MONEY GOES TO THE CLIENT. THIS IS FINE IN MANY CASES SINCE THAT IS THE ONLY WAY MANY ACCIDENT VICTIMS CAN RECEIVE QUALITY HEALTH CARE. BUT THERE IS A DANGER. WHEN MONEY IS NOT COMING OUT OF YOUR POCKET, YOU MAY BE WILLING TO ENGAGE IN MORE MEDICAL CARE THAN YOU REALLY NEED, THEREBY BUILDING UP THE LIEN WHICH, BY DEFINITION, MEANS LESS MONEY IN YOUR POCKET AT THE END OF THE CASE. ALSO, IF YOU LOSE THE CASE, YOU WILL STILL OWE THE DOCTOR THE MONEY INCURRED BY YOU IN TREATMENT.

Usually, lawyers will not take contingency fee cases unless they believe the case is "winnable" (they can secure a beneficial settlement or court verdict) and "collectable" (they can collect money once it has been awarded). Thus, lawyers will often want proof of insurance or other assurances that their efforts will bear fruit should they succeed. Personal injury cases, malpractice cases and large real estate cases are often handled on a contingency fee.

HOURLY FEES

Clients usually want a contingency fee since they feel their risk of out of pocket losses are minimized by the fact that the lawyer receives no fees if no money is collected. However, since the types of cases in which lawyers are willing to "gamble" on a contingency fee are limited, many clients must pay their lawyers based on an hourly fee. People who are getting divorces, who have property disputes and who hire lawyers to give business advice or negotiate and draft contracts typically pay by the hour.

An hourly fee is just what the name implies: the lawyer is paid an agreed upon price per hour for his or her services. The current price of lawyer hours ranges from about $75 to $250, depending on the locale and type of case involved.

With so much money at stake, it is essential that you pay close attention to your fees in order to keep as much money in your own pocket as you can. In that regard, remember the following:

Always get your agreement of representation in writing.

It is not unusual for clients and their lawyers to have a misunderstanding about how the client is to be billed. The chances that this will happen to you will be reduced if you get your fee agreement with your lawyer in writing. This written contract is often called a **retainer agreement** and it will set forth the nature of your case, your lawyer's duties to you and the way you will be billed.

When discussing whether to retain a lawyer, always review AND MAKE SURE YOU UNDERSTAND the retainer agreement before you sign on the dotted line (and not after!). When doing so, look for the following issues and ask the lawyer you are thinking about hiring the following questions:

Are there minimum billing units?

A **minimum billing unit** is a measure of time lawyers use for convenience in billing. These are usually in 6 minute increments, which are billed as tenths of an hour. Thus, if a service takes 4 minutes 30 seconds, it will be billed at one tenth of an hour as will a charge for work that takes 7 minutes.

However, you should be aware that some lawyers use minimum billing units to increase the time they can bill against your case. Here's how this little scheme works. In the contract, a clause similar to the following will appear:

CLIENT ACKNOWLEDGES THAT ALL PHONE CALLS WILL BE BILLED AT A MINIMUM OF .3 HOURS.

In real people's language, this means that the minimum charge for all phone calls will be *18 minutes* (.3 x 60 minutes = 18 minutes)! The effect of this, of course, is to raise the actual rate you are being charged since you will be paying for time that may not have actually been spent on your case! For your pocketbook's and fairness' sake DO NOT AGREE TO A MINIMUM BILLING UNIT OF MORE THAN 6 MINUTES (.1 hour).

Do you pay extra for the lawyer to go to court?

Some lawyers charge an hourly rate but have a different charge for going to court. For example, the following language might appear in the proposed retainer agreement:

CLIENT AGREES TO PAY LAWYER $200 PER HOUR FOR SERVICES RENDERED. IN THE EVENT THAT LAWYER MUST ATTEND COURT ON CLIENT'S BEHALF, THE MINIMUM CHARGE WILL BE 4 HOURS.

In this case, the lawyer might be in court for only 30 minutes, yet still legally charge the client for 4 hours.

Some lawyers defend this practice on the basis that by being away from the office, they do less work and thus "lose money" by going to court. However, we believe that an hour is an hour is an hour and that you should only be charged for time actually spent on your behalf and not be forced to pay a premium because your case goes to court.

Under what circumstances can the fee be raised?

Some lawyers will take your business for one fee and then, sometime later, send you a letter advising you that the fee has been raised. Before you agree to hire a lawyer based on an hourly rate you believe you can accept, be sure to discuss whether the rate of charge can be raised and, if so, under what circumstances.

What activities are billed?

Clients are often amazed at the broad range of activities that a lawyer performs on their behalf (and charge to their billing ledger). Here is a partial list:
- telephone calls to the client, witnesses, adverse counsel, etc.
- writing letters, reading letters
- legal research, reviewing documents
- office conferences with the client, witnesses, investigators, etc.
- preparing court documents (pleadings), reviewing court documents
- going to court, going to depositions, conferences outside the lawyer's office
- review of file, preparation for trial, preparation of court orders

As we said, that's just a partial list. If you have any questions about what services are or are not to be billed, make sure you talk about it with your lawyer before you retain him or her and put the understanding that is reached in writing in the retainer agreement.

Which of the lawyer's business expenses will I be responsible for?

Many lawyers charge you money in addition to their fees and court costs (see discussion above on costs). They also ask you to agree to pay for expenses, such as parking fees, mileage charges, photocopying, messenger services, postage, long distance phone calls,etc. We believe that some of these costs, such as postage and mileage, should be considered part of the lawyer's overhead and not chargeable to you. Be sure the issue of expenses is clearly agreed upon in writing between you and your lawyer so that there is no misunderstanding.

Does the lawyer charge for "travel time"?

Most lawyers charge for time spent traveling on your behalf. You do need to reach a specific agreement about this aspect of billing (hopefully with a lower rate for travel time) before you agree to be represented by the lawyer.

Intra-office conferences between lawyers

If you hire a law firm, more than one lawyer and/or law clerk may work on the case. Find out if you are charged for intra-office communication about your case and beware of double billing (where all personnel charge one file for the intra-office conference).

> **CONSUMER ALERT: BEFORE YOU AGREE TO GO FORWARD WITH A LAWSUIT, BE SURE YOU GET AN ESTIMATE FROM THE LAWYER IN WRITING AS TO WHAT THE TOTAL OUT OF POCKET EXPENSES WILL BE - *BOTH FEES AND COSTS*. AND MAKE SURE THE LAWYER IS INSTRUCTED TO ADVISE YOU IN WRITING IF THE CHARGES ARE GOING TO EXCEED THE ESTIMATE AND, IF SO, WHY THEY ARE.**

Find Out if You Will Have to Pay a Retainer Fee

It is common for lawyers to charge a lump sum fee when they agree to take the case. This is called the **"retainer fee."** For example, let's say you are retaining a lawyer to represent you in a divorce. The lawyer and you agree that you will pay $150 per hour for his or her services. The lawyer may also request that you pay a fee. Let's say it is $2,500. The $2,500 is the retainer fee.

You also want to make sure that when you pay a retainer fee, it is applied against work performed on your case. In other words, that the initial work your lawyer performs is billed against the retainer (i.e. $2,500 would pay for the first ten hours work at a billing rate of $250 per hour) rather than having to pay the fee without having it applied to the initial work.

> **CONSUMER ALERT: IT IS OFTEN DIFFICULT TO GET A LAWYER TO NEGOTIATE THE AMOUNT OF HIS OR HER HOURLY FEES. HOWEVER, THEY WILL OFTEN NEGOTIATE THE AMOUNT OF THE RETAINER FEE. SO, IF YOUR LAWYER ASKS FOR $2,500, DON'T BE AFRAID TO COUNTER OFFER A FEE OF $1,000.**

> **CONSUMER ALERT: YOU WILL NOT BE ASKED TO PAY A RETAINER FEE IN A CONTINGENCY FEE CASE. HOWEVER, WHETHER A CASE IS BASED ON A CONTINGENCY FEE, AN HOURLY RATE OR SOME OTHER FORM OF BILLING, YOU MAY**

BE ASKED TO DEPOSIT MONEY IN YOUR LAWYER'S CLIENT TRUST ACCOUNT (AN ACCOUNT SET ASIDE TO HOLD CLIENT MONEY AND WHICH MUST BE KEPT APART FROM THE LAWYER'S PERSONAL FUNDS) TO PAY FOR COSTS. THIS IS PROPER, SO LONG AS YOUR FUNDS ARE NOT INTERMINGLED WITH THE LAWYER'S AND SO LONG AS YOU RECEIVE A FULL ACCOUNTING OF YOUR FUNDS SPENT FOR COSTS.

Always Insist on Receiving a Detailed Monthly Billing Statement

Imagine if you went to a restaurant and they gave you a check that merely stated, "Charges for food eaten, $125." If you were a smart consumer, you wouldn't pay such a check but would insist that you review the method by which the charge was determined. If that is true when it comes to the relatively small charge you incur at a restaurant, then isn't it even more important that you demand a detailed monthly bill from your lawyer, where thousands of dollars may be at stake?

Your detailed monthly billing statement should contain the following information:

• *the dates within which the bill applies*

• *the date each service was rendered or charge incurred*

• *the time spent on each service*

• *the total amount of money charged for each service rendered and the nature of each cost expense incurred*

• *the total amount charged during the billing period*

• *the total amount owed or credit remaining in your account*

CONSUMER ALERT: EACH LAWYER'S BILL WILL LOOK A LITTLE DIFFERENT. WHEN YOU HIRE A LAWYER, ASK HIM OR HER TO SHOW YOU A SAMPLE BILL AND EXPLAIN IT TO YOU SO THAT YOU WILL UNDERSTAND YOURS WHEN IT ARRIVES IN THE MAIL.

Once you receive your monthly bill, be sure to review it for accuracy! When doing so, look out for the following billing errors:

Charges For Services That Were Not Rendered

Overbilling For example, if you have had a telephone call with your lawyer that lasted 15 minutes and you are charged for 20 minutes.
Mathematical errors Yes, they do happen.
Any charge that you find questionable Just because you don't know the exact reason you believe a charge is in error, that does not mean it is not, in fact, in error.

If you find a mistake in your bill, you should take immediate steps to correct the problem. This can best be done by telephoning your lawyer's bookkeeper, secretary or the lawyer to discuss the problem. Whether you are right or wrong, *make sure that you are not charged* for the time it takes to investigate and correct your bill.

Once a billing error has been admitted, be sure that it gets corrected. Part of doing this is writing a confirming letter which details the promises that were made to you about correcting your bill. Here is a sample:

MARCH 4, 1992

MARY GOODLAWYER
1221 BIGBUCKS AVENUE
LITIGATION, MICH. 33333

RE: CORRECTION OF STATEMENT

DEAR MS. GOODLAWYER,

THE PURPOSE OF THIS LETTER IS TO CONFIRM OUR TELEPHONE CONVERSATION OF MARCH 3, 1992. AT THAT TIME I POINTED OUT THAT I HAD BEEN BILLED 2 HOURS FOR AN OFFICE CONFERENCE THAT TOOK ONE HOUR. DURING OUR CONVERSATION YOU AGREED THAT A MISTAKE HAD OCCURRED AND THAT IT WOULD BE CORRECTED ON MY NEXT MONTHLY STATEMENT. ACCORDINGLY, I AM ENCLOSING A CHECK TO PAY FOR MY LAST MONTH'S SERVICES BUT HAVE SUBTRACTED THE AMOUNT THAT I DO NOT OWE.

THANK YOU FOR YOUR COURTESY IN THIS MATTER.

VERY TRULY YOURS,

HARRY SUPERCLIENT

STATUTORY OR COURT ORDERED FEES

The fees that are charged to clients in some areas of the law are set by the legislatures by statute or are left up to judges to decide. For example, when the estate of a deceased person goes through probate, most states set the lawyer's fees based on a percentage of the value of the estate being probated. In other cases, a judge decides how much the lawyer is to receive. Typically, court ordered fees are found in the areas of workers compensation, conservatorships and guardianships.

FLAT RATE FEES

On occasion, lawyers will quote one set price for the services they render. Most often, this type of fee quote will come in the field of criminal law. If your lawyer quotes you a flat fee, you should still get a retainer agreement to protect you from the lawyer saying, "Oh, that fee was to take care of the case before trial. Now, I need another $3,000 to take the case to court.

WHAT TO DO IF YOU ARE UNHAPPY
WITH YOUR REPRESENTATION

Many clients feel impotent when working with a lawyer because they believe they are not sufficiently trained to judge the quality of their own lawyer's work. This turns them into "uh huh" clients, who hear what their lawyer tells them and then say, "Oh, uh huh." This "uh huh" attitude can be bad for the client's legal health (and the patient's physical health, and the general consumer's financial health, etc.) as well as their pocketbooks.

JUDGING YOUR LAWYER'S WORK

Lawyers and their clients work very closely together on matters which are frequently of great import to the client. Thus, it is easy to build a personal relationship with your lawyer and to come to think of him or her as a "friend". However, it is very important to remember that your interaction with your lawyer is, first and foremost, of a *business nature*. And in that business relationship, you are the employer and the lawyer is the hired brain (or mouth).

This being so, it is important that you stay on top of what is happening with your own case so that you can judge the work of your hired professional. Have no fear, you can do this. Here are some tips to help you with that task:

Never Be Afraid to Ask Questions

One of your lawyer's most sacred duties to you is to keep you informed as to what is happening with your case, the applicable law and the tactics to be used. If you don't understand any aspect of your lawyer's representation, ask questions. (However, remember that in hourly rate cases you will be charged.)

Make Sure You Receive Copies of Your Own Written File

Just as armies "travel on their stomachs," so do legal matters travel on their paper work. Letters, pleadings, documents, etc. are all a part of the world of law and lawyers.

In order to completely understand your own case, you should receive copies of most of the important paper work so you can set up your own working file about your own case. Thus, be sure to instruct your lawyer to send you copies of your own pleadings and correspondence. (If you receive paper work you don't understand, be sure to ask your lawyer to explain it to you.)

Review Your Lawyer's Performance

While you do not have the legal training or experience that your lawyer has, you can still evaluate the quality of his or her work. In doing so, look at the following issues:

Is your lawyer prepared? Your lawyer's work on a case can be compared to a baseball player's performance on the field. The more preparation before the game, exercising, reading scouting reports, taking batting practice, the more likely he is to hit a home run. So too with your lawyer: the more he or she prepares for the legal service to be performed, the more likely he or she is to do a good and professional job on your behalf.

Is your lawyer's work done in a timely manner? One of the reasons many lawyers find their work to be stressful is that they are often working under strictly enforced time deadlines. (If your lawyer is late, you may lose a case based on that fact alone.) Also, if your lawyer always seems to be working on your file in a frenzy of last minute activity, he or she may not be doing the best job possible.

Does your lawyer seem to be in charge of events? The world of law in general and lawsuits in specific can be a very rough place where it seems that the rules of the jungle apply despite the seeming dignity of the surroundings of plush offices or dignified court rooms. This being the case, you want a lawyer who can stand up to the tides of legal life and fight for you when that is necessary. You also want a lawyer who is at the cause of the course of events and not at the effect of them.

Does your lawyer seem to have a solid grasp of the case? Nothing is more disturbing to a client than when his or her lawyer seems to be floundering over the issues and strategies of his or her case. Thus, if your lawyer seems to have difficulty remembering the facts of your case or the law that applies as he or she has previously explained it to you, you may want to point out to your lawyer that you are spending good money and a lot of it on professional services and that you expect to have a lawyer who is familiar with your case.

Are things "going well?" No lawyer can win every case. And, in fact, a lawyer can do everything right and still lose. However, if you are dissatisfied with the course of events, you may wish to sit down with the lawyer and get a solid briefing about what went wrong and why.

If You Are Unhappy, Do Something About It

One of the most disturbing things that can happen to a client is to be unhappy with or distrustful of his or her own lawyer. In such cases, clients have been known to fall into despair and a feeling of helplessness and impotence that virtually destroys their ability to "take care of business." Many are left embittered and angry, feeling betrayed and abused by the very person they paid to help them. This situation is not healthy for clients and lawyers alike.

But be of good cheer. There are concrete and positive steps you can take to prevent such a client horror story from happening to you.

Talk to your lawyer: Many clients seem to believe that lawyers are mind readers, that somehow the lawyer will know by osmosis that the client is unhappy. This is not true. Lawyers often complain among themselves that their clients don't tell them how they feel.

•If you are unhappy about anything, *speak up*! And the sooner the better.

•If you are going to speak with your lawyer regarding something you are unhappy about, *be specific*. Be able to identify your cause of concern and show him or her in a logical manner why you are unhappy. (Once you have spoken your piece, be sure to *listen*. You are not trying to "win" something but to communicate.

•You should also *take notes* about what your lawyer tells you. In this way, you can digest what he or she tells you at your leisure and think about how you feel.

•After the matter has been cleared up, *write a confirming letter* to your lawyer setting forth the specifics of what was discussed and the conclusions that were reached. A confirming letter not only serves as an explanation point to the discussion but it sets the terms of the discussion in concrete in the event of a later dispute.

Here's a sample confirming letter for you to use as a model if you need to write one to your own lawyer:

MARILYN MOUTHPIECE, ATTORNEY AT LAW
5656 CHARGE A LOT PLACE
LEGAL CITY, MARYLAND 43434

RE: OUR CONVERSATION OF 5/8/92

DEAR MS. MOUTHPIECE:

THE PURPOSE OF THIS LETTER IS TO CONFIRM THE UNDERSTANDING WE REACHED OVER THE BILLING DISPUTE I BROUGHT TO YOUR ATTENTION IN MY LETTER TO YOU DATED APRIL 16, 1992. SPECIFICALLY, WE AGREED AS FOLLOWS:

1) YOU WOULD RESCIND THE RATE INCREASE UNTIL SEPTEMBER 1, 1992. ON SEPTEMBER 1, YOUR HOURLY FEE WILL BE INCREASED TO $175 PER HOUR. UNTIL THEN, IT WILL REMAIN AT $160 PER HOUR.

2) YOU WILL REMOVE THE CHARGES FROM MY LEDGER FOR PHOTOCOPYING MY FILE. WE ALSO AGREED THAT IN THE FUTURE, IF THERE IS VOLUMINOUS PHOTOCOPYING TO BE DONE, I WILL TAKE IT TO A PHOTOCOPY STORE AND WILL PAY FOR THE REPRODUCTIONS RATHER THAN PAY YOUR FIRM 50¢ A PAGE. YOU WILL PROVIDE COPIES OF PLEADINGS AND CORRESPONDENCE TO ME IN THE FUTURE AT NO CHARGE.

3) WE AGREED THAT YOU ARE PERMITTED UNDER OUR REPRESENTATION AGREEMENT TO CHARGE FOR TRAVEL TIME. HOWEVER, IF YOU CONDUCT BUSINESS BY CAR PHONE ON OTHER CLIENTS' CASES, THE TIME SO SPENT WILL BE DEDUCTED FROM THE TRAVEL TIME YOU CHARGE TO MY FILE.

THANK YOU FOR YOUR COOPERATION IN RESOLVING OUR MISUNDERSTANDING AND FOR EXPLAINING YOUR BILLING PROCEDURES TO ME. I LOOK FORWARD TO A CONTINUING AND MUTUALLY ADVANTAGEOUS ATTORNEY-CLIENT RELATIONSHIP.

VERY TRULY YOURS,

HENRY T. NODUMMY

CONSUMER ALERT: IF YOU DO NOT FEEL COMFORTABLE COMMUNICATING OVER THE PHONE OR IN PERSON WITH YOUR LAWYER ABOUT YOUR DISPLEASURE, WRITE A LETTER OF COMPLAINT. IN THAT WAY, YOU CAN TAKE YOUR TIME TO GATHER YOUR THOUGHTS AND PUT THEM ON PAPER IN A WAY THAT ACCURATELY COMMUNICATES THE MESSAGE YOU WANT TO SEND. IN YOUR LETTER, BE COURTEOUS, BE SPECIFIC AND ASK FOR A RESPONSE TO YOUR CONCERNS. AND THANK THE LAWYER FOR ALL OF THE GOOD WORK HE OR SHE HAS DONE FOR YOU.

Get a second opinion Sometimes when things go wrong, you may not know whether it is your lawyer who has gone wrong or the "Fates." If you find yourself in this position, the time may have come to get a second opinion about the case.

When you go to a second lawyer for an opinion, you should take the same steps you originally took when looking for your original lawyer. You should also tell the lawyer that you are getting a second opinion and that you may or may not be thinking of changing lawyers (see below). You should also be sure to bring as much of the file as you have in your possession with you to the lawyer and you should instruct your original lawyer to cooperate in the second lawyer's review by answering questions and providing documents. (Your original lawyer should not resent this if he or she truly cares about your legal and emotional welfare.)

It is true that a second opinion costs money. But failing to seek assistance out of the loop of your original attorney/client relationship could end up costing you even more: more money, more anguish and more legal problems if your case goes sour.

Fire your lawyer It is a sad commentary on the intimidation some clients feel when dealing with their own lawyers that they are not even aware that they have the right to fire their own attorney. They can, of course, and every day many do just that.

You don't have to have a reason to fire your lawyer. You can do so for any reason you want to, whether real or imagined. However, this is not a decision to take lightly. There are very real consequences to this act which you must be aware of:

•It will cost you money: Firing your lawyer is probably going to cost you money in the short run. In an hourly fee case, you will have to pay your new lawyer to read the file and otherwise become familiar with the case. Even in a contingency fee case there may be expenses, such as the lawyer asking you to repay advanced costs.

> CONSUMER ALERT: IF YOU CHANGE LAWYERS IN A CONTIN-
> GENCY FEE CASE, YOU CAN ONLY BE COMPELLED TO PAY ONE
> CONTINGENCY FEE. YOU CANNOT BE FORCED TO PAY TWO
> FEES. IN SUCH A CASE, THE LAWYERS INVOLVED IN THE CASE
> ARE EXPECTED TO DIVIDE THE FEE BETWEEN THEMSELVES.
> IF YOU FIND YOURSELF CAUGHT BETWEEN LAWYERS IN A
> CONTINGENCY FEE CASE, DEMAND YOUR SHARE OF THE
> MONEY. THEY DO NOT HAVE A RIGHT TO HOLD IT UP.

•It will impede progress on your case: When you change legal horses in midstream, you will impede the progress of your case. It will take time for the new lawyer to become familiar with the intricacies of your case and he or she will have to fit you into his or her "schedule." Thus, once you make the decision to change lawyers, do it sooner rather than later!

> CONSUMER ALERT: IT IS ESPECIALLY DANGEROUS TO CHANGE
> LAWYERS JUST BEFORE A TRIAL. GOING TO TRIAL TAKES A
> GREAT DEAL OF PREPARATION, AND IF YOUR NEW LAWYER IS
> FORCED INTO THE BREACH BEFORE HE OR SHE IS REALLY
> READY, YOU COULD LOSE THE WAR.

•The impact on your life: When you change lawyers, your life will not go on as usual. You are going to have to take whatever time it takes to assist your new legal representative to come up to speed on your case. That may mean hours of conferences and telephone calls when you would rather be spending time with your children.

Once you have decided to fire your lawyer, all you have to do is write him or her a letter stating that you no longer desire their representation. If you are involved in a lawsuit, you will also have to make sure that the court and the other parties to the case are informed. Most courts have forms for that purpose and your old lawyer will usually prepare the document and file it with the court for you. You will also have to make sure you get a copy of the file. If you are replacing one lawyer with another there will be less hassle in your life since it will be your new attorney's job to make sure that all forms are prepared and filed and that your file gets into his or her hands.

Sue your lawyer If your lawyer's representation is beneath the standard of care of other lawyers in the community, that is, if he or she makes mistakes that are considered "negligence" and if those mistakes cost you money, you can sue for **malpractice**.

Most lawyers have malpractice insurance from which judgments and settlements can come. That means they will have lawyers to represent them so you will probably need a lawyer of your own to pursue the case on your behalf (most malpractice lawyers take cases on a contingency fee).

Suing for malpractice is a complicated procedure. Plus, it may be a little difficult to find a lawyer willing to sue a colleague, especially in smaller communities. However, if you believe you have been the victim of negligence, and that the negligence has cost you a significant amount of money, you should definitely look into asserting your rights by bringing a malpractice case.

> CONSUMER ALERT: HALT PUBLISHES A DIRECTORY OF LAW-YERS WHO ARE WILLING TO SUE THEIR COLLEAGUES FOR MALPRACTICE. TO RECEIVE A COPY, CONTACT HALT IN WASHINGTON D.C. (SEE THE CONSUMER ALERT AT THE END OF THIS CHAPTER.)

Report your lawyer If your lawyer's conduct is unethical (stealing your money, abandoning your case, lying about mistakes, etc.) you can and should report him or her to your State Bar Association in the hopes that the lawyer will be disciplined. Discipline can include disbarment or suspension from practice and/or an order to compensate you for your out of pocket losses, among other actions.

If you are forced to report a lawyer, be sure to be very specific with your complaints and try to back up what you say with documents, witness statements or other "hard" evidence which supports your claim. Bar associations are often reluctant to act unless they are sure misconduct has occurred and if you cannot prove the case they are likely to give your lawyer the benefit of the doubt.

> CONSUMER ALERT: IF YOU HAVE LOST MONEY BECAUSE OF A LAWYER'S MISCONDUCT, YOU MAY BE ABLE TO RECOVER ALL OR PART OF YOUR OUT OF POCKET LOSS. MOST STATE BAR ASSOCIATIONS MAINTAIN A *CLIENT SECURITY FUND* TO REIMBURSE CLIENTS WHO HAVE LOST MONEY AT THEIR OWN LAWYER'S HANDS. FOR DETAILS IN YOUR STATE, CON-TACT YOUR STATE BAR ASSOCIATION.

GIVE YOURSELF A RAISE:
HOW TO SAVE MONEY WHEN
YOU ARE "WITH LAWYER"

Lawyers cost an awful lot of money, so anything you can do which can keep some greenbacks in your own pocket without hurting your case should be pursued. Keep the following in mind whenever you are involved professionally with a lawyer:

Organize Your File Ahead of Time

A significant amount of a lawyer's time can be spent organizing the papers and documents of a file when he or she takes on a case. In hourly fee matters, you pay for this organization. Thus, it will save you a great deal of money if you organize and label your file ahead of time, thereby saving your lawyer some time consuming work. You should also have a typed list of witness names and addresses and a list of all evidence you believe the lawyer needs to know about.

Be Prepared

When you are going to visit a lawyer in his or her office or talk with him or her over the phone, be sure you are well prepared in advance. That means having all of your documentation organized and all of your questions written down ahead of time. After all, the more efficient you are in doing your job as a client, the less time it will take at your lawyer's office and the more money you will keep in your own pocket.

Do Some of the Tasks Yourself

A good way to save money is to do some of the "grunt" work of the case yourself. For example, you may wish to photocopy voluminous documents yourself at 5¢ a page at a photocopying service because your lawyer might charge you 25¢ or even 50¢ a page. If something has to be dropped off or picked up, you could volunteer instead of paying for the lawyer, a law clerk or a paralegal to do the work.

Negotiate the Retainer Agreement

Before you hire the lawyer, don't be afraid to try and negotiate a better deal. For example, you may get the lawyer to lower the percentage of the contingency fee, the hourly rate or the retainer fee.

Watch Out For Billing Abuses

Be on the lookout for billing abuses, such as charging for secretarial time, charging excessive minimum billing units and charging more time than a service actually took (sort of a lawyer's answer to a butcher putting his or her thumb on the scale.)

> **CONSUMER ALERT: IF YOU ARE UNHAPPY WITH YOUR BILL, SPEAK UP AND DON'T ALLOW YOURSELF TO BE INTIMIDATED INTO PAYING MONEY YOU DO NOT BELIEVE YOU OWE. MOST STATES HAVE *ATTORNEY/CLIENT FEE DISPUTE ARBITRATION* PROGRAMS WHICH ALLOW CLIENTS TO ARBITRATE THEIR FEE DISPUTES WITH THEIR LAWYERS AT LITTLE OR NO COST. CLIENTS CAN USUALLY REPRESENT THEMSELVES IN THESE INFORMAL HEARINGS.**

Keep An Eye on Costs

As you now know, there is a difference between fees and costs. Costs can run into the thousands of dollars in a lawsuit and are often a significant part of the total expense of litigation. Instruct your lawyer to keep costs to a minimum and tell him or her to get your approval before incurring a cost in excess of $250.

Don't Make Unnecessary Phone Calls

Some clients get understandably nervous about a case and tend to call their lawyers when there is nothing to talk about. An occasional call to see what is going on is fine but repeated phone calls that accomplish nothing only cost you money. Besides, if you have instructed your lawyer to keep you informed, you should rarely be in the dark.

Ask Your Lawyer to Allow Law Clerks or Paralegals to Handle the "Easy" Work

Much of law is basic stuff. One way you can save money is to hire a lawyer who uses law clerks or paralegals to perform the simpler tasks under the lawyer's supervision. You save money because the time law clerks and paralegals spend on a file are billed at a lower amount than your lawyer charges.

Go Without a Lawyer

While it is often true that "he who represents himself has a fool for a client," there are some relatively simple legal matters that can often be handled without the assistance of an attorney. Thus, if your budget is tight and you feel you have the ability, time and interest to handle these matters on your own, you might want to give it a try.

> **CONSUMER ALERT: IF YOU DECIDE TO TAKE CARE OF YOUR OWN LEGAL PROBLEM, THERE IS AN ABUNDANCE OF RESOURCES AVAILABLE TO ASSIST YOU. MOST COMMUNITIES HAVE LEGAL LIBRARIES YOU CAN GO TO FOR REFERENCE TO LAWS AND LEGAL FORMS. THERE ARE ALSO MANY BOOKS AVAILABLE TO HELP YOU. ONE IS *YOU DON'T ALWAYS NEED A LAWYER*, BY CRAIG KUBEY, *ET AL* (1991, CONSUMER REPORTS BOOKS, YONKERS, NY). THE LARGEST PUBLISHER OF SELF HELP LAW BOOKS IS NOLO PRESS, BASED IN BERKELEY, CALIFORNIA. WHILE MANY OF THEIR BOOKS ARE AIMED AT THE CALIFORNIA MARKET, MANY ARE ALSO USEFUL TO PEOPLE IN OTHER AREAS OF THE NATION. FOR A COPY OF THEIR CATALOGUE, CONTACT THEM TOLL FREE AT 1-800-445-NOLO (IN CALIFORNIA) OR 1-800-992-NOLO, (THE REST OF THE U.S.).**

There is a consumer organization called HALT: An Organization For Legal Reform, which you may want to investigate joining. The purpose of HALT is to reform the justice system so that all people can dispose of their legal affairs in a simple, affordable and equitable manner. HALT works to improve the quality, reduce the cost and increase the accessibility of the civil justice system.

In addition, HALT publishes a series of CITIZENS' LEGAL MANUALS and the EVERYDAY LAW SERIES to increase consumers' ability to handle their legal affairs and allow them to be informed users of legal services. HALT's quarterly magazine, THE LEGAL REFORMER, is a magazine that discusses major legal reform efforts.

HALT also pursues legislation at the state and federal levels seeking to reform laws concerning the unauthorized practice of law and tort reform.

While we believe that some of HALT's agenda goes too far and moves into the area of restricting victims' rights, we do recommend that legal consumers consider joining this consumer protection organization. For more information, contact: HALT, 1319 F Street NW, Suite 300, Washington D.C. 20004, (202) 347-9600.

Chapter Seven

PHYSICIANS "R" US

YOU AND YOUR HEALTH CARE

There is an old saying which states, "If you have your health, you have everything." This statement is one of the world's truisms, as anyone who has ever suffered a prolonged period of ill health will tell you. Unfortunately, good health often depends on access to quality health care, and quality health care usually costs money -- either your own, a friend's or relative's, or payments from a health insurance company or the government.

This chapter will deal with you and your doctor, how you can be empowered in the physician/patient relationship, how you can work effectively with your doctor (which helps your doctor help you) and how you can save money in many of the areas of health care. (This is no small issue. 13% of the nation's gross national product went for health care in 1991, according to the U.S. Department of Commerce.)

THE WORLD OF HEALTH CARE

DOCTORS

The "glamour" group of health care professionals is, of course, the doctors. Doctors spend a lot of years preparing for their work - four years of college, another four years of medical school, one year of internship and then several years in "residency" while they pursue a "specialty."

The word "specialty" is a generic one and doesn't really tell you what you need to know about a doctor's expertise. The words you really want to look for when determining a physician's expertise are words such as "**Board Certified**" and "**Board Qualified**." The "boards" in question are the national medical boards which govern the various fields of physician endeavor. To become "Board Certified" means that a doctor has become an M.D. and then gone on to receive residency training (work in a hospital in a particular field under a supervising physician) in his or her medical field of choice. Then, the doctor has also been in active practice, taken additional courses and passed a national test to achieve the "certification" of the board. (To be board qualified means that a doctor is eligible to take the test. It may also mean that the doctor took it and did not pass it.)

> **CONSUMER ALERT: ANY DOCTOR CAN CLAIM THEY "SPE-CIALIZE" IN ANY FIELD OF MEDICINE. FOR EXAMPLE, WE HAVE HEARD OF AN OBSTETRICIAN WHO CLAIMS TO "SPE-CIALIZE IN PLASTIC SURGERY." THUS, THE TERM "SPECIALTY" IS ACTUALLY MEANINGLESS AND CAN BE USED TO IMPLY**

EXPERTISE THAT DOES NOT EXIST BY TRAINING OR EXPERI-
ENCE. THUS, THE CORRECT QUESTION TO ASK A DOCTOR
WHEN INVESTIGATING HIS OR HER CREDENTIALS IS *"ARE YOU
BOARD CERTIFIED?"* NOT "ARE YOU A SPECIALIST?"

NURSES

If doctors are the glitz of medical care, nurses are the foot soldiers. Nurses do far more than people realize. Nurse practitioners are permitted to give physical exams, order and interpret tests and manage common illnesses. Certified nurse midwives deliver babies under normal childbirth circumstances. And of course, the Registered Nurse provides hands on care to hospitalized patients and provides much of the "humanity" of the health care system, as do Licensed Vocational Nurses.

PHARMACISTS

Pharmacists dispense drugs and medicines as prescribed to you by your doctor. But used to his or her fullest potential, a pharmacist offers many other vital health care services, such as providing important patient education about the drugs being taken, acting as a fail safe against physician mistakes (yes, they happen) and preventing a patient from taking several drugs that may be fine when taken alone but toxic when taken together. Pharmacists can also help you select over the counter medicines for less serious maladies that do not require a doctor's prescription.

> CONSUMER ALERT: IF YOU CAN, USE ONE PHARMACY TO FILL ALL OF YOUR PRESCRIPTION NEEDS. AND ALWAYS MAKE A POINT OF ASKING THE PHARMACIST WHAT THE POTENTIAL SIDE EFFECTS OF A MEDICINE MIGHT BE AND WHETHER A PRESCRIPTION WILL CAUSE A HEALTH PROBLEM IF TAKEN WITH OTHER PRESCRIBED OR NONPRESCRIBED DRUGS YOU ARE TAKING.

> CONSUMER ALERT: THERE IS A NEW TREND IN MEDICINE TODAY WHERE SOME DOCTORS ARE DISPENSING THEIR OWN PRESCRIPTIONS. THIS CAN SAVE YOU MONEY. HOWEVER, IT DOES REMOVE THE FAIL-SAFE PROTECTION PROVIDED BY A PHARMACIST. IN ADDITION, IT MAY NOT BE A GOOD IDEA FOR A DOCTOR TO HAVE A FINANCIAL INCENTIVE TO PRESCRIBE MEDICATIONS.

CHIROPRACTORS

Chiropractors believe that good health depends to a large degree upon a well functioning and balanced nervous system. This balance depends, according to this view, on the correct alignment of the vertebrae and related nerve centers.

Chiropractors "adjust" the spine to keep it aligned through physical manipulations, most often associated with the relief of back and head aches. Chiropractors also use heat, ultrasound and other forms of treatment to assist patients in distress. Chiropractors can give physical exams, order x-rays, diagnose certain ailments and treat a wide scope of ailments such as nonallergic asthmas, spastic colon and headache. They can not, however, prescribe medications, engage in "invasive procedures," treat all ailments or, in most cases, hospitalize patients.

We, of course, have not run the gamut of the health care professionals. There are physical therapists, X-ray technicians, podiatrists (health care professionals who treat ailments of the feet), osteopaths (equivalent to M.D.s but who also use spinal adjustments) and many others.

HOW TO FIND THE RIGHT DOCTOR

Finding the right doctor to assist you is vital to your health - both physical and financial. But how to go about it? Many people don't know.

As with any consumer empowered activity, you need an organized approach.

CHOOSE THE RIGHT KIND OF DOCTOR

It is important that you receive your treatment from a doctor who is board certified (or working under a doctor who is) in the field of medicine that you need. If you have a doubt about what kind of doctor to select, ask your primary care physician or an internist (adults) or pediatrician (children) for assistance.

FIND A DOCTOR THAT MEETS YOUR PERSONAL NEEDS

When looking for the right doctor for you, keep in mind the " 5 A's" as recommended by a spokesperson for the Los Angeles Medical Association. The 5 A's are:

Ability

Ability is the threshold question each patient should be concerned with above all other considerations. Ability deals with the doctor's professional and clinical skills. For example, what are the doctor's credentials in your field of need? Has the doctor continued to receive education on the ever evolving field of medical care? In short, is he or she a "good" doctor?

Availability

Even a doctor who is the best that money can buy is not going to do you much good if he or she is not available to help you. Thus, if the doctor does not keep convenient office hours, is too busy or is not reachable by phone in time of need, he or she is not going to do you much good.

Accessibility

This "A" concerns itself with finding a doctor who practices in a place you can "get to." For example, if you have a disability and you must depend on a bus to get around, you will probably not want to select a doctor whose office is ten blocks from the nearest bus stop. Thus, with rare exceptions, such as dealing in a highly specialized field, you are probably better off finding a doctor who you can get to when you need to.

Affordability

The term "affordable doctor" may seem like an oxymoron but it is an issue that you must consider. There are several ways to request a doctor to work within your financial means which we will discuss.

Affability

No, this does not refer to your doctor having a good sense of humor but it does deal with the "art of medicine," that is, the ability of your doctor to communicate with you in a manner that makes you comfortable and which you can comprehend.

FINDING THE CANDIDATES

Finding a good doctor should be approached in a methodical and careful manner. Your best bet is to get referrals. The following are probably the best sources for the names of good doctors:

Other Doctors

If you need a doctor, another doctor can be an excellent source of names, since most doctors know the reputation of their colleagues in a given community. Your primary care physician should be an especially important source for referrals to sub-specialists. However, in order to avoid being trapped in a "mutual referral society," or tennis partner referral or other situation where a doctor makes a recommendation for reasons other than medical excellence, ask the following questions:

•Why have you recommended this particular doctor over all of the other physicians in town?

•What are the doctor's credentials?

•Are there others with whom I can talk about this particular doctor's reputation and medical skills?

•Have you ever referred a family member to this particular doctor?

It might also be a good idea to ask the doctor for the name of three referrals so that you can compare and contrast the candidates to find the right doctor for you.

Nurses and Other Medical Personnel

Nurses, office managers and others who work closely with doctors and in hospitals often know a lot about the quality of care being offered by the local medical community. Thus, these people are an excellent source of names and/or sources of information about a name you may have obtained from other sources. You can also ask them to ask their bosses for a referral or an opinion of a doctor you have had recommended to you.

Family and Friends

We are very strong believers in the benefit of using other consumers as sources of information about products and services. This holds true for doctors and, in fact, referrals from satisfied patients are a major source of business for doctors. Thus, when looking for a doctor, do not hesitate to go to the recipient of medical services for referrals to good doctors and the names of those physicians who should be avoided.

Local Medical Societies

Most medical associations have computerized referral services available to you at little or no cost. A referral will usually consist of several names and include useful information about the doctors' education and credentials (i.e. board certification, etc.). However, remember that the names available will only be those doctors affiliated with the association and with rare exceptions, the doctors are names on a list only, that is, the association will not have screened the names for excellence.

Hospital Referral Services

Many hospitals' marketing departments operate physician referral services, using names of doctors who are "on staff" (i.e. permitted by the hospital to hospitalize patients).

MAKING THE CHOICE

You can not possibly make an intelligent selection of a doctor if you do not get a "feel" for the man or woman behind the white coat and stethoscope. This means that you should strive to meet the doctors you are thinking of retaining face to face if you can, or at the very least, by telephone. (Obviously, emergency situations do not allow for this luxury.)

When you set up a meeting, you should be prepared to pay a small price, since few doctors give free initial consultations. (However, it never hurts to ask.) You should ask ahead of time what the tab will be so that you do not have any unpleasant surprises.

When you meet the doctor, it is a good idea that you bring with you some or all of the following:

Proof of Health Insurance

Unfortunately, many doctors will not consider taking you as a patient if you do not have a good health insurance policy.

Your Past Medical Records

Your doctor needs to know as much about you as possible, so any records you have will be helpful.

> **CONSUMER ALERT: MOST STATES GIVE YOU THE ABSOLUTE RIGHT TO HAVE COPIES OF YOUR OWN MEDICAL RECORDS. THUS, YOU SHOULD ALWAYS ASK FOR YOUR OWN RECORDS AND KEEP THEM IN A SAFE PLACE IN THE EVENT OF NEED.**

A List of Allergies and Medications

Any doctor will need to know if you have any allergies or if you are taking any medicines. Better yet, bring your medicines along with you to show the doctor.

Be Prepared to Discuss Your Family's Health History

One of the most important pieces of information a doctor needs about you is the health history of your immediate family, since many diseases seem to "run in families" as do some health breakdown propensities.

Write Down Why You Are Consulting the Doctor

You will want to discuss with the doctor, in detail, why you are consulting him or her. A good way to prepare for this patient task is to write down your symptoms, fears and questions, ahead of time so that you will be able to be efficient in your meeting.

Be Prepared to Ask Questions

You need to ask your doctor intelligent questions if you are to make an intelligent decision about your health care. Among the questions we recommend are the following:

What are your credentials? As we discussed, the most important attribute you want in a doctor is ability. One measure (not the only one) of ability is credentials; board certification, medical school, place of residency, fellowships, (i.e. F.A.C.S. for Fellow of the American College of Surgeons, an honorary credential above board certification), etc.

In which hospitals do you have staff privileges? Hospitals conduct screening procedures when a doctor applies for staff privileges (some hospitals are tough, others lax). If your doctor is accepted at all of the major hospitals in your community, it may mean that he or she is highly regarded. If your doctor is only accepted at one or two of the less well thought of hospitals, it may mean that the doctor is not well regarded in the medical community.

What kind of continuing education activities do you pursue? It is imperative that your doctor maintain a continuing course of education to keep up with the ever changing face of medicine. If your doctor says that he or she knows so much that no further education is required, you don't need his or her services.

What is my care going to cost? Many people don't talk money before the fact. This can be a mistake. You have a right to know what your care is going to cost and how it is billed. You should also talk about matters of health insurance and payment for that portion of the bill that is not covered by health insurance and whether your doctor will accept monthly payments.

> **CONSUMER ALERT: IF YOUR INSURANCE IS GOING TO PAY A HEFTY AMOUNT FOR SERVICES RENDERED, ASK YOUR DOCTOR IF HE OR SHE WILL ACCEPT THE INSURANCE PAYMENTS AS YOUR PAYMENT IN FULL. MANY WILL AND THAT CAN SAVE YOU HUNDREDS OF DOLLARS. BUT REMEMBER, THE TIME TO ASK THAT QUESTION IS BEFORE, AND NOT AFTER, HEALTH CARE SERVICES HAVE BEEN RENDERED.**

Who is going to "cover" for you? No doctor can be available 24 hours a day, 365 days a year. Thus, when a doctor is not going to be available, he or she will arrange with another doctor to "cover" their patients while they are away. It is important that the covering physician and your regular doctor have equivalent capabilities. You should also be prepared to ask questions about your medical condition and the course of treatment that the doctor believes should be pursued. Then and only then (in nonemergencies) will you truly be able to make an intelligent decision about your health care.

> **CONSUMER ALERT: IF YOU HAVE A MEDICAL CONDITION, IT IS VITAL THAT YOU LEARN AS MUCH ABOUT IT AS YOU CAN. THAT IS NOT TO SAY THAT YOU SHOULD BE THE DOCTOR BUT THAT IS TO SAY THAT YOU CAN BETTER TAKE CARE OF YOURSELF AND BETTER ASSIST YOUR DOCTOR TO TREAT YOU IF YOU COME INTO MEDICAL CARE FROM A POSITION OF KNOWLEDGE RATHER THAN IGNORANCE.**

TOWARD AN EMPOWERED RELATIONSHIP WITH YOUR DOCTOR

Too many people put doctors on pedestals, believing that they, as "mere" patients, have no right to question their physician's authority nor judge the quality of the work that is performed. This attitude is a prescription for disaster, for not only is it your body and health that are the subjects of the relationship but you are the one who is going to have to live with the results of your medical care.

With so much at stake, it is important that you take charge of your health care. This isn't as hard as it may seem. All it takes is a little gumption, a dash of knowhow and the realization that you can do it. Here's how:

DOCTORS

When you need medical treatment, the decision as to which way to go and how to get there, must ultimately be *yours*. It is your body we are talking about and it is your life.

But, you ask, isn't it your doctor's job to do whatever he or she thinks is best for you? Aren't you, as a patient, supposed to give yourselves over in complete trust to those who have spent years training to be the healers we need to take care of our problems? In short, aren't you supposed to trust doctors?

The answer, of course, is that at some point you will have to trust your doctor. But that trust should not be blindly given. Like respect, trust should be earned and earned because of the information your doctor presents to you and not because he or she has a fancy diploma hanging on the office wall.

Informed Consent

It is your legal right to shape your medical care. The decision you make, in theory, in fact, should be based on a full disclosure of the *pros and cons* of moving forward with tests or treatment and the consequences of not doing so. Once you have been fully informed, then *you decide* what to do or what not to do. This concept is embodied in the terms, **informed consent** and **informed refusal**.

> **CONSUMER ALERT: NEVER TRUST A DOCTOR WHO SAYS SOMETHING LIKE, "WHEN YOU GO TO MEDICAL SCHOOL, THEN I'LL ANSWER YOUR QUESTIONS. EITHER YOU TRUST ME OR YOU DON'T." THIS IS ARROGANCE AT ITS WORST.**

> **CONSUMER ALERT: NEVER BE AFRAID TO ASK YOUR DOCTOR TO SPEAK IN REAL PEOPLE'S LANGUAGE. AFTER ALL, YOUR DOCTOR'S JOB IS TO COMMUNICATE WITH YOU *IN A WAY YOU UNDERSTAND*, NOT THE WAY HIS MEDICAL COLLEAGUES DO. FOR EXAMPLE, IF YOU ASK YOUR DOCTOR WHY YOUR HEAD STILL HURTS AND HE OR SHE SAYS THAT THERE IS "AN IDIOPATHIC CAUSATIVE AGENT INVOLVED," WHAT IS REALLY BEING SAID IS, "I DON'T KNOW."**

Staying Informed

After having given informed consent (or refusing treatment), you have the absolute right to be kept current with the ongoing course of your care and your health. In other words, you have the right to know what is going to happen to you, step by step.

Here's an example of what we mean. Assume you have agreed to take a prescribed medication for an infection. Your doctor should tell you how long to take the drug, what to look out for in terms of benefits and/or problems, what side effects may be expected (i.e. drowsiness, nausea, etc.) and what food, drink or other medications to avoid. Likewise, if you are going to have surgery, you should have the entire procedure laid out to you so that you will know what is happening each step of the way.

You also have the right to the prompt return of test results. Nothing is more stressful than taking a medical test and waiting on the fence for the results. In order to reduce the strain of waiting for the results, we suggest that you ask how long the test will take and then, make an appointment to receive the results, either in person or by phone.

The Importance of Second Opinions

Any doctor will tell you that patients shouldn't feel funny about seeking a second opinion. Medicine is, at best, an inexact science. No doctor has a monopoly on wisdom. Thus, a second opinion can be a vital component of effective medical care.

But how do you tell whether you need a second opinion? Often, it will be your own doctor who will suggest it. Even when that isn't true, you should get a second opinion before serious surgery (nonemergency), when diagnosed with a serious ailment or when told that your seemingly significant symptoms are relatively harmless or if you feel uncomfortable with the course of your treatment or your doctor's approach to your care.

Judging Your Doctor's Service

Many doctors are hard working, dedicated, ethical professionals who pride themselves on their medical skills and their ability to help their patients. That does not mean that they do not make mistakes. Nor does it mean that all doctors are deserving of such praise.

But, you are a patient. You haven't gone to medical school. How can you judge your doctor's performance on your behalf? Here are some helpful pointers:

Educate yourself about your body We should all know as much as we can about our own bodies and about the ailments that may afflict us. For example, it is important to know the "Seven Warning Signs of Cancer" as published by the American Cancer Society. If you have diabetes, you should learn as much as you can about your disease (with the aid of your doctor, among other sources such as the Diabetes Association). *This is not the same as self diagnosis*, which is never a good idea. But the more you know, the better able you will be to judge the quality of your care.

Notice the way in which your doctor answers your questions Your doctor's ability to answer your questions in a direct and understandable way, can give you a good idea as to how much he or she really knows about what is going on. Of course, that is not to say that the answer will always be known instantly or that the answer will always be known. But that is to say that if the answer isn't known, your doctor can tell you why and/or can tell you the steps he or she can take to find out, ranging from referring you to a sub-specialist, to consulting the books or performing more tests.

Be Aware of Your Doctor's Attitude If your doctor resents your involvement with your own care, if he or she becomes angry or agitated at the thought of a second opinion, if your doctor doesn't seem to think you or your problems are important, you may have the wrong doctor.

Be Aware of Your Health The reason you pay doctors to treat you is to help you maintain good health or to seek assistance for medical problems that may arise. If you are unhappy with the way the course of your health seems to be going, it may not be a problem with your doctor, but then again, it might be. So, if you find that you are having unanticipated setbacks, new problems that your doctor didn't warn you about or if your health simply is not improving despite your doctor's best efforts, you may wish to discuss the matter with your doctor and see if another approach or the involvement of another physician, is warranted.

Be Aware of Your Doctor If your doctor is frequently unavailable to you or seems to be under emotional distress or seems to be frequently ill, you may not be receiving optimum care.

Listen To Your "Inner Voice" Sometimes we just "have a feeling" when things are not right. Call it instinct, call it your guardian angel, call it Fred for all we care, if you feel things are not the way they should be, don't ignore yourself! At such times dig deeper into the cause of your discomfort. Discuss it with your doctor. Solicit a second opinion. In other words, respect yourself enough to be willing to walk the extra mile to make sure you are being well cared for.

Explore Alternative Health Care More and more people are exploring alternatives to traditional medical care. If you choose to join this group, be careful and research alternative therapies very carefully before you accept treatment. You should also discuss the issue with your doctor. A useful book on this subject is *The Other Medicines*, by Richard Grossman (1985, Doubleday, N.Y.)

What to Do If You Are Unhappy With Your Doctor

The last thing any patient wants is to be unhappy with their own doctor. After all, it's bad enough to have a health problem but to come to realize that your "knight in shining armor's" armor is tarnished, well that is a prescription for being unhappy, indeed.

If you find yourself in that miserable circumstance, don't allow yourself to become paralyzed with fear and anguish. Take action to protect yourself!

Talk To Your Doctor The key to solving any problem is communication; communication that is forthright and honest. Thus, the first step to solving your problem is to schedule a meeting with your doctor to "clear the air." When you meet with your doctor to discuss your unhappiness, be sure to:

•*Prepare for the meeting* When you are talking about any important issue, it is always a good idea to write down what you want to talk about ahead of time so that you will not forget in the heat of the moment or because you get nervous or your doctor gets defensive.

•*Be specific* Your doctor cannot correct the problem or help you to understand that there is not a problem, if he or she doesn't know exactly what the trouble is from your point of view.

•*Avoid emotionalism* This isn't easy. After all, it is your health and thus, your happiness, you will be talking about. But by staying calm and reasonable, you will be better able to communicate, which, as we said, is the key to solving your difficulty.

•*Write down what you are told* Write down what your doctor tells you. Remember, you are dealing in matters of great concern about which you may have little or no training. Thus, you will want to be able to digest what your doctor tells you and perhaps investigate it further.

•*Get a second opinion* If the dispute concerned the quality of your care or diagnosis, after having listened to the doctor, get a second opinion. As we have discussed, no doctor should ever be offended if you want a second opinion, and you will undoubtedly feel better if an independent voice verifies the correctness of your doctor's approach. If the second opinion conflicts with what your doctor told you, sit down and discuss it with him or her and see if a new approach is the way to go.

Change Doctors Only you can decide when and if the time has come to change doctors. Maybe you aren't getting well. Maybe you don't feel you are being treated with the courtesy you deserve. Maybe your doctor has too many other patients to give you adequate attention. Whatever the reason, if you believe the time has come to find new blood to handle your health care, keep the following in mind:

•*Maintain continuity of care* Never fire your old doctor until you have found another one to take his or her place, especially if you are suffering from an illness or condition that requires ongoing care. Failure to maintain **continuity of care** could cause you to have a problem without a doctor 'on call' to handle it.

•*Choose your new doctor well* If you are changing once, you do not want to have to do it again. So, take your time and choose your new doctor carefully. After all, you want the best health care available and you are the one responsible for finding it. Do your job right and you should be able to avoid an unpleasant *deja vu*.

•*Have your medical records forwarded* Your new doctor will need a complete record of your medical history. The two may also have to consult with each other so that the new doctor can get up to speed on your case. Thus, don't hesitate to give him or her your former doctor's name, address and phone number so that can be accomplished.

•*Tell your old doctor why you left* While your relationship with your physician is not a personal one but is professional, there are very real intimate and personal aspects to it. As a matter of courtesy, politely explain to your old doctor, by mail if you wish, why you felt a change was necessary.

Report Your Doctor If you believe your doctor has acted unethically, report your doctor to the State Medical Examiner's Office. The following are some of the things that can get your doctor in hot water with the medical licensing authorities:

•Incompetence
•Gross Negligence
•Repeated Negligent Acts
•Falsifying Medical Records (yes, it does happen)
•Mental or physical illness which substantially impairs the doctor's ability to practice medicine
•Prescribing dangerous drugs without a medical exam
•Intoxication while attending a patient
•Abuse of drugs or alcohol

> **CONSUMER ALERT: IDEALLY, YOUR STATE MEDICAL BOARD SHOULD BE IN THE BUSINESS OF PROTECTING THE PUBLIC AGAINST THE BAD APPLES IN THE MEDICAL COMMUNITY BARREL. UNFORTUNATELY, THESE AGENCIES ARE OFTEN UNDERFUNDED, BOGGED DOWN IN BUREAUCRATIC DELAYS AND ARE OTHERWISE INEFFECTIVE.**

You can also complain about a doctor to local medical associations and hospitals where he or she is on staff, your health insurance company (asking them to stop payment) or your doctor's medical group. (Complaints to the medical board, hospitals and group all have the potential to impact the doctor's livelihood, so be sure you are accurate in what you say and be sure you have as much evidence as you can to support your side of the story.)

Sue Your Doctor If your doctor's care falls beneath the standards of care in the local medical community and if that deficient treatment injured you, you can sue for malpractice. Do not take this step lightly. It will be a grueling and difficult process where you may feel like a loser even if you win.

> **CONSUMER ALERT: MANY STATES HAVE RESTRICTED YOUR RIGHT TO BRING MALPRACTICE SUITS AND HAVE THROWN TECHNICAL LEGAL REQUIREMENTS IN YOUR WAY OF DOING SO. THUS, IF YOU BELIEVE YOU HAVE A MALPRACTICE CASE, BE SURE TO CONSULT A LAWYER WHO IS EXPERIENCED IN**

THE FIELD, AND DO IT SOONER RATHER THAN LATER, SINCE SOME OF THE TECHNICALITIES HAVE TO DO WITH THE PASSAGE OF TIME.

HOSPITALS

No one likes to have to be admitted to a hospital. After all, what fun is it to wear gowns which are drafty in the rear? But for most of us, sooner or later that day arrives when we or a loved one must do so because of illness, the need for surgery or for extensive medical testing.

If you are like a lot of consumers, you may feel you have little or no consumer power when it comes to hospitals. Not so. It just takes some know-how and a measure of assertiveness in order to choose the right hospital for you and to make sure that you have the best stay possible under your individual circumstances.

When you choose a hospital, look for two basic criteria; medical excellence and the quality of the hotel function.

Medical Excellence

Receiving top-notch medical care is obviously the most important aspect of your hospital stay. Included in the concept of medical excellence are:

•The equipment, personnel and facilities to treat the problem presented;

•The ability to deal with any complications that may arise; and

•Sanitary conditions that effectively prevent secondary problems, such as staph infections, from arising.

The Hotel Function

Comfort and pleasantness of surroundings are also important considerations, although usually less so than the quality of medical care provided. Are the rooms well lit and nicely decorated? Is the food nutritious? (Good hospital food, another oxymoron.) In other words, is the facility managed in such a fashion that you or your hospitalized loved one will be made as comfortable as possible under the medical circumstances?

It is your job as a patient to select, and the obligation of your doctor to recommend, a hospital that best combines the hotel and medical functions to best meet your specific needs. For example, if you are undergoing major surgery, the quality of the intensive care unit will count for far more than whether the hospital serves steak tartar.

Choosing a Hospital

Most people go to the hospital recommended by their doctor. This is fine, so long as the reason for the hospitalization is that the *hospital selected is the best one to care for your particular problem.*

Before agreeing to a particular hospital, you are well advised to ask questions.

We don't mean to nag but asking questions is a very important part of effective consumerism. That is how you know the score and equally important, how you let others know you know the score. Some of the questions to ask your doctor about the hospital(s) recommended to you are:

Why this particular hospital over all of the others? Your doctor should be able to give you a more intelligent answer than, "Because."

What is your personal experience with this hospital that makes you believe it is the right choice? Hopefully, the answer will allude to the quality of the nursing staff or the excellence of post-operative care.

Does this hospital have what it takes to care for me if things go wrong? More than one patient has been admitted to one hospital only to have to be transferred to another by ambulance when complications arise. One way to avoid this problem is to make sure that the hospital can handle whatever crisis may come along or can transport you to an appropriate hospital promptly.

Does the hospital have a problem with hospital acquired infection? Unfortunately, a problem exists in some hospitals concerning patients becoming ill due to exposure to infectious agents while hospitalized. Thus, this is a very important question to ask about the hospital. After all, who wants to be in a hospital that makes you sick instead of helping you get better?

Research the Hospital

You should not view your hospital choice as selecting a "pig in a poke." There are ways to look into the quality of care offered at each hospital in your community:

Find out what the JCAH rating is. JCAH stands for *Joint Commission on the Accreditation of Hospitals*. The sole purpose of this commission is to encourage and enforce the attainment of uniformly high standards of institutional medical care. They do this by periodically inspecting each hospital and then issuing a report which describes the good, the bad and the ugly aspects of care in the facility. The JCAH will give an accreditation ranging from three years (best) to probation. The report is a public document and you have the right to, and should, ask to read it or have it explained to you. We note, however, that some consumer activists contend that JCAH is often not as tough as its stated goals.

Contact your State Department of Health. If an unhappy consumer complains about a hospital to the state Department of Health, generally the agency will conduct an investigation to see whether the complaint has merit, and if it does, will require that corrective measures be taken. As an informed health care consumer, you should contact your health department and ask what they can tell you about the hospital(s) you are considering. (NOTE: The Department of Health is a licensing public agency while the JCAH is a private accrediting commission.)

Ask your friends. If you have had friends, acquaintances or relatives who have been hospitalized in the hospital(s) you are considering for your own hospital stay, ask them if they were pleased or displeased with the quality of their care and the comfort of the facility.

Inspect the Hospital

If a doctor you trust has recommended a hospital, there is full JCAH accreditation and the health department has had no major complaints, there is only one other thing you can do to protect yourself - take a tour and inspect the facility for yourself.

Walking through the hospital will give you a pretty good idea about how the place really operates when no big wigs from the JCAH or heath department are expected. Look to see if the halls are clean. Do the nurses seem frazzled and overworked or calm and in control? Is the atmosphere one of quiet and friendly competence or can you cut the hostility with a scalpel. Is the place quiet and conducive to healing and recovery? As they say, a picture is worth a thousand words.

**CONSUMER ALERT: BEFORE AGREEING TO A HOSPITALIZA-
TION IN ANY FACILITY, CHECK YOUR HEALTH INSURANCE
POLICY! MANY POLICIES COMPEL YOU TO GO TO PARTICU-
LAR HOSPITALS IN YOUR COMMUNITY IN ORDER FOR YOU TO
RECEIVE FULL HEALTH INSURANCE BENEFITS. THUS, GOING
TO AN UNAPPROVED HOSPITAL (IN A NONEMERGENCY) *CAN
COST YOU A LOT OF MONEY!***

Your Rights as a Patient

People frequently feel powerless when they are flat on their back or in a wheel chair while confined in a hospital. Happily, you have rights as a patient when you are hospitalized, thanks in large part to years of effort put in by health care consumer advocates.

The following is a list of patient rights. In many states most or all of these have been codified into state law:

•You have the right to exercise your rights without regard to sex or cultural, economic, educational or religious background or the source of payment for your care.

•You have the right to be treated with respect and consideration by all hospital personnel.

•You have the right to know the name of the physician who is in charge of coordinating your care (known as the attending physician) and the names and professional relationships of other physicians who will consult with the attending physician. (Often the attending physician will be your own doctor).

•You have the right to receive from your attending physician, information about your illness or malady, course of treatment and prospects for recovery, *all in terms you can understand*.

•You have the right to give your informed consent or to make an informed rejection of treatment and to otherwise actively participate in your own medical care.

•You have the right to privacy and the right to be told the reason that any individual might be present during your treatment or care.

•You have the right to reasonable compliance with requests you make for service.

•You have the right to leave the hospital at any time, even against the advice of your physician (known as a discharge against medical advice).

•You have the right to continuity of care.

•You have the right to be advised if your care will be given in conjunction with a medical research project and to refuse to participate in the experimental care, if you so desire.

•You have the right to know how to best continue your health care after your discharge.

•You have the right to a clear, easy-to-understand, detailed bill, regardless of the source of payment, and a detailed explanation thereof. (More on that below.)

•You have the right to know the rules and hospital policies that apply to your conduct as a patient.

Of course, knowing what your rights are and enforcing them may seem to be two different things. But it's not so tough. Just follow these simple suggestions:

•Choose a friend or family member to serve as your personal advocate When you are hospitalized, you are often too sick or have too little energy to be able to put your best foot forward in protecting your rights and making sure you get the optimum in service and care. Thus, we suggest that you designate a friend or relative as your standard bearer for you. Introduce this person to your doctor and the nurses and let them know that he or she will be serving as your liaison regarding issues of comfort and quality of care.

•*Confront the person causing the problem* If there is an individual who you are unsatisfied with, before making a major case out of the problem, either talk or have your personal advocate talk with him or her to see if the problem can be straightened out.

•*Go to the Nursing Supervisor* If one-on-one discussion doesn't turn the trick, ask to see the nursing supervisor. He or she should be able to handle most any difficulty that may have arisen.

•*Contact the administration* If you still have not been able to achieve satisfaction with your problem, go right to the administration.

•*Bring your doctor into the act* If you need to and if the problem concerns the quality of the medical care you are receiving, call in the big gun - your doctor. The hospital will care very much about what your physician thinks since they need him or her to hospitalize patients in the facility in order to make money. Thus, if your doctor complains, to paraphrase the old commercial, the administration listens.

•*Appeal to the Director of Medicine* If two doctors disagree on your course of treatment, bring in the hospital's director of medicine to sort out the dispute.

Reviewing Your Hospital Bill

The day finally arrives. You finally get to do that one thing you have wanted to ever since you were admitted to the hospital - you get to leave it. Free at last, free at last, thank God almighty, you're free at last!

But are you? There's still one small matter to attend to: the bill.

Did we say "small?" Well, that's not really the right word to use when describing a hospital bill. "Huge" comes to mind. So does "outrageous" and "exorbitant." One day in a semi - private room costs hundreds of dollars. And if you have to stay in more "deluxe" accommodations such as the intensive care unit, then you are going to know what financial hemorrhage is all about.

What your bill includes Your basic room rate includes one hospital bed, a night stand, a television (usually), three meals a day, basic nursing services and housekeeping. That's just about it.

What isn't included in your bill Reread the passage directly above. Virtually everything else provided by the hospital and which are not set forth in "what your bill includes" - those things you have to pay for the use of separately. Items such as aspirin, (sold by the pill), oxygen, bandages, monitoring equipment usage, these items and more get billed in addition to your daily standard rate. As any of you who have been hospitalized know, these "optional extras" make the price of your hospital stay add up fast.

Keeping from being overcharged You will usually receive your hospital bill a few days after your discharge. (Obviously, you will want to make sure your health insurance has been sent a copy so they can pay their fair share. This will have been arranged when you were admitted.)

Before he founded Voter Revolt and wrote Proposition 103 in California, Harvey Rosenfield started a project in affiliation with Ralph Nader, called "The Bills Project." (Contact The Bills Project at P.O. Box 1736, Santa Monica, CA, 90406.) This worthwhile endeavor researches ways in which consumers are overcharged. According to Rosenfield's research, there are six areas in which hospitals are likely to overcharge their patients. Be on the lookout for the following:

•*Indecipherable bills* Some hospitals send bills which itemize by computer number rather than listing the service or product. Since you cannot possibly know what the computer numbers mean, you cannot have any idea what and why you were charge. Also, look out for the infamous "Miscellaneous" charge.

•*Unitemized bills* You are entitled to know the basis of all charges made on your bill. This is basic to being able to determine whether the bill is accurate. If you get a bill that merely charges you "$44,550 for hospital stay June 1-13," (or for a too-general category within a bill) complain loudly and clearly!

•*Overcharging* If you have been billed for an item in an amount that you think is in excess of its value, speak up. After all, it's one thing to pay one dollar for two aspirin, but six?! (Yes, it has happened.) Of course, you may not know what the fair market value of a product or service actually is, but the only way to know if you have been overcharged is to ask.

•*Billing Fees* Some hospitals actually have the gall to bill you for preparing your bill! Talk about adding insult to injury! In our opinion, if a charge is found on the bill for "processing fee" or "handling expense," make a fuss. Adding up your bill should be part of the hospital's overhead expenses which your daily room rate should have already covered.

•*Mistakes* When you receive a bill that is twenty pages long, and your eyes glaze over, it is difficult to find errors in your bill. But, the bill was prepared by human hands and thus mistakes can happen. For example, you might find a bill for an EKG that you did not receive or you might be charged twice for the same service or product. So, take the time to review the bill. It could save you money. You should also send the bill to your insurance company for review.

•*Interest Charges on Mistakes* On occasion, when hospitals correct errors in their billing, they will continue to charge you interest on the unpaid balance, even if the mistake was their fault. This is a big "no, no." Thus, when you have errors corrected, make sure that any interest charges on the bill charged against your account for money you did not, in fact, owe, are also removed from your bill.

If you believe that there is a billing error on your hospital statement, we have two key words for you, words that could save you a lot of money - CHART AUDIT. A chart audit involves a line by line comparison of your bill with your actual medical chart. Thus, if you are charged for a service that your chart shows was not performed, that item will be taken off of your bill.

Of course, mistakes will never be caught if you don't ask that corrections be made. As with all business transactions, such requests are best done in writing. Here's a sample letter you can use:

MAY 23, 1992

HIGH ROLLER MEMORIAL HOSPITAL
ATTN: PATIENT ACCOUNT REPRESENTATIVE
3333 COSTS ALOT LANE
PAYMUCH, WYOMING 44444

RE: ACCOUNT NUMBER 43567 - I. M. FRUGAL

DEAR SIR OR MADAM:

I WAS HOSPITALIZED IN YOUR INSTITUTION FROM MAY 8, 1992 - MAY 13. MY ATTENDING PHYSICIAN WAS DR. BERNARD SHOTGIVER. I WAS ALSO SEEN BY A CONSULTING DOCTOR, MARY STETHOSCOPE, CONCERNING AN INFECTIOUS PROBLEM.

I RECEIVED MY HOSPITAL STATEMENT ON MAY 18. UNFORTUNATELY, I BELIEVE I HAVE FOUND SEVERAL ERRORS THAT I WOULD LIKE YOU TO CORRECT. THEY ARE AS FOLLOWS:

MAY 8 - $55 FOR EKG. I HAD AN EKG AT MY DOCTOR'S OFFICE BEFORE MY ADMISSION AND HE HAS BILLED ME FOR IT. I DO NOT BELIEVE THAT THE HOSPITAL ADMINISTERED ONE TO ME.

MAY 10 - OXYGEN. I WAS NEVER GIVEN OXYGEN. I DID NOTICE THAT THERE WAS OXYGEN IN MY ROOM BUT IT WAS ALREADY THERE WHEN I WAS ADMITTED.

MAY 10 - $15 FOR ASPIRIN. I TOOK TWO ASPIRIN THAT DAY FOR A HEADACHE. I CANNOT BELIEVE THAT THEY COST $7.50 APIECE.

MAY 13 - WHEELCHAIR RENTAL - $25. I WAS WHEELED OUT OF THE HOSPITAL BUT AM I SUPPOSED TO BE CHARGED FOR THIS SERVICE?

MAY 13 - MISCELLANEOUS - $125 I CANNOT PAY FOR A CHARGE THAT I DO NOT UNDERSTAND. PLEASE SPECIFY WHAT PRODUCT OR SERVICE THIS IS TO PAY FOR.

WOULD YOU PLEASE CONDUCT A CHART AUDIT ON MY FILE AND ADVISE ME IN WRITING AS TO THE RESULTS. AND PLEASE REVERSE ANY INTEREST CHARGES THAT HAVE ACCRUED ON ANY INCORRECT BILLINGS THAT MAY BE DETERMINED.

THANK YOU FOR YOUR COOPERATION. YOU HAVE A VERY NICE HOSPITAL.

VERY TRULY YOURS,

I. M. FRUGAL

CC: TO YOUR HEALTH INSURANCE COMPANY

CONSUMER ALERT: THERE IS A BOOK THAT IS AN INVALU-ABLE SOURCE OF CONSUMER EMPOWERMENT FOR THOSE WHO ARE GOING TO BE HOSPITALIZED. ITS TITLE IS *TAKE THIS BOOK TO THE HOSPITAL WITH YOU* (1985 RODALE PRESS,

EMMAUS, PENNSYLVANIA) IT WAS WRITTEN BY CHARLES B. INLANDER, (THE EXECUTIVE DIRECTOR OF THE PEOPLE'S MEDICAL SOCIETY) AND ED WEINER.

HEALTH INSURANCE

A discussion of doctors and our medical system would not be complete without at least a brief description of the important issues surrounding health insurance. An unfortunate truism in the United States is that those without adequate health insurance frequently receive, almost by definition, inadequate health care.

There are three basic types of health insurance in the country; fee for service, health maintenance organization and government benefits.

Fee For Service Health Insurance

Most people are familiar with fee-for-service insurance. There are three basic parts to a traditional health insurance policy: Surgical/Medical, Hospitalization and Major Medical. *Surgical Medical* Surgical/medical portions of your health insurance will typically pay for treatment you receive in a doctor's office and for surgical procedures. Here's how it usually works:

•There is **a deductible**: A deductible is the money you pay up front before insurance benefits are owed. In traditional health insurance, the deductible is usually based on a calendar year and will run anywhere from $100 - $1,000. The higher the deductible, the lower your premium should be so if you find that you are paying too much for health insurance, investigate this way of saving premium dollars.

•You will owe a **copayment**. A copayment is the percentage of the doctor's bill that you pay. Typically, you will pay 20 percent and the health insurance will pay 80 percent, although those numbers are certainly not carved in stone. There will usually be a cap on your copayment obligation. If, for example, your cap is $5,000 per calendar year, then after that amount has been paid by you, the insurance company covers the rest of the year's bills in full.

CONSUMER ALERT: OFTEN, HEALTH INSURANCE COMPANIES PAY LESS THAN THEIR FULL OBLIGATION OF THE AMOUNT BILLED BY YOUR DOCTOR. THE WAY THEY DO THIS IS TO PROMISE TO PAY THE "USUAL, CUSTOMARY AND REASONABLE" CHARGES THAT ARE BILLED. OFTEN, WHAT THE DOCTOR CHARGES AND WHAT THE INSURANCE COMPANY CONTENDS ARE USUAL, CUSTOMARY AND REASONABLE ARE TWO VERY DIFFERENT THINGS, WHICH COULD RESULT IN YOUR PAYING MORE. SOME POLICIES EVEN ALLOW THE INSURANCE COMPANY TO JUDGE THE "APPROPRIATENESS OF CARE" AFTER THE FACT. IN THESE CASES, IF THE COMPANY DOES NOT BELIEVE THE CARE YOU RECEIVED WAS APPROPRIATE, THEY MAY REFUSE TO PAY ANY BENEFITS AT ALL.

ONE WAY AROUND THIS DILEMMA IS TO ASK THE DOCTOR TO ACCEPT WHAT THE INSURANCE COMPANY DEEMS A REASONABLE FEE AS THE FEE THAT YOU WILL BE CHARGED. ANOTHER IS TO ASK THE DOCTOR TO ACCEPT MONTHLY PAYMENTS FOR THE AMOUNT YOU OWE.

Cost containment provisions to watch out for Most fee for service health policies contain provisions that restrict their benefits if you don't "follow the rules." The most common of these rules are the following:

•*Same day admission for surgery* Presidents and members of Congress still have the luxury of going into the hospital the night before surgery. Often, you do not. Thus, if your policy requires admission into the hospital on the morning of surgery and you go in the night before, the first day's payment may be on you.

•*Pre-admission testing* It is less expensive for the insurance company if tests that must be taken before admission to a hospital are made on an outpatient basis. As a result, most policies now require you to undergo pre-admission testing in non-emergency situations.

•*Outpatient surgery* There is a growing trend for insurance companies to insist that minor surgeries be performed on an outpatient basis. This means that all recovery is done at home.

•*Second opinion requirements* In nonemergency situations, many insurance companies require you to get a second opinion before submitting to surgery in order for you to receive full benefits. Since studies have found that many surgeries are unnecessary (particularly hysterectomies and caesarean sections), being forced to get a second opinion may do you a very big favor, in addition to saving you and the insurance company some money.

•*Incomplete coverage for preventive care* One of the down sides of traditional health insurance is that it often does not cover the preventive medical care that everyone needs to pursue in order to avoid serious illness or catch potentially life threatening conditions such as cancer, while they are still "young" and thus more susceptible to treatment. Thus, routine physicals, mammograms, cholesterol screening, pap smears and other such procedures are often not covered.

Hospitalization The hospitalization portion of your traditional health insurance is designed to pay for hospital services, such as a semi-private room, the use of the surgical suite, outpatient services and the like.

Most hospitalization plans pay for most of the usual services rendered by hospitals. However, you, as an alert consumer, will want to watch out for the following limitations which could end up costing you a lot of money:

•*Indemnity plans* An indemnity plan is one that pays a specific amount of money per day. These kinds of plans are usually not that comprehensive and often don't pay a large percentage of the total bill. Of course, they are usually cheaper to purchase but the coverage is almost always inadequate.

•*Waiting periods* If your hospitalization plan requires a waiting period before coverage begins, you could end up in big financial trouble. Most hospital stays are relatively short and they have become even shorter in recent years thanks to insurance company pressure to keep costs down. Thus, if your policy contains a three-day waiting period and you are in the hospital for four days, you will receive only one day's worth of benefits.

•*Short periods of coverage* At the other end of the hospitalization spectrum are policies that cover only brief periods of hospitalization. These policies are dangerous because they do not protect you against worst case scenarios.

•*Maximum payments that are too low* Some policies are deceptive in their appearance. On one hand they will set a seemingly high maximum number of days permitted to be paid under the policy. Then, on the other, they limit their maximum financial exposure to $10,000 or $25,000. Talk about giving with one hand and taking away with the other! If you have a policy such as this, you are very poorly protected against catastrophic needs.

Restricted payment for specialty care Specialty care might be an intensive care unit or a rehabilitation unit or other such venue of specialty care. In these settings the patient receives a lot of attention, attention that could mean the difference between a life and death or quality and despair. This intensity of treatment comes at a cost: frequently double the hospital's normal daily charge. If your policy restricts payments for specialty care, you may find your pocketbook in need of an intensive care unit.

Limitations on hospitals Many hospitalization policies now require you to be hospitalized at a specifically identified hospital that has contracted with the health insurance company to provide care for you at reduced rates. These hospitals are called **contract hospitals** and failure to use them for your nonemergency hospital needs may be hazardous to your finances since your hospitalization benefits would be substantially reduced.

Prior consent for hospitalization Some policies will not pay full benefits for hospitalization unless the insurance company agrees ahead of time that it is required under the circumstances (in nonemergency situations).

CONSUMER ALERT: USUALLY THERE WILL BE MORE THAN ONE CONTRACT HOSPITAL IN YOUR COMMUNITY. THUS, YOU SHOULD STILL GO THROUGH THE PROCESS OF INVESTIGATING WHICH HOSPITAL TO GO TO, EVEN THOUGH THE NUMBER OF HOSPITALS YOU CAN CHOOSE FROM MAY BE LIMITED BECAUSE OF YOUR HEALTH INSURANCE POLICY.

CONSUMER ALERT: THE NEW COST CONTAINMENT SCHEME IS "MANAGED CARE" WHERE YOU HAVE TO GET PRIOR PERMISSION FOR MUCH OF YOUR MEDICAL CARE IN ORDER TO RECEIVE FULL BENEFITS. IF YOUR HEALTH INSURANCE USES THIS PROCESS BE VERY SURE YOU UNDERSTAND THE PROCEDURE AND FOLLOW DIRECTIONS WITH REGARD TO CONSULTATION WITH THE INSURANCE COMPANY.

Major Medical Another key element of a good overall health insurance protection package is that part which protects you from the incredibly high cost of treating catastrophic illness or injury. Major medical coverage, as it is usually called, is designed to supplement your basic medical/surgical and hospitalization coverage in order to pay for just about everything you will need should you be hit hard with a long term or truly serious medical condition. The benefits provided by major medical include:
•A high total benefit package
•Extended hospital stays
•Extended periods of in-home care
•Durable medical equipment benefits
•Skilled nursing home care
•Prescription costs

CONSUMER ALERT: SUZIE MATZ, A REGISTERED NURSE WHO WORKS AS DISCHARGE COORDINATOR FOR A REHABILITATION CENTER IN CALIFORNIA, SAYS THAT THE MAJOR MEDICAL PORTION OF YOUR HEALTH INSURANCE POLICY MAY BE THE MOST IMPORTANT OF ALL. SHE KNOWS, SINCE SHE MUST DEAL WITH PATIENTS REQUIRING CATASTROPHIC CARE EV-

ERY WORK DAY. SHE SAYS THAT IN THE EVENT YOU ARE SERIOUSLY INJURED AND WITHOUT MAJOR MEDICAL PROTECTION:

1) THE DAYS YOU CAN SPEND IN REHABILITATION MAY BE LESS THAN YOU WOULD NEED TO HELP YOU WITH YOUR PARTICULAR PROBLEM.

2) YOU MAY BE UNABLE TO AFFORD EXPENSIVE HIGH TECH DURABLE MEDICAL EQUIPMENT, SUCH AS ELECTRONIC WHEEL CHAIRS AND EQUIPMENT TO ASSIST YOU WITH PERSONAL HYGIENE.

3) THE ALL IMPORTANT PHARMACEUTICALS WHICH HELP MAKE LIFE WORTH LIVING AND WHICH A CATASTROPHICALLY ILL OR INJURED PERSON CANNOT LIVE INDEPENDENTLY WITHOUT.

4) IN HOME THERAPY, OUTPATIENT THERAPY, ATTENDANT CARE AND OTHER HUMAN SERVICES MAY HAVE TO BE DONE WITHOUT.

SO DON'T BE PENNY WISE AND POUND FOOLISH. GET A MAJOR MEDICAL POLICY IF YOU CAN AFFORD THE PREMIUMS.

Health Maintenance Organizations

Health maintenance organizations (HMOs) are gaining in popularity as the years go on and the cost of health insurance rises. The point of an HMO is to provide you with all of the necessary medical services you need in a way that controls costs so that your premium can remain at a reasonable level.

In a sense, HMOs are a form of socialized medicine, capitalism style. In socialized medicine, taxes help pay for the cost of all citizens' health care. Beyond the money paid to the government (which can be quite a chunk), there are few health care costs that have to be paid out of the citizen's personal pocket. In theory, this takes care of all of the important health needs of the populace.

This is similar to the way an HMO operates. Instead of the government, you (or your employer in the case of group plans paid as a benefit of employment) pay the tab directly to the HMO (which may be profit or nonprofit). In return, all of your health care needs are taken care of by the HMO at little or no extra cost to you. Thus, you need not worry about deductibles, significant copayments and the like. *This control of extra out of pocket expenses is one of the chief benefits of HMO membership.*

"Sounds good," you say, "but what's the catch?" Well, yes, there is a catch. You give up freedom of choice. You are limited as to which doctors and/or hospitals you can use for your heath care, that is, *you are only allowed to use the doctors and facilities authorized by the HMO*, or you receive no health insurance benefits (except in life threatening emergencies).

This lack of choice can cause problems. While most HMOs have a wide selection of primary care physicians, they usually have far fewer subspecialists who are authorized to handle specialized care (meaning that the subspecialist may not be the best one in the community) and it may be difficult to get your doctor and/or plan to authorize a referral due to the efforts to keep such extra treatment costs at a minimum. (Cost containment efforts sometimes pressure doctors to keep costs low, it is alleged, at the expense of the patient.) In addition, you only can use HMO authorized or operated hospitals.

HMOs put heavy emphasis on cost cutting because their profits or financial viability come from doing less rather than more. Some HMO members complain that this makes it more difficult to receive all of the care required, especially in out of the ordinary matters. On the other hand, HMOs provide coverage for preventive care not usually paid for by standard health insurance which may help you avoid that unusual illness or condition in the first place.

There are three types of HMOs:

The IPA (Independent Physician Association) model An IPA is a group of doctors who, for the limited purpose of working as part of an HMO medical plan, form a legal entity that contracts with the HMO to provide covered services. In other words, doctors who are in private practice and who handle traditional fee for service patients, may also be a part of an HMO. The HMO will also contract with local hospitals to care for plan members. The plan member can only use doctors or hospitals listed as approved by the HMO, but they generally go to a doctor's private offices just as they would if they were insured by traditional health plans.

The group model For you history buffs, the first group model HMO was established in 1929 at a cooperatively owned hospital in Elk City, Oklahoma by Dr. Michael Shadid. However, the most famous group model is probably Kaiser/Permanente, located in California and several other states. Group model HMOs are essentially partnerships among the Medical Plan, a large number of doctors who limit their practice to work within the HMO and sometimes hospitals (as with Kaiser) who restrict their services to plan members (except in life threatening emergencies). In a group model, the medical plan will only refer you to doctors and hospitals that are part of the group. The doctors will work in Plan clinics and hospitals rather than a private office. (Sometimes, this can present a problem of convenience if it is a long distance between your home and the HMO clinic or hospital).

Staff model HMOs In a staff HMO, the doctors are not equal partners of the Medical Plan, but employees of it. This means the plan has a lot of power (the inherent power of an employer) over how patients are treated. Most treatment in a staff model HMO is performed at Plan owned clinics and/or hospitals. As employees, the doctors cannot generally have private practices beyond the work they perform for the HMO.

HMOs continue to be controversial. Here is a brief "pros and cons" summary of HMOs.

PRO:

Lower premiums. As stated, HMOs generally charge less for their coverage than do traditional health insurance policies.

No copayments or deductibles. This allows you to limit your out of pocket medical costs to a degree not possible in traditional health insurance plans.

Prescriptions are paid. Usually, HMO members do not have to pay for prescription medicine or, if they do, the expense is a nominal sum. The same cannot always be said for traditional fee-for-service health insurance.

You can choose your own primary care physician. While your choice of doctors will be limited to those authorized by the HMO, there are usually enough authorized doctors on their list to enable you to choose a good PCP.

Preventive health care is covered. Unlike fee for service policies, basic life saving preventive health care is covered by an HMO.

Your records are always available in group and staff model HMOs. Because doctors at group and staff HMOs take care of their patients from the HMO facility itself, the patient's records will always be available quickly, even when the patient's PCP may not be.

CON:

Insufficient testing. Some plan members complain that it is hard to get the HMO to adequately test them regarding their health care complaints. (Of course, traditional health insurance companies complain that doctors order too much testing!)

Difficulty in getting nonplan emergency room treatment. If you have a sudden onset of a medical problem, your first instinct is to "get thee to the nearest emergency room." However, if you are an HMO member and the nearest emergency room is not an authorized hospital, you could have to wait long periods to get authority for treatment (agreement by the plan to pay the emergency room), which is often refused in non-life threatening circumstances.

Difficulty in getting authorization for treatment outside the plan area. As of the date of this writing, there is no national HMO. That can present problems for you if you travel outside of your community, where authorization for treatment may be slow in coming or difficult to obtain at all in non-life threatening circumstances.

Difficulty in getting specialists. If you have a medical condition that requires a specialist, you may have difficulty getting a referral. You may also find that you are not allowed the best specialist that money can buy because he or she may not be part of the list of authorized physicians. (This can create a conflict between a plan member and an administrator that may cause the member to seek help elsewhere and pay for it him or herself.)

You may have to change doctors if you join an HMO. If you change from one fee for service insurance company to another, chances are you will not have to change doctors. However, you will have to change doctors if you join a staff or group model HMO (and may if you join an IPA model). This could force you to leave a doctor who you are very happy with and who knows your body, for one that, will take time to know you and your individual health quirks.

The decision as to whether an HMO or traditional health insurance plan is best for you is, well, up to you. Each person has their own individual health care needs and preferences. Studies seem to indicate a high level of satisfaction with HMOs by plan members. In fact over thirty million Americans are now serviced by over 600 different HMOs. On the other hand, there are increasing reports of dissatisfied HMO members complaining about poor quality control and we note that there have been some bankruptcies in the HMO industry. We can say that if you do decide to join an HMO, you should be prepared to be the squeaky wheel that gets the grease if you do not feel you are getting sufficient medical attention or proper HMO care.

CONSUMER ALERT: UNLIKE TRADITIONAL INSURANCE, THE STATE OVERSIGHT OF HMOS IS USUALLY CONDUCTED BY THE DEPARTMENT OF CORPORATIONS RATHER THAN THE DEPARTMENT OF INSURANCE.

Preferred Provider Organizations

Many of the traditional health insurance companies have responded to the high cost of medical care by creating a hybrid form of health insurance called a preferred provider organization (PPO).

A PPO works as follows: Your health insurance company, employer, union, or other deliverer of group health protection signs contracts with doctors, hospitals and other health service providers to supply health care at a discount rate. In return, the service providers receive monthly payments (called capitation) for each person serviced by the PPO. If the cost of care exceeds the capitation fee, the doctors will be paid extra money, usually at a discounted price.

That's nice, you say, but what is the bottom line to me? The answer: *less money out of your pocket*. The premiums are usually lower than traditional insurance. Moreover, if you use a PPO authorized physician or hospital, the health care provider will accept your insurance benefits as payment in full (after you have paid the deductible). On the other hand, using doctors or health care facilities that are not authorized by the PPO will cost you money because you will receive less in benefits (except in life threatening emergencies) and thus have a large copayment obligation.

> CONSUMER ALERT: ONE WAY TO SAVE MONEY ON HEALTH INSURANCE IS TO JOIN A GROUP THAT CAN NEGOTIATE FOR LOWER PRICES, OR, AS IN THE CASE OF MANY EMPLOYERS AND UNIONS, WILL PAY FOR THE ENTIRE INSURANCE PREMIUM. IF YOU ARE NOT COVERED BY A GROUP POLICY, SEE IF A PROFESSIONAL ASSOCIATION OR OTHER GROUP OFFERS A GROUP RATE AS ONE OF THE BENEFITS OF MEMBERSHIP. ALSO, LOOK FOR INSURANCE BROKERS WHO SOMETIMES BUY HMO MEMBERSHIPS AT DISCOUNT RATES AND WHO THEN SELL THEM TO YOU BELOW THE PRICE YOU COULD OBTAIN FROM THE HMO ITSELF.

Medicare

Medicare is a form of national health insurance offered by the government to senior citizens and others, such as those who are disabled and those with kidney failure.

Medicare comes in two parts, cleverly called "Part A" and "Part B." Here's how the two parts work:

Part A Part A protects Medicare recipients from the costs associated with hospitalization. Here are the important features of these important health benefits;

•*Coverage is free* If you are eligible for Medicare (age 65 and older and eligible for Social Security retirement benefits for most beneficiaries) you receive hospitalization without charge. (If you are age 65 and ineligible for Medicare, you can pay for Part A coverage, but it costs plenty).

•*What is covered* Medicare will pick up a large portion of your hospitalization expenses. There will be a deductible that changes from year to year. After you pay the deductible, days 1 - 60 are paid in full by Medicare. In days 61 - 90, you will have a considerable co-payment, which goes even higher between days 91 and 365. (Contact your Social Security office for the current amount of copayments after the first 60 days.) Part A also protects you for a limited time of skilled nursing home care, a brief period of home health benefits and hospice care (a truly excellent benefit for the terminally ill and their families). For more details contact your local Social Security office.

•*Beware of DRGs* One fly in the Part A ointment, is the Diagnosis Related Group program (DRGs) of cost containment. This program has doctors complaining that their patients are being forced to leave hospitals "sooner and sicker" than ever before.

DRGs allow Medicare to pay hospitals at a predetermined flat rate for illnesses based on the patient's diagnosis. For example, if you are hospitalized with an ailment that the requires an average of 5 days worth of hospital care to treat, then the hospital will receive payment for five days worth of care. This means, that the *hospital's financial benefit* requires that you leave the hospital as soon as is medically possible. Many claim that this financial incentive has hospitals planning the patient's discharge literally from the moment that the patient is admitted.

Defenders of the DRG system point out that the discharge date under the law is to be setermined on the basis of the Medicare recipient's medical needs alone and not on the amount the hospital receives in payment. That indeed, is the law. However, what is true ideally and in real life are often two different things altogether.

That being so, you need to know how to fight back if you feel as if you (or a loved one who is on Medicare) are receiving the bum's rush to leave the hospital. Remember:

•You do have the right to receive all of the hospitalization your condition requires.

•You do have the right to be fully informed about decisions affecting your Medicare coverage and your medical treatment. Get these decisions in writing whenever possible and get copies of your medical records if you believe a dispute concerning your hospitalization is brewing.

•You have the right to **appeal** written notices you receive from the hospital or Medicare stating that hospitalization will no longer be covered. If you decide to appeal, don't delay. You will be dealing with an entity called a Peer Review Organization that is charged with reviewing decisions regarding hospitalization coverage.

CONSUMER ALERT: IF YOU AND YOUR DOCTOR BELIEVE IT WILL HARM YOUR HEALTH TO LEAVE THE HOSPITAL, DO NOT LEAVE BUT APPEAL THE DECISION TO WITHDRAW COVERAGE FROM YOU. IF YOUR APPEAL IS SUCESSFUL, YOU WILL HAVE YOUR HOSPITALIZATION PAID FOR PURSUANT TO MEDICARE GUIDELINES. IF IT FAILS, YOU WILL HAVE TO PAY THE ADDITIONAL HOSPITALIZATION YOURSELF, BUT YOU WILL HAVE PROTECTED YOUR HEALTH.

CONSUMER ALERT: IF YOU ARE ASKED TO LEAVE THE HOSPITAL, BE SURE TO ASK YOUR DOCTOR TO PRESCRIBE IN-HOME HEALTH CARE IF IT IS MEDICALLY WARRANTED. THIS TOO, WILL BE COVERED BY MEDICARE FOR A TIME AND CAN MAKE A BIG DIFFERENCE IN THE QUALITY OF YOUR RECOVERY.

Part B This portion of Medicare is a voluntary major medical health insurance that is charged for, but the price is a very reasonable buy, indeed. Part B pays for services such as surgery, office visits, diagnostic testing and the use of durable medical equipment. Like fee for service health insurance, Medicare recipients pay a deductible and copayments (Medicare pays 80 percent and the patient 20 percent). Unfortunately, Medicare does not pay for most routine preventive treatment and there is usually no benefit for prescribed medications.

Payments to physicians under Part B are made on the basis of the "reasonable charge." Understanding this concept and using a physician who **accepts the assignment** of Medicare benefits is key to saving money on Medicare. Simply put, a doctor who accepts the assignment receives his or her payments directly from Medicare and in return, agrees to accept the amount Medicare states is a reasonable charge as the amount to be billed. A doctor who does not accept the assignment must bill the patient but the patient does not receive the cost control feature and can be charged what the market will bear.

CONSUMER ALERT: MEDICARE PUBLISHES A LIST OF MOST OF THE DOCTORS IN YOUR AREA WHO WILL ACCEPT THE ASSIGNMENT. THESE DOCTORS ARE KNOWN AS MEDICARE PARTICIPATING PHYSICIANS AND THE LIST IS CALLED THE *MEDICARE PARTICIPATING PHYSICIAN/SUPPLIER DIRECTORY*. IT IS AVAILABLE THROUGH MOST LOCAL SENIOR CITIZEN ORGANIZATIONS OR YOUR LOCAL SOCIAL SECURITY OFFICE.

Part B also covers services such as outpatient hospital care, ambulance services, durable medical equipment, administered drugs (as opposed to prescribed), outpatient therapy such as speech therapy and in limited circumstances, chiropractic care.

CONSUMER ALERT: BECAUSE MEDICARE DOES NOT TAKE CARE OF A LARGE CHUNK OF A SENIOR'S HEALTH CARE COSTS, IT IS A GOOD IDEA TO PURCHASE SUPPLEMENTAL INSURANCE KNOWN AS MEDI- GAP POLICIES. FOR THE LATEST INFORMATION ON MEDI- GAP INSURANCE, CONTACT YOUR LOCAL CHAPTER OF THE AMERICAN ASSOCIATION OF RETIRED PERSONS (AARP) OR YOUR LOCAL SOCIAL SECURITY OFFICE.

CONSUMERS' AGENDA

The health care delivery system in the United States is out of control. Costs are skyrocketing, 37 million people are without insurance at all and matters seem headed for worse times and not better. Clearly, something needs to be done.

We believe the answer is some form of national health insurance. Many people may not know it, but the United States is the only industrialized nation (other than South Africa) which does not provide health care for all of its citizens. Germany has it. Japan has it. France, Israel, Sweden, Finland, Holland and Belgium all have it. Our neighbor to the North, Canada, has it. Why not the United States?

There are several plans "on the drawing board" for some form of national health insurance in the United States. The American Medical Association and Senator Edward Kennedy (D-Massachusetts) envision a form of compulsory health insurance in which, employers would be compelled by law to provide adequate health coverage for all full time employees. State pools would be created to assist smaller businesses obtain group health insurance at reasonable rates. For those individuals not working or unqualified for employer provided insurance, the rules concerning Medicaid (a joint health program for the very poor funded by the Federal government and the states) would be standardized, providing for minimum benefits throughout the nation.

There are other proposals available too which are beyond the scope of this book. But there is one statement that is at the core of this book: get involved. This issue will not be placed on the front political burner if you don't take a stand.

You can also join or found local organizations such as the Champaign County Health Care Consumers Organization, which supports national health insurance and seeks to keep health care services in the local area working at an optimum level. The CCHCC believes in promoting collective action by citizens everywhere. They encourage each of you to contact them and receive their assistance in establishing like minded organizations where you live. If you are interested, contact: Champaign County Health Care Consumers Organization, 44 Main Street, Suite 208, Champaign, Illinois, 61820, (217) 352-6533.

GIVE YOURSELF A RAISE

If there is an area of consumer involvement that cries out for economic relief, the field of health care is it. The following are some money saving suggestions that we hope will keep more money in your pockets and working on behalf of yourself and your family.

KNOW THE COST CONTAINMENT PROVISIONS OF YOUR HEALTH INSURANCE

As we have briefly touched upon in this chapter, virtually all health insurance policies have "cost containment" clauses (which we would call restrictions on benefits for the benefit of the insurer). Be sure you take the time to understand those contained in your policy, either by reading the policy and the explanatory brochures that your company provides or by speaking with your health insurance company representative or group plan administrator.

JOIN A GROUP

If you can find a way to obtain a group insurance rate, do it. It could save you a lot of money in the price of premiums due to the bargaining power of large numbers. Group health insurance can be found at places of employment, through unions and through professional and personal interest associations. Moreover, you can usually (but not always) get *better coverage* through a group, such as:

No Preexisting Condition Exclusions

Often individual (and increasingly, small group) policies will exclude preexisting health conditions from coverage. For example, one consumer complained that her health insurance company refused to cover any expenses related to her female organs because of minor surgery she had undergone.

No Waiting Periods

Group policies often allow for quick coverage once you are eligible for group coverage. Individual policies often have lengthy waiting periods or periods excluding preexisting conditions from coverage for months or even years.

Lower Deductibles and Better Benefits

Group coverages frequently cover more for less money, and call for lower deductibles. This keeps more money in your pocket and out of the health care system.

CONVERT GROUP HEALTH INSURANCE INTO YOUR OWN NAME IF YOU LOSE EMPLOYMENT BENEFITS

In these lean economic times, some of you may be losing your jobs. This tragedy is compounded when you also lose your group health insurance which was provided by your employer or union.

However, all is not lost. You can convert your group health insurance into your own name (at your own expense) for a period of time thanks to the provisions of Federal law known the Congressional Omnibus Reconciliation Act (COBRA) and a subsequent omnibus bill (OBRA).

If you are a widow or dependent child of a covered worker, if your spouse or parent becomes eligible for Medicare, if you or your spouse has been laid off, if you are the divorcing spouse of a covered worker, COBRA is probably for you.

If you are eligible for the right to convert group health insurance into your own name, we suggest you take advantage of this provision for the following reasons:

•You will continue to be protected by health insurance with no break in coverage.

•You will be able to get health insurance at a price probably not otherwise obtainable.

•You will not have to worry about preexisting condition exclusions or waiting periods.

•You will give yourself some breathing room to find and become eligible for other group plans (from 18 months to 36 months depending on your specific circumstances.)

It is vital that you understand your COBRA rights to continued health insurance. For more information, contact your group plan administrator or member of Congress.

INCREASE THE SIZE OF YOUR DEDUCTIBLE AND/OR COPAYMENTS

If you find that your health insurance premiums are simply too high to pay, look into increasing the size of the up-front money (the deductible) you pay before the health insurance company has to pay any benefits. By doing so, you may be able to lower the size of your premium into an area you can afford. You can also try increasing the size of your copayment responsibility. Whatever you do, try not to go without health insurance. Otherwise, your only health care may be found at a public hospital or free clinic.

JOIN AN HMO OR PPO

If you cannot afford or do not desire a traditional fee for service policy, look into health maintenance organizations and/or preferred provider organizations which can often provide for your health care for less money.

ASK YOUR DOCTOR TO ACCEPT HEALTH INSURANCE BENEFITS AS PAYMENT IN FULL

If your bill is high, your doctor may be willing to take the payment made by your health insurance company as payment in full. The only way to know is to ask. But be sure to do it before and not after the treatment is rendered so that there are no hard feelings created between you and your doctor.

MEDICARE PATIENTS - ONLY USE DOCTORS WHO "ACCEPT THE ASSIGNMENT."

As we discussed, the difference between having a doctor who will accept the Medicare assignment and one who will not can be hundreds, if not thousands, of dollars per year.

USE GENERIC DRUGS WHEN MEDICALLY APPROPRIATE

Often a prescription drug sold as a "brand name" will cost more than the same medication sold by its generic name. Usually, there is little or no difference between a brand name drug and a generic drug other than price. In fact, The Public Citizen Health Research Group (HRG) estimates that the average savings per prescription of using generic drugs is $7.50! According to the HRG, if older adults alone switched most of their prescriptions to generic drugs, the total savings could amount to *1.8 billion dollars a year*! Thus, if you are prescribed medication, ask your doctor and your pharmacist whether a generic drug will fit the prescription as well as a brand name. Usually (but not always) it will, if the original patent has expired.

> **CONSUMER ALERT: AN EXCELLENT BOOK FOR ASSISTING CONSUMERS WITH THEIR USE OF PRESCRIPTION DRUGS, BOTH AS TO SAFETY AND ECONOMY, IS *WORST PILLS BEST PILLS* BY DR. SIDNEY WOLFE, ET AL (1988, PUBLIC CITIZEN HEALTH RESEARCH GROUP, P.O. BOX 19404, WASHINGTON, D.C. 20036, $12.00 PER COPY.)**

COMMUNITY HEALTH CLINICS

There are hundreds of community clinics around the country which can provide decent medical care to those who may not be able to afford a personal physician.

MAKE USE OF FREE CLINICS

Many communities have "free clinics" where volunteer doctors assist those in need. If you do not have the money for health care or if you do not have health insurance, these clinics may be your best bet for treatment of ailments that do not require hospitalization.

TAKE CARE OF YOUR OWN HEALTH

At one time in human history, our health was attacked primarily by forces that were not fully understood and pretty much outside of an individual's control to prevent. Diseases such as tuberculosis, polio, smallpox, plague, measles and even influenza were the killers and maimers that people feared most. Why in 1918, the flu epidemic of that year killed 548,000 people in this country alone!

Today, thanks to an unrelenting medical war against contagious diseases and the improvement in medical care in general, things have changed. Polio no longer scares millions of children and their parents, as it did as recently as the 50's. Tuberculosis still strikes, although now it is usually curable. Best of all, smallpox, that feared killer, has been virtually wiped off the face of the globe.

Unfortunately, these diseases have given way to a new generation of maladies that work unceasingly to shorten the length and quality of life. Diseases of the heart, cancer, and now AIDS, strike and destroy in frightening numbers.

The good news in all of this is that much of this death and suffering is avoidable, since many of the afflictions that plague mankind as we approach the end of the 20th Century are created by the way we live our lives. Thus, much of the misery can be reduced or eliminated by simple changes in lifestyle.

Smoking

Most health authorities blame smoking for contributing to a large percentage of heart attacks and for up to 85 percent of lung cancers! The United States Surgeon General reports that over a thousand deaths a day are directly or indirectly related to smoking.

Excessive Drinking

The excessive use of alcohol is a major cause of death and disability in this country. Drinking can injure your health by causing cirrhosis of the liver for example and its abuse creates horrible problems ranging from family dysfunction to automobile accidents, which takes thousands of lives each year in the United States.

Drug Abuse

A popular music lyric of the 60s said, "Speed kills." Indeed it does, as do heroin, crack, cocaine and a host of other drugs. Substance abuse can also cause severe mental and emotional illness, creating havoc in your personal life and leading to stress and disease. Exchanging "dirty" needles when injecting drugs can spread AIDS or hepatitis.

Diet

A proper diet is a key ingredient to a healthful life. The intake of too much fat, for instance, can raise cholesterol levels, leading to vascular disease and heart attack or stroke. Fat has also been connected with colon cancer. Too much salt may lead to high blood pressure. It pays to eat well and properly, for as the old saying goes, when you have your health, you have everything.

Sexual Practices

There is an epidemic of venereal diseases in this country which are severely affecting people's health. The most notorious, of course, is AIDS. But AIDS is not alone among sexually transmitted diseases. Syphilis still attacks tens of thousands, so does gonorrhea, and herpes hasn't abated either. These diseases are mostly preventable by using proper care or practicing abstinence, depending on the circumstances.

Safe sex is 1) no sex (abstinence), 2) mutual monogamy with an uninfected partner, or 3) sexual practices that do not involve the exchange of bodily fluids. Safer sex means using a condom every time during sexual intercourse. CONDOMS ARE NOT FOOLPROOF protections, but they are certainly better than engaging in unprotected sex, at least as far as disease prevention is concerned.

> **CONSUMER ALERT: IF YOU WOULD LIKE MORE INFORMA-TION ON AIDS AND ITS PREVENTION, CALL THE NATIONAL AIDS HOTLINE AT 1-800-342- AIDS OR YOUR LOCAL HEALTH DEPARTMENT.**

The People's Medical Society is a consumer protection organization you should consider joining. As a member, you will receive a free subscription to the People's Medical Society Newsletter. You will also be entitled to substantial members-only discounts on health action kits, health bulletins, special reports and best selling books.

Among the publications available through this fine consumers' organization are the following:

- Medicare Made Easy
- Take This Book to the Hospital With You
- How to Evaluate and Select a Nursing Home
- A Book About Menopause
- 150 Ways to Lower Your Medical Costs

The philosophy of the People's Medical Society is as follows:

1) To give people the information they need to protect themselves in their daily lives; and

2) To bring thousands of people together as a social and political force strong enough to stand up to the medical establishment.

For more information, contact the People's Medical Society, 462 Walnut Street, Allentown, PA 18102, (215) 770-1670.

Another consumers' group you should consider is the Public Citizen Health Research Group (HRG). Founded in 1971 by Ralph Nader and Dr. Sidney Wolfe, the HRG is active on issues relating to food and drug safety, patients' rights, health planning and health care financing. Health Letter *is a monthly newsletter featuring articles on important health problems, telling what HRG is doing about them and suggesting ways to protect yourself and your family.*

For more information, contact Health Research Group, 2000 P Street, NW, Washington, DC 20036, (202) 833-3000.

Chapter Eight

THE INSURANCE CONNECTION
SAVING MONEY AND GRIEF
ON INSURANCE

Insurance is big business - and we mean BIG! "How big is it?" you ask? Well, it's so big that according to the Insurance Information Institute, 453 BILLION dollars were spent on insurance premiums in 1989 the United States alone, and that number has only gone up since then! It is so big, that 12 percent of the spendable income of Americans is spent on insurance. (According to the National Insurance Consumer Organization (NICO), if you are part of an average American family, you and your loved ones spent $2,972 in 1988 for direct premiums and a total of $4,459 in indirect payments.) In fact, the insurance industry is so big that more is spent on insurance by Americans than on their own personal federal income taxes, excluding social security. Now, that's big!

We believe that too much of your money is going into insurance company coffers. We are convinced that with a little motivation and some good information, you can save hundreds of dollars a year or more on your auto insurance, life insurance, homeowners insurance and health insurance. There are also many types of insurance that NICO (and we) recommend that you do not buy, thereby saving even more money, money that can be put to good use in other, more productive areas of your life.

HOW TO BUY INSURANCE

Many people spend more money on insurance than they really have to. Why? Certainly not because they want to contribute to the insurance executives' relief fund. No, people spend too much, in our view, because the insurance industry is "seller-based" instead of "consumer-based." By that, we mean that the overall tendency in the industry is away from consumer-sensitive competition toward selling you a bill of goods, based on what *they want to offer* you rather than on what they *should offer* in policy terms and service in order to earn your business.

For example, advertising: You rarely see an insurance company advertising on television, radio or in print, "Buy from us because we have the lowest prices in 8 out of 10 areas in the state according to the statistics of the State Insurance Department." Nor do you hear them tell you, "Buy from us, we have the lowest complaint ratio of any company in the state." And you certainly never hear, "Buy from us. Our policy is better than the competition because we promise you your rates won't be raised when you have a claim that was not your fault." Instead they advertise name recognition, through pretty jingles, stolid images of stags and rocks and catchy slogans. These are designed to get you to remember the company but they do not tell you one thing you need to know as a consumer to help you decide what to buy.

The only way this dismal state of affairs is going to change is if you and millions of other insurance consumers "take the stag by the horns" and force insurance companies to earn your business instead of expecting you to more or less passively give it to them. Here's how:

STEP 1: DO YOUR HOMEWORK

Before you can be a smart shopper, you should prepare yourself for the task by learning as much as you can about what you are buying. In order to do so, you will need detailed information about the ins and outs of the type of insurance you plan to purchase (i.e. life, health, auto, etc.). You will also need information about the various companies who sell the kind of insurance you want to buy.

Luckily, there is a veritable cornucopia of information available to you - if you know where to look. Take advantage of the information provided by the following resources in researching insurance companies.

Consumer books and articles

There are many books and articles written about insurance each year. Your local library should have many in their stacks and others can be found at your local book store if you want to purchase any for your own book collection at home. Here are just a few examples:

Winning the Insurance Game by Ralph Nader and Wesley J. Smith. (1990, Knightsbridge Publishing, New York).
Taking the Bite Out of Life Insurance by James Hunt. (1988, National Insurance Consumers Organization, Alexandria, Virginia). This helpful guide can help save you money on life insurance.
Life Insurance: How To Buy the Right Policy at the Right Price. The editors of Consumer Reports and Trudy Lieverman. (1988, Consumer Reports Books, Mount Vernon, NY). This fine book from the good people at Consumers Union can empower you and save you money.
The Complete Guide to Health Insurance: How to Beat the High Cost of Being Sick. (1988, Walker and Company, New York.) This well-written book explains health insurance in an easy-to-understand manner.
Health Insurance Made Easy ... Finally by Sharon L. Stark. (1989, Stark Publishing, Shawnee mission KS). Sharon Stark's empowering guide can give you plenty of helpful information at a reasonable price.

There are also many articles both in newspapers and magazines which can help you learn about insurance. Of particular interest to consumers are the several issues of Consumer Reports that have dealt with areas such as auto and homeowners insurance. (The address for Consumer Reports is 101 Truman Ave, Yonkers NY 10703-1057 or they can be reached by phone at (914) 378-2000.)

National Insurance Consumer's Organization (NICO)

NICO is a nonprofit national organization whose sole purpose is to be an advocate for, and provide assistance to, insurance consumers. Founded and headed by a former federal insurance administrator and casualty actuary, J. Robert Hunter, NICO can provide you with manuals that give you valuable details about your insurance. Depending on the type of insurance, NICO may also be able to recommend specific companies to you that are doing a good job in giving the insurance consumer value and quality for his or her premium dollar. *We urge you to join NICO* for a $30 tax deductible donation. For more information, contact NICO, 121 Payne Street, Alexandria, Virginia 22314, (703) 549-8050.

Industry Organizations

The insurance industry has established several organizations to promote consumer education (often from the industry perspective). One such organization is the Insurance Information Institute. In addition to providing consumer pamphlets and materials, they offer a toll free consumer hotline to help you with questions you may have about property/casualty insurance (auto, homeowners, etc.). That number is 1-800-221-4954. There are also organizations of insurance agents that offer consumer information. One such organization is National Association of Professional Insurance Agents in Washington, D.C.

Insurance Company Representatives

There is no question that you should use these insurance professionals as valuable sources of information but at the same time, remember that most of them earn their living by selling insurance on commission, i.e. no sale, no money in their pockets. Thus the old lawyer term *caveat emptor* (buyer beware) definitely applies.

Your State Department of Insurance

Most state insurance departments provide useful consumer information about the various types of policies sold under their jurisdictions. Some state departments of insurance can also give you *information, such as price comparisons and consumer complaint ratios, about specific companies selling in your state.*

STEP 2: SHOP AROUND

The biggest mistake many insurance consumers make when they buy insurance is that they take the first good-looking policy that comes along, often basing their buying decision on the name recognition that comes from watching 10,000 commercials for the company on television. This is unfortunate, for there are frequently wide variations in price and sometimes in product. Here are just a few tips on finding the best buy:

Compare Agents

Choosing the right insurance professional to assist you with your purchase is vital to an effective insurance buying strategy (with the exception of those times that you can safely buy through the mail, which we shall discuss). The professional should be courteous, knowledgeable and should get the sale based on price and the quality of the product, company and service it provides, rather than high pressure salesmanship. Remember, when selecting an insurance agent, you are looking for a professional to serve you over the years and not just for the immediate transaction.

You should talk both with **"captive agents,"** those who work for only one company and **"independent agents,"** those who represent many. By doing so, you give yourself an additional bonus: an increased exposure to the many companies in the market. By taking a week or so to allow the insurance professionals to do their thing, you will have given yourself a solid grasp of what is available on the market and at what prices.

CONSUMER ALERT: ACCORDING TO JAMES QUIGGLE, DIRECTOR OF THE NATIONAL ASSOCIATION OF PROFESSIONAL INSURANCE AGENTS, THIS IS THE BEST WAY TO FIND A GOOD INSURANCE AGENT:

1) *SHOP AT LEAST THREE AGENTS (WE SAY FIVE).* COMPARE THEM TO SEE WHICH ONE OFFERS THE INSURANCE PACKAGE THAT BEST MEETS YOUR NEEDS. THIS MEANS COMPARING THE POLICIES, PRICES AND SERVICES TO DETERMINE THE TOTAL VALUE OF THE PACKAGE.

2) *CHECK OUT THE AGENT.* CALL THE BETTER BUSINESS BUREAU TO SEE IF THE AGENT HAS A HISTORY OF COMPLAINTS. CALL THE STATE INSURANCE DEPARTMENT TO SEE IF THE AGENT IS LICENSED OR HAS DISCIPLINARY ACTIONS ON RECORD. ASK FRIENDS AND NEIGHBORS FOR REFERRALS TO AGENTS WITH WHOM THEY'VE PERSONALLY DONE BUSINESS.

3) *VISIT THE AGENCY BEFORE DOING BUSINESS.* DOES IT APPEAR WELL MANAGED AND PROFESSIONAL? DO THE PERSONNEL APPEAR TO BE COURTEOUS AND HELPFUL?

4) *EDUCATE YOURSELF ABOUT THE KIND OF INSURANCE YOU WANT.* THIS MEANS, UNDERSTANDING WHAT VALUE MEANS WITH REGARDS TO PRICE, SERVICE AND QUALITY OF COVERAGE.

5) *TALK WITH THE AGENT FACE TO FACE.* DOES THE AGENT APPEAR INFORMED AND COURTEOUS? CAN THE AGENT EXPLAIN THE TERMS OF THE POLICY AND ANSWER YOUR QUESTIONS IN PLAIN TERMS THAT YOU CAN UNDERSTAND? DOES THE AGENT APPEAR TO *WANT* TO HELP YOU? DOES THE AGENT ASK PROBING QUESTIONS TO HELP UNCOVER YOUR INSURANCE NEEDS?

CONSUMER ALERT: ALL AGENTS ARE NOT CREATED EQUAL! WE'VE TOLD THIS TRUE STORY BEFORE BUT IT IS WORTH REPEATING BECAUSE IT ILLUSTRATES THE MONEY-SAVING POWER OF COMPARISON SHOPPING. WESLEY J. SMITH WAS SHOPPING FOR AUTO INSURANCE A FEW YEARS AGO. FOR TWO CARS, HE WAS QUOTED A PRICE RANGE FROM $3,000 TO $4,200 PER YEAR! (AND HE AND HIS WIFE HAD NO TICKETS OR ACCIDENTS!) UNDAUNTED, HE CHECKED WITH AN AGENT WHO REPRESENTED A COMPANY KNOWN FOR LOW RATES, FROM WHOM ANOTHER AGENT HAD ALREADY QUOTED THE $3,000 PRICE. THE SECOND AGENT TOOK EXTRA TIME TO LOOK INTO THE APPLICATION AND DISCOVERED THAT THE APPLICANTS OWNED THEIR OWN HOME. BASED ON THE AGENT'S SUPERIOR PRODUCT KNOWLEDGE AND THE WILLINGNESS TO WALK THE EXTRA MILE FOR A CLIENT, HE WAS ABLE TO GET THE SAME COVERAGE FROM THE SAME COMPANY AS THE $3,000 QUOTE AT A SAVINGS OF MORE THAN $900 PER YEAR!

Compare Policies

You will want to compare what each company is offering you for the premium it is demanding. Frequently, this information is supplied in computer printout comparison sheets. In comparing, look at the following:

Price How much are you going to pay? Does the company allow you to pay periodic payments over time and if so, is there a surcharge?

Coverage Limits How deep and how wide is your insurance umbrella? In other words, does the coverage protect you against *catastrophic* loss (worst case scenarios) and is it *comprehensive* enough to protect you against a wide range of losses that may occur.

What are the deductibles, if any? The term deductible means the money you have to pay up front before the insurance company comes to your financial assistance in the event of a claim. Deductibles are usually expressed in terms of dollars but they can also be expressed in time, i.e waiting periods before benefits are payable. The higher the deductible, the less likely your company will have to pay benefits and the lower your rates should be.

What are the exclusions? Exclusions specifically carve out areas that are not covered under the policy. For example, a standard homeowner's policy excludes earthquake damage from protection, thereby compelling homeowners who want this protection to purchase earthquake coverage at an extra price.

Compare the Intangibles

There are other areas you should look at. One of these is the ease of making claims. Some companies make this all important process easy on the consumer and others make it more difficult. Also, ask your friends and neighbors who may have insurance from the companies you are looking at whether they are happy or unhappy with the quality of service. Finally, listen to what your gut says. Sometimes a "feeling" is the best friend a consumer can have.

Compare the Finalists

At some point, three or four finalists will stand out as offering the policies you believe will best suit your individual needs. Once you have limited your search to the finalists, take a little extra time to look into the following for each:

Their rating for financial soundness It does you no good to pay for insurance only to have a company go out of business just as you are about to make a claim. This being so, you will want to check into the financial condition of the companies who have made your list of finalists.

Happily, you will not have to get a degree in corporate accounting practices to do this. There are several publications which rate the financial condition of insurance companies for you. The best known of these is *Best's Insurance Reports*, which gives companies ratings ranging from A+ on down. There have been some complaints in recent years that *Best's* may be a little too generous in their decision making (a complaint that *Best's* vigorously denies) about ratings. Thus, it is a good idea to also check *Standard and Poor's* and/or *Moody's* when looking into the financial condition of the companies. Your agent or local librarian should have that information for you close at hand.

The complaint rates of the companies As was stated earlier, many insurance departments keep records on the number of complaints they receive from consumers against the companies that do business in the state.

CONSUMER ALERT: IF YOU RUN INTO TROUBLE WITH YOUR INSURANCE COMPANY IT IS IMPORTANT TO COMPLAIN TO THE STATE DEPARTMENT OF INSURANCE IF THE SITUATION WARRANTS. NOT ONLY MAY YOU RECEIVE ASSISTANCE BUT YOUR COMPLAINT WILL BE COUNTED AS A MARK AGAINST THE COMPANY, WARNING OTHER CONSUMERS AND PERHAPS ACTING AS AN INCENTIVE FOR THE COMPANY TO CLEAN UP ITS ACT.

The recommendations of consumer advocates Consumer protection organizations such as NICO and Consumers Union often publish specific recommendations and/or comparisons of insurance companies and policies. Not that you should base your buying decision solely on what consumer advocate tell you, but if you trust the messenger you should probably pay a lot of attention to the message.

Now that you have come this far, you should know the following about each of the policies you are comparing:
- The depth and breadth of coverage
- The price
- The complaint record of the company
- The financial well-being of the company

Then, by factoring in matters such as ease of claims services and the availability of an easy payment plan, you should be able to make an informed decision about which policy you wish to purchase.

A NUTS AND BOLTS GUIDE
TO DIFFERENT POLICIES

There is an old saying that knowledge is power. This is especially true when it comes to buying insurance, since there is financial danger everywhere you look as a consumer. On one hand, if you don't buy based on a sound knowledge of what you are purchasing and if you don't learn to take advantage of discounts and other money saving avenues, you may be wasting your good money on premiums that are higher than they need to be or on purchasing more insurance than you really need. On the other hand, if you are underinsured or don't have insurance at all, you could be courting financial disaster if you suffer a loss and have no financial net to catch you. For many consumers, finding the right balance is, to quote Rogers and Hammerstein, "a puzzlement." The following will fill in most of the pieces for you.

AUTO INSURANCE

Not too many years ago, reading about auto insurance would have been a sleep prescription for an insomniac. Prices were generally low, most people could get insurance, and the issue of uninsured motorists had not reached the problem stage that it has reached today.

But then, things changed. Prices skyrocketed in many parts of the country. Most states passed mandatory financial responsibility laws which had the effect of compelling car owners to purchase auto insurance whether they wanted to or not. The insurance industry began to lobby for "reform" of the civil justice system under the moniker, "no-fault insurance." Trial lawyers and others fought back to preserve the current system and soon the entire field of auto insurance and the law of torts took on the air of a battlefield.

All of this has left consumers a bit shell-shocked and more in need of positive information than ever before about their auto insurance needs. But take heart. Auto insurance is understandable and it can be made more affordable if you know how to go about finding the best rates.

Who is Covered?

There is some confusion in many people's minds as to exactly who or what is covered by their auto insurance policies. The answer to that question is that both "who's" and a specific "what" are exactly what is being protected. The "what," of course, is specifically identified. People, known in the jargon of the industry as "the insureds," are also covered under the policy. There are generally three different categories of people who can qualify as an insured under your automobile policy:

The person(s) who owns or leases the vehicle You, your spouse and specifically named family members who reside with you are covered under the policy and are known as the **named insureds**.

Those you allow to use the vehicle If you allow someone to drive your car, they are known in the insurance biz as **permissive users** and will be covered under the policy.

Others who can be held legally responsible for accidents in which your vehicle is involved There are other times when another may be legally liable for your driving mistakes.

What is Covered?

An auto insurance policy, whether in a fault or no-fault state, is really several different coverages wrapped up into one package. Some of the coverages are mandatory and some optional. All are priced separately and then totaled to come up with your ultimate premium price.

Liability The issue of **liability** is the most controversial aspect of auto insurance and the most expensive to purchase. Liability is designed to pay the costs of personal injuries that your negligent driving causes to another.

In an auto insurance policy, there are three separate problems that an automobile accident may create: your financial responsibility to pay for damages related to the bodily injury of others, to the damaged property of others, and the costs of defending a lawsuit brought against you.

•*Bodily Injury* If your driving negligence causes the injury or death of another, you are responsible under the law for the damages that result from the accident. Since our form of justice does not permit "an eye for an eye, a tooth for a tooth or a whiplash for a whiplash," you will have to pay monetary damages for the injuries you cause. This includes items such as medical bills, loss of wages and compensation for the uncompensatable, and what lawyers call "pain and suffering" (in other than no-fault states).

When you purchase liability insurance as part of an auto insurance policy, you are protecting yourself from the expense of paying such damages. You have the power to choose how much protection from liability you want to buy. Usually, this protection is expressed in terms of a **split limit amount**, e.g. $25,000 per person, $50,000 per accident.

Under this form of protection, the most that one severely injured person could receive from your insurance would be the amount stated "per person," or $25,000 in the example above. This is known in the personal injury lawsuit trade as the **policy limits**. If the actual damages were more than $25,000, you could be forced to pay the difference out of your own pocket. That is why you should be sure to protect yourself sufficiently if you have a great deal of assets to lose in a lawsuit.

> **CONSUMER ALERT: SOME COMPANIES OFFER COVERAGE THAT IS EXPRESSED AS SINGLE LIMIT AMOUNTS, *PER ACCIDENT*. THUS, IF YOU HAVE A TOTAL LIABILITY COVERAGE OF $300,000, YOU HAVE MORE REAL PROTECTION IN THE EVENT A PERSON WAS SEVERELY INJURED THAN YOU WOULD IF YOU HAVE A $100,000/$300,000 POLICY.**

•*Property Damage* If your driving damages another person's property, be it another vehicle, a fence or whatever, the property damage portion of your auto insurance pays the tab.

Like coverage for personal injury, your auto policy will set forth the maximum benefits that your insurance company will have to pay if you damage someone else's property. Many states require a minimum of $10,000 worth of coverage but with the cost of auto repair being what it is, it is probably better to be covered by a minimum of $25,000 worth of protection or preferably more, if you can afford it.

Coverage for property damage is based on fault.

•*The Cost of Defense* A very important part of your liability protection package is the obligation of your insurance company to pay for your legal defense if you are sued for damages. Lawyers costing what they do, without this protection, you might not have to worry about paying damages for liability since the cost of defense alone could very well bankrupt you. Your insurance company's obligations go beyond just paying the lawyer. It must also pay your costs of defense, including the payment of expert witnesses, filing fees and other similar expenditures. Thus, this important protection will literally save you thousands, or tens of thousands, of dollars if you are sued on account of an auto accident.

Medical Pay This portion of your automobile insurance is optional, that is, there is no state law compelling you to have it. However, it is relatively inexpensive and is well worth the money, especially if you do not have health insurance.

Medical pay protection has no relation to who caused the accident. As such, it is a form of no fault insurance. It is designed to pay for the cost of medical care and/or funeral expenses for the following: *the insured and family members who live in the same household* and *any passenger injured while in the "covered vehicle."*

> **CONSUMER ALERT: MEDICAL PAY LIMITS APPLY PER PERSON, NOT, AS IN PERSONAL INJURY LIABILITY, PER ACCIDENT. THUS, IF YOUR POLICY PROTECTED YOU FOR $6,000 IN MED PAY AND FOUR PERSONS COVERED UNDER THE POLICY WERE INJURED, THE INSURANCE COMPANY COULD BE RESPONSIBLE FOR UP TO $24,000 WORTH OF BENEFITS.**

Collision and/or Comprehensive Another important part of your auto insurance policy is the optional coverage you can take out to protect the value of your vehicle and/or its contents. This is broken down into two different coverages, **collision** and **comprehensive**.

• *Collision* Collision is usually defined as the "upset of your auto or its impact with another vehicle or object." Translation: That means there is an impact between your car and some other solid thing. If that unfortunate event should happen to your car and it is damaged, the optional collision coverage is designed to pay for the repair and/or replacement of the vehicle.

• *Comprehensive* Loss caused by flying objects, theft, fire, windstorm, hail, riot, hitting an animal, etc. is covered by the comprehensive aspect of your policy. Comprehensive is also optional.

Here are some other things you need to know about comprehensive and collision coverage:

• Both are separate and must be taken out and paid for separately.

• There are deductibles. Most deductibles run around $200, but if you want to reduce the cost of the premium, you can raise that amount.

• Your company has a lot of power deciding how to pay for your loss.

1) The amount necessary to repair the vehicle or replace property that was lost. This method of determining loss is relatively simple - if the repair cost is $1,500, then they owe $1,500 less the deductible.

2) The cash value of the stolen or damaged property. This is a little trickier and it is here that a lot of people complain about getting the shaft from their own insurance companies. Under the terms of the policy, the insurance company may elect to "cash you out" of your car rather than repair your vehicle. This sounds good, but the kicker is that they get to deduct for depreciation and adjust for the deteriorated physical condition of your car. As a result, many people who have their cars "totaled," receive less than it will take to replace the car.

> **CONSUMER ALERT: IF YOUR CAR IS GOING TO BE TOTALED, AND YOU ARE UNHAPPY WITH THE AMOUNT OF MONEY THE INSURANCE COMPANY WANTS TO PAY YOU, FIGHT BACK! LOOK IN THE CLASSIFIED ADS AND SEE WHAT CARS LIKE YOURS ARE SELLING FOR. IF IT IS MORE THAN THE COMPANY IS OFFERING, PHOTOCOPY THE ADS AND SEND THEM TO YOUR INSURANCE COMPANY WITH A LETTER POINTING OUT THAT THE ADS ARE EVIDENCE OF THE REAL FAIR MARKET VALUE. ALSO, BE SURE TO TELL YOUR COMPANY IF YOU HAD EQUIP-MENT IN THE CAR THAT SHOULD CONSTITUTE CAUSE TO INCREASE ITS VALUE.**

• Collision is not based on fault.

• Your collision policy will pay benefits for vehicles you don't own. If you are driving a car you do not own and are in an accident or the car is stolen while in your possession, you collision coverage will pay benefits for the loss. However, this protection will not apply if you drive the car on a regular basis.

• If you have comprehensive and are therefore covered for theft, there is a transportation benefit. If you have to rent a car, for example, you may be entitled to receive partial reimbursement for the expenses.

Uninsured Motorist Imagine the horror of being involved in a serious auto accident and having the other driver run away from the scene or find that the driver is bankrupt and without insurance. *Uninsured motorist protection is an optional coverage designed to pay for your personal injury damages* (including wage loss and pain and suffering) if you are hurt by such an uninsured motorist or hit and run driver.

This protection is based on fault. If you caused the accident and the other car is not insured, you receive no benefits under the uninsured motorist coverage no matter how badly you are hurt. (In such a case, your med pay protection will pay benefits.) However, if you would have been entitled under your state's law of negligence to damages from the driver of the other car, you can receive the same amount of benefits up to the policy limits.

Three groups are covered under your uninsured motorist protection. These three are, the insured, members of his or her household and any other person legally entitled to recover damages. The coverage also applies to injuries sustained by the insured or householders who are injured as pedestrians by an uninsured motorist.

The policy limits are expressed in terms similar to a split limit liability protection. Thus, there will usually be a be a maximum coverage per person and per accident (i.e. $25,000/$50,000).

> CONSUMER ALERT: SOME COMPANIES ALSO OFFER AN *UNDERINSURED* MOTORIST PROTECTION AT EXTRA COST ABOVE UNINSURED MOTORIST COVERAGE. IF YOU CAN AFFORD IT, LOOK INTO THIS PROTECTION. IT CAN MAKE A BIG DIFFERENCE IF YOU ARE SERIOUSLY HURT BY SOMEONE WHO HAS INSURANCE BUT DOES NOT HAVE ENOUGH INSURANCE TO PAY FOR ALL OF YOUR DAMAGES.

Miscellaneous Coverages There are many smaller coverages which can pay you benefits that you need to understand. These include rental car reimbursement and towing. Ask your insurance agent for details.

Give Yourself A Raise by Saving Money on Auto Insurance

People all over the country are beginning to scream about the increasing cost of auto insurance. Things have gotten so bad that several states, such as Pennsylvania, New Jersey and California are trying to pass laws to halt the reign of premium surges currently being waged against consumers by many auto insurance companies.

The outcome of these battles and those yet to come is uncertain. However, there are some specific things you can do now to hold the line against high insurance premiums.

Shop around Taking the time to shop around can be the most valuable couple of hours you invest in saving yourself money on auto insurance. Due to the lack of clear comparative price information, it takes a little digging to find the best value.

> CONSUMER ALERT: SOME STATE INSURANCE DEPARTMENTS PUBLISH PRICE COMPARISON SURVEYS THAT MAY BE ABLE TO TELL YOU THE LOWEST PRICED COMPANIES IN YOUR AREA. FOR EXAMPLE, A 1988 CALIFORNIA SURVEY REVEALED THAT IN ONE AREA OF CALIFORNIA, THERE WAS AN $819 DIFFERENCE IN PREMIUMS CHARGED FOR SIMILAR POLICIES WITH EQUAL COVERAGE AMONG THE VARIOUS COMPANIES

IN THE MARKET. SO TAKE THE TIME TO LOOK AROUND. IT COULD KEEP HUNDREDS OF DOLLARS IN YOUR WALLET EVERY YEAR.

Be a good driver *Your driving record is the key to keeping down the price of your auto insurance no matter what state you live in.* Without a good record, there is little you can do other than choose between paying exorbitant or outrageous premiums or joining a poor risk insurance pool where you will really be forced to feel the financial heat.

Drive a car subject to a lower rate Your insurance company does not look at all cars as distinctions without a difference. No, they look at the crashworthiness, the price and other factors when deciding how much to charge for each model on the market. This being so, it behooves you to have a chat with your agent regarding the price of premiums when you are in the market for a new car. He or she will be able to tell you the auto insurance consequences that you will experience based on which car you obtain. Warning: That Super 12 Turbo metal animal on wheels that goes from 0 to 80 in 6 seconds may cost you as much to insure as your monthly payments on the car.

Adjust your current coverage As with most kinds of insurance, you can lower your premiums by increasing the risk of loss that you will absorb yourself. In other words, you can save more now, but if you have a claim, you will have to pay more later. Here are some of the adjustments you can make:

•*Raise your deductibles*. Many of the benefits paid by auto insurance companies for claims are for relatively low cost collisions. If you agree to absorb most or all of these smaller claims by raising your deductible, you can save some dollars in your premiums.

•*Lower the maximums*. This is more risky than raising your deductibles because it reduces your protection against worst case scenarios.

•*Refuse optional coverages*. The liability portion of your insurance policy is mandatory in many states, although you have a wide latitude over how much protection you wish to take out. (Other states permit you to post a bond or otherwise prove financial responsibility in lieu of insurance.) However, as we said, much of the auto insurance package is optional, which means you can save money by doing without.

•*Take advantage of discounts*. Many insurance companies offer discounts which can save you money. Here is a list of many discounts available from most major companies:

•Multi-car discount. If you have more than one car to insure, most companies offer discounts for all vehicles insured.

•Multiple-policy discount. Some companies offer discounts if you buy more than one type of policy from them, i.e. auto and homeowners.

•Driver education discount. Some states require, and many companies offer, discounts for drivers who have successfully completed driver's education courses.

•Nonsmoker's discount. Any way you look at it, it costs to smoke and not only in terms of your health.

•Anti-theft devices. Companies in a few states will give you a discount on your comprehensive premium if you install anti-theft devices in your car to discourage car thieves.

•Passive restraints discount. Some companies will give you a break on your no-fault and/or med pay discount if your car has airbags. Airbags save lives and prevent serious injuries.

•Good driver discount. Many companies give discounts if you have not been convicted of a moving violation or been in an accident over the term of the policy.

•Good student discount. If you are under 25, especially if you are male, you are going to get it in the neck when it comes to auto insurance premiums. However, if you are a good student, some of this high cost may be mitigated by a well earned discount.

•Mature driver. If you are over 50, don't be quiet about it. Your age may save you up to 10 percent on your auto insurance.

•*If you have no-fault insurance, coordinate your PIP coverage with your health insurance.* No fault insurance has a portion of coverage called personal injury protection coverage, otherwise known as PIP. The PIP coverage pays for all of your medical bills whether or not you cause the accident (as opposed to fault states where the only protection for personal injuries you sustain in an accident you cause will be your med pay). If you live in a no-fault state, you can direct that the first benefits to be paid for your health care will come from the health insurance rather than your auto insurance. If you do, according to Consumers Union, you can save money.

•*Purchase optional coverage.* Sometimes, it is not the insurance you do not buy that saves money but that coverage you do purchase. Thus, if you have special equipment or have other items you want included in your insurance protection which are excluded from protection in the standard auto insurance policy (such as CBs or customized equipment), you may want to purchase extra protection called an **endorsement**. Ask your agent for more details.

RESIDENTIAL INSURANCE

Most of you who are reading these words, whether a renter or a property owner, have or should have residential insurance. As with auto insurance, residential insurance consists of several parts:

Protection of Your Property (homeowner's insurance)

Residential insurance protects against up to five specific areas of your property:
•The dwelling itself
•Other structures on the property
•Personal property
•Loss of use of your property
•Miscellaneous coverages
Let's look at each in turn.

The dwelling (homeowner's coverage) This consists of your living structure, known in real people's language as your house, along with structures attached to it such as your garage.

The protection provided by your policy is to rebuild or repair your dwelling should it be destroyed or damaged. This means that you do not need to insure to the sales value of the house but to the *replacement value* of the premises. (For example, if you could sell your house for $300,000 but could rebuild the structure for $200,000, you do not need to insure up to $300,000.)

> **CONSUMER ALERT: SOME BANKS AND OTHER LENDERS COMPEL THE DEBTOR TO TAKE OUT HOMEOWNER'S INSURANCE IN AN AMOUNT EQUAL TO THE MORTGAGE OR TRUST DEED DEBT. IN OTHER WORDS, THEY MAY FORCE YOU TO OVERINSURE YOUR PROPERTY. THE TIME TO LOOK AT THAT ISSUE IS WHEN YOU ARE NEGOTIATING YOUR LOAN.**

CONSUMER ALERT: A BIGGER POTENTIAL PROBLEM THAN OVERINSURING, IS UNDERINSURING. IN ORDER FOR YOUR PROTECTION TO BE COMPLETE, THE COVERAGE YOU TAKE OUT MUST BE AT LEAST 80 PERCENT OF THE ACTUAL REPLACEMENT COST TO REBUILD YOUR HOME. FAIL TO DO THAT, AND YOU WILL NOT RECEIVE FULL BENEFITS IF YOU HAVE A LOSS.

•*Which perils are protected against?* In insurancespeak , a peril is something that can create a loss, i.e. fire in homeowner's insurance or theft in auto insurance. Some policies cover more than others. The best policies have a general protection clause which protects you against all perils except those specifically excluded in the policy.

•*What is excluded from coverage?* That last clause raises the important issue of exclusions in homeowner's policies. Every policy has some, many of which can be overcome by purchasing extra protection. Ask your agent for details.

CONSUMER ALERT: IF YOU LIVE IN AN AREA WHICH IS COVERED BY THE GOVERNMENT-SUBSIDIZED FLOOD INSURANCE PROGRAM, LOOK CAREFULLY INTO PURCHASING THIS LOW-COST PROTECTION. IF YOU LIVE IN AN EARTHQUAKE DANGER ZONE, BE SURE TO LOOK INTO THE PRICE OF EARTHQUAKE INSURANCE. EARTHQUAKE INSURANCE WILL PAY FOR REBUILDING YOUR HOME ALTHOUGH THERE IS A DEDUCTIBLE, USUALLY OF 10 PERCENT OF THE VALUE. THE COVERAGE IS EXPENSIVE IN MANY AREAS BUT THE RISK OF LOSS IS SO PROFOUND IT IS PROBABLY WORTH PICKING UP IF YOU CAN AFFORD IT.

The dwelling (renter's insurance) You renters out there in readerland don't have to worry too much about the structure since you do not own it and its protection is up to your landlord. However, if renters have improved the premises by affixing permanent improvements to the property (known as fixtures), the landlord's insurance may not cover the additions. If that happens to you, your renter's policy should cover the loss if 1) the improvement was paid for by you, the insured tenant, and 2) it was used exclusively by you.

The dwelling (condominium owner) Condominiums are an interesting variation on the theme of home ownership. When you purchase a condo, you are, in essence, buying two things at the same time:

•You are buying sole ownership of your "home space." Thus, the risk of loss to the inside of your condo is yours and yours alone.

•You are also buying a small piece of the whole complex, known as the "common areas," such as lawns, swimming pool, walkways, etc. This ownership comes with a price tag in that you are proportionately responsible for the maintenance of the common areas of the condominium and are assessed a monthly charge for that purpose. You can also be charged a **loss assessment** if extra money is needed for complex upkeep, say a new roof.

This presents some interesting insurance issues. The governing body of the condominium complex, called the condominium association, must decide about issues of obtaining insurance for the complex and the terms of that insurance. You should involve yourself in these discussions since one way or the other, *you will pay for the decisions that are made*; shelling out for your share of the premium and/or a loss assessment slapped on you if the condo complex suffers a loss and it is underinsured.

Your individual condominium insurance will cover the following physical property in the condo complex:

•*The property you own* The complex policy should cover damage to the physical space you live in but if it does not, your policy should fill in the empty spaces.

•*Portions of the common area* Your individual policy will also provide protection for your obligations to repair the common area, up to $1,000 under the basic policy.

When looking at individual condo insurance, you need to ask yourself, your condo association and your sales agent three questions to make sure you are adequately protected against dwelling and other structural loss:

•Do I have adequate protection of my home space? Many association policies underinsure in that they only provide for the rebuilding of the structure should it be destroyed. But there is more to a home than the four walls enclosing it. There are fixtures, built-ins, etc. If you association policy is not enough to completely restore your home in the event of loss, you should either work to improve the association's policy or make sure your individual policy will take up the slack.

•Are improvements I have made to my home space covered by the association's policy? Again, if the answer is no, think about getting the association to improve its policy or improve your own.

•Am I covered for loss assessments? You should make sure your individual policy provides adequate protection against the rude financial intrusion of a loss assessment required by an inadequate association policy.

Protection of personal property (all) Your personal property will also be protected by a standard residential insurance policy. And this property (stereos, furniture, clothes, etc.) is protected against loss anywhere in the world so long as it is owned or used by the insured. The personal property of others can also be covered if it is located in a residence occupied by the insured.

The actual amount available to you for that will be limited. In addition, specific types of property will also have limited benefits (for example, jewelry is only protected against loss up to a maximum of $1,000 and property used for business purposes is only covered for up to $2,500). Thus, when you are purchasing your residential insurance, be sure you go over this important aspect of coverage to see whether it is in your financial interest to purchase additional protection for your personal property.

> **CONSUMER ALERT: IT IS A GOOD IDEA TO MAKE AN INVENTORY OF YOUR PERSONAL PROPERTY AND KEEP IT IN A SAFE PLACE. YOU SHOULD ALSO TAKE PICTURES OF THE MORE VALUABLE ITEMS TO PRESENT TO YOUR INSURANCE COMPANY IN THE EVENT YOU HAVE TO MAKE A CLAIM FOR THE LOSS OF PERSONAL PROPERTY.**

Liability Another important protection you buy with your residential insurance premiums is protection against liability. As with auto insurance, the liability portion of your policy protects you against damages you might have to pay for your negligent acts against another person's property or body and the cost of defense in the event you are sued. There is also a medical pay provision which covers persons injured on the insured location with your permission under many conditions. As with all liability policies, it is important to know the limits of coverage and if they are inadequate to protect you, you should consider increasing them or purchasing an umbrella policy.

> **CONSUMER ALERT: IF YOU ARE UNABLE TO OBTAIN A RESIDENTIAL INSURANCE POLICY BECAUSE YOU LIVE IN A HAZARDOUS AREA, LOOK INTO THE *FAIR PLAN* (FAIR ACCESS TO INSURANCE REQUIREMENTS), A SUBSIDIZED PROPERTY INSURANCE PROGRAM DESIGNED TO GUARANTEE THAT HIGH RISK PROPERTIES HAVE ACCESS TO INSURANCE PROTECTION. FOR THOSE IN HIGH CRIME AREAS WHO CANNOT GET PROTECTION, THE FEDERAL GOVERNMENT HAS A *CRIME INSURANCE* PROGRAM THAT YOU MIGHT BE INTERESTED IN. ASK YOUR LOCAL INSURANCE AGENT FOR DETAILS.**

Give Yourself A Raise on Residential Insurance

The cost of residential insurance is not as burdensome to most consumers as is auto insurance. But even so, that does not mean that there aren't significant opportunities for you to save money over that which you may currently be spending on this important insurance protection.

Shop around At the risk of sounding like a broken record, we must reemphasize the importance of taking the time to sample the market when you buy insurance. There is simply no short cut if you want to get the best value.

Don't overinsure You can save money by making sure you have not overinsured your property. In that regard, look at the following:

•*Too-low deductibles* The typical deductible in a homeowner's policy is $250. If you are willing to risk paying more up front money in the event of a claim tomorrow, you can raise that figure and save money on your premiums today.

•*The size of the liability protection* If you are an average middle class consumer, you probably don't need super-high levels of liability protection.

•*The amount of money to replace your home* As we said earlier, one common mistake consumers make is to take out homeowner's insurance in an amount equal to the sales value of the entire property, including the land, rather than the replacement value of the dwelling. Next time you are speaking with your agent, ask him or her if you are overinsured in this area.

Don't underinsure On the other hand, you want to make sure your insurance is sufficient to protect you. You must have the dwelling insured to at least 80% of its replacement value or you will suffer a reduction in benefits.

Exclude coverage for wind and hail It might be risky, but if you live in an area known for damage caused by wind and hail, you can save a lot of money from the cost of insurance by agreeing to take care of such damage yourself. Only you can decide whether the money saved is worth the risk of loss you will assume by deliberately excluding these perils from your insurance protection.

Investigate discounts As with auto insurance, there are many discounts that you may qualify for to save you money. Here are some of the most common:

•Multiple-policy discount
•Safety device discount (i.e. smoke alarms, etc.)
•Nonsmoker's discount
•Fire-resistant material discount
•Mature owner discount

Work to prevent losses Even if you have adequate insurance protection, a loss is likely to cost you a lot of money. Thus, you should take steps to protect yourself from having to make a claim at all, such as the following:

•*Take steps to foil burglars* Your local police department and homeowner's insurance agent should be able to give you some ideas on how to keep yourself from being a property crime victim.

•*Make your home as fire safe as possible* Your local fire department will have tips on avoiding fire hazards in the home. So will your local insurance agent. Here's another suggestion: Enlist the help of your kids. And don't forget to install fire detectors.

•*Be prepared for natural disasters* The time to prepare for a storm, earthquake or other natural disaster is before it occurs, not when it is barreling down upon you. Talk with your community preparedness agencies about what steps you can take to keep your property and family safe in the event of a natural disaster.

•*Look for hazardous conditions upon your property* If someone is injured while on your property, you will feel bad and it may cost you money. Why not avoid the problem in the first place by correcting hazardous conditions as you discover them?

LIFE INSURANCE

Life insurance: most of us don't really like the subject because it deals with the subject of death. Plus, there is the life insurance agent, who, while providing a valuable service, sometimes seems as likely to bore you (or "guilt" you) into signing up for a policy than to sell you one based on the merits. Finally, there is the question of those earnings projection charts that are virtually guaranteed to make your eyes glaze over and short circuit the synapses in your brain. Still, life insurance is a vital part of most families' financial security and so it is a subject that must be reckoned with.

Life insurance has several purposes, depending on the kind of policy you select.

Protection of Beneficiaries

The most obvious reason to purchase life insurance is to protect those named to receive the proceeds should the insured "shuffle off this mortal coil," as Shakespeare so artfully put it. Those who receive the proceeds are called **beneficiaries**. People name beneficiaries for many reasons, including the following:

Income protection The most common and most important reason to buy life insurance is to protect a family against the loss of the income earned by the breadwinner(s).

Payment of debts Some people take out life insurance to make sure that specific debts are paid in the event of their death.

To resolve potential business disputes Partnerships and other business entities often take out life insurance to pay the family of a deceased principal.

As an investment Some forms of life insurance accrue monetary worth over the years and thus are deemed investments. The amount of money a policy is worth is known as the **cash value** of the policy.

As a tool of estate planning For people with larger estates, life insurance trusts and life insurance is often used as a method of avoiding estate taxes and to otherwise plan for the distribution of an estate upon the demise of the insured.

The Kinds of Life Insurance

Life insurance comes in three basic types: the **term policy**, the **cash value** policy and the **annuity**, (which is primarily an investment vehicle rather than a life insurance policy and so will not be discussed). We will take a look at both term and cash value policies below.

One of the issues that puzzles life insurance consumers is which kind to buy. As we shall see, both have their pros and cons, and so ultimately, you will have to be the one to decide which way you want to go.

> **CONSUMER ALERT: LIFE INSURANCE COMPANIES MAKE A HIGHER PROFIT ON CASH VALUE POLICIES THAN THEY DO ON TERM POLICIES. THEY ALSO PAY AGENTS HIGHER COMMISSIONS ON CASH VALUE POLICIES. THUS, IT IS IN THE FINANCIAL INTEREST OF THE LIFE INSURANCE INDUSTRY TO SELL YOU CASH VALUE LIFE INSURANCE. AS A RESULT, A LOT OF ENERGY MAY BE PLACED IN A SALES DISCUSSION TO GET YOU TO BUY A CASH VALUE POLICY.**

Term life insurance Term life insurance can be defined as life insurance that is in effect for a period of time specified in the policy. If the insured passes away during that time period, the face amount of the policy is owed to the designated beneficiaries (known as the death benefit). If the death occurs after the term has expired, no benefits are owed. *Term policies do not accrue any cash values.*

Unless you only want term insurance for a short period of time, *it is essential that you buy a policy that is guaranteed to be renewable.* That means you can renew the policy even if you are on death's doorstep. Otherwise, if the company caught wind of any serious health problems you might be having, they would refuse to continue to insure your life.

The *price of term life insurance will go up every time you renew.* That is because with each year you age, the statistical chance that you will die increases, and therefore, your premium does also.

> **CONSUMER ALERT: SOMETIMES CONSUMERS WANT TO PURCHASE CASH VALUE POLICIES BUT CANNOT AFFORD THE HIGHER PREMIUMS WITHOUT UNDERINSURING THEMSELVES. THE INSURANCE INDUSTRY RECOGNIZES THIS AND SOME TERM POLICES ARE SOLD WITH THE *CONVERTIBILITY* CLAUSE, THAT IS, THE RIGHT TO CONVERT TO A CASH VALUE POLICY IS GUARANTEED IN THE LIFE INSURANCE CONTRACT.**

Term life insurance has several pros and some cons. The following are some of the advantages of buying term life insurance over cash value:

•*It costs less.* Cash value life insurance premiums are more expensive than term premiums because you have to pay higher charges that go to the company and/or the sales agent. Thus, each premium dollar purchases more life insurance face value than does each cash value life insurance premium dollar. According to NICO, annual renewable term insurance provides the most coverage for the least cost.

•*You can probably earn more money by investing your money yourself than you can in a cash value policy*. A major part of the cash value life insurance sales pitch is the line that your premium is working for you. And this is true. However, if you buy term life insurance and invest the difference in the premium costs between cash value and term yourself, you will probably earn more.

•*If there is a claim, the entire benefit comes out of the life insurance company's coffers and not your beneficiary's pocket*. If you die and have a $100,000 term insurance policy, your beneficiary will receive approximately $100,000. Same thing goes for unencumbered cash value polices of course, except for one small catch. Assume your cash value policy was worth $15,000 when you died. Your beneficiary would get $115,000, right? Wrong! The check would be for $100,000 - meaning that "your" $15,000 simply disappears.

> **CONSUMER ALERT: SOME COMPANIES WILL PAY BOTH THE CASH VALUE AND FACE VALUE OF A CASH VALUE TYPE POLICY. BUT IN RETURN, THEY EITHER CHARGE A HIGHER PREMIUM OVER THEIR BASIC POLICY OR THE POLICY ACCRUES VALUE AT A SLOWER RATE THAN IT OTHERWISE WOULD.**

•*Term insurance meets the primary purpose of life insurance*. THE MOST IMPORTANT PURPOSE OF LIFE INSURANCE FOR THE AVERAGE CONSUMER IS THE PROTECTION OF THEIR FAMILY. Term insurance meets this purpose at a lower cost than cash value insurance.

> **CONSUMER ALERT: MOST CONSUMER ADVOCATES IN THE FIELD, INCLUDING NICO AND CONSUMERS UNION, RECOMMEND THAT THE AVERAGE CONSUMER PURCHASE ANNUAL RENEWABLE TERM INSURANCE OVER CASH VALUE. ALL OTHER THINGS BEING EQUAL, WE AGREE. (FOR THE ARGUMENTS IN FAVOR OF CASH VALUE, SEE BELOW.)**

There are several questions you should ask when looking into term life insurance, including the following:

•Do I have enough protection? Whether you are buying cash value or term insurance, this is the key question that you need to have a "yes" answer to. There are all sorts of different ways to determine how much you should buy to adequately protect your family, but we like the approach of the actuary-founder of NICO, J. Robert Hunter.

•*Multiply the yearly income of the person being insured by 5*. Mr. Hunter believes that the best balance between the protection provided by life insurance and the cost of the premiums is to multiply the yearly income of the breadwinner being insured by a factor of five. Thus, if that amount was $40,000, then the base amount of life insurance face value should be at least $200,000.

•*Next, add in the cost of special expenses*. If you wish to make sure that special expenses, such as your children's college tuition, are provided for by your life insurance, then add that amount to the base amount of the face value.

•*Then, factor in any debts that need to be paid*. If you have any major debts, such as a second trust deed or large credit card debt, you should now add the amount owed into the equation.

•*Provide for an emergency fund*. It never hurts to provide a little extra, say $10,000 or so for emergencies to the base amount.

•*Finally, include the price of your funeral.* This is a little ghoulish, but funerals can cost a lot of money. This being so, it is a good idea to plug that expense into the total of the benefit to be paid after you are gone.

Here's how that might look on paper:

	$200,000 (5 times income)
+	80,000 (college tuition for two)
+	25,000 (trust deed payoff)
+	10,000 (emergency fund)
+	10,000 (funeral)
TOTAL:	$325,000 in face value coverage

Of course, you are free to provide for more than this amount if you choose. However, it is probably not a good idea to take out less coverage than provided in this formula, unless you cannot afford the premiums.

•What is the maximum premium I will have to pay in the future? If you are shopping for some form of renewable term insurance, your sales agent will probably show you a projection chart telling you what future premiums are likely to cost if you continue to renew your policy. Any projections that are mere estimates do not bind the company to charge that amount. In addition to an estimate of future premium charges, you will want to receive a *maximum premium guarantee* which sets the highest amount you can be charged under the policy.

•For how long is the policy guaranteed to be renewable? You do not need life insurance for the rest of your life if, that is, you live to a ripe old age. No, your primary concern should be to provide for a growing family. Thus, you will want to make sure that you have the absolute right to renew your term policy at least until your chicks have left the nest.

•Are there any special coverages that I should pick up? As with most insurance, you can buy extra protection (called a **rider**) for extra premium dollars. One such coverage is the right to convert to a cash value policy. Another is the right to have your premium suspended during times of disability, called a waiver of premium rider. Have your agent explain the available riders to you and why he or she thinks they may be worth the money.

Cash value policies Cash value polices come in several different varieties for your shopping confusion, er - perusal. The scope of this book does not allow us to go into minutiae which illustrate the differences among the competing forms of the genus. However, we can go into the similarities.

•*Cash value policies accrue worth over time.* In addition to providing a death benefit like a term policy, a cash value life insurance contract provides for the policy to accrue worth.

•*Cash value policies have flexibility.* One of the big selling points of cash value policies is that there is more to them than merely paying premiums. For example, in many policies you can direct your cash value to be used to pay the premiums thereby eliminating a bill from your budget.

•*Cash value policies can be borrowed against.* When a policy has accrued sufficient value, that worth can be used as collateral to borrow against. Note, however, that if too much money is taken out, the policy can fail; that is, the amount in the account will not be enough to pay the death benefit. If that happens and the insured dies, the beneficiaries will not benefit. If, the insured dies and the policy has not failed, the amount owed will be taken out of the death benefit. It is also important to remember that the insurance company will charge you interest on the money borrowed in an amount greater than you are earning from your policy.

CONSUMER ALERT: SOME COMPANIES ALLOW YOU TO ACCRUE HIGHER CASH VALUES IF YOU DO NOT BORROW AGAINST YOUR POLICY. THIS SYSTEM IS CALLED DIRECT RECOGNITION . IF YOU DON'T EXPECT TO BORROW AGAINST YOUR POLICY, LOOK INTO THIS FEATURE.

•*Cash value policies have level premiums.* Unlike term policies, most cash value policies are structured so as to not increase their premiums over time. (Of course, the increased cost of the mortality charge has already been factored in when setting the initial premium.)

•*There are significant tax advantages to cash value policies.* Another big selling point stressed by life insurance agents are the tax benefits available to policy holders of cash value policies. And, it is true - there are some tax breaks that can be of real benefit:

•The amount of money that is accrued in cash value every year is tax-deferred. Assume you earned $500 in interest in a savings account where you bank. Uncle Sam would quickly congratulate you for your thrift as he reached into your wallet to take his income tax share. On the other hand, if you accrue the same amount in life insurance cash value, he will leave you alone and tell you he'll collect his share later.

•The tax is waived if the cash value is paid as part of a death benefit. If you win your bet with the life insurance company and die forcing them to pay your beneficiaries, then Uncle Sam forgives the taxes owed on any accrued cash value so long as it has been consumed by the death benefit.

•You can deduct the premiums from the value you have accrued when you take out your cash value. If you remove the cash value, by taking it out or cashing in your policy, you owe income tax just as if you had accrued the money in a savings account. However, unlike a savings account, you have the right to deduct the premiums you paid from the amount of the cash value, thereby significantly reducing your tax or sometimes, eliminating it altogether.

NOTE: THIS BOOK DOES NOT PURPORT TO GIVE TAX ADVICE. IN ORDER TO BE SURE HOW YOUR LIFE INSURANCE AFFECTS YOUR TAXES INDIVIDUALLY, CONSULT YOUR ACCOUNTANT OR LAWYER.

Here are some of the pros of cash value policies:

•If you don't die during the time the policy is in effect, you still have an investment with a cash value policy.

•In later years, cash value policies do not increase in the size of the premiums. This is not so with term insurance, which can be very expensive in later years.

•Life insurance policies sold by mutual companies (companies owned, in theory, by the policy holders) pay dividends to policy holders or on behalf of their policies. The dividends paid on cash value policies will be higher than those paid to the owners of term policies.

•Inflation eats up the true worth of term policies more readily than cash value policies. If inflation reduces the real value of the death benefit, some cash policies allow the accrued cash value to be rolled over into a policy with a higher death benefit. Not so, term policies.

•Cash value polices have excellent tax benefits which are not present in term policies.

Buying cash value policies If you decide that a cash value policy is for you, you will run into the dreaded **earnings projection chart**. The purpose of the earnings projection chart is to prove to you what a great investment you will be getting if you buy the policy being pedaled to you. Here's what one looks like. This is an actual chart prepared for Wesley J. Smith, then a 40 year old nonsmoker, in good health. The death benefit of the quote is $150,000.

CASH VALUE PROJECTION CHART

PROJECTED VALUES

GUARANTEED VALUES

AGE	END OF YEAR	ANNUAL OUTLAY	CASH VALUE	SURRENDER VALUE	CASH VALUE	SURRENDER VALUE
41	1	$1,791	$1,382	$0	$1,299	$0
42	2	1,791	2,881	1,005	2598	878
43	3	1,791	4,488	2,604	3,933	2,286
44	4	1,791	6,236	4,336	5,290	3,714
(AGES 45 - 63 OMITTED)						
64	24	1,791	117, 901	117,901	27,898	27,898

Guaranteed values: Based on guaranteed interest rate of 4 percent and the guaranteed cost of insurance
Projected values: Based on the current cost of insurance, which is subject to change, and the following interest assumptions of 9.54 percent.

Let's take a look at what all of that means:
•Note, the annual premium is $1,791. That's almost $150 per month. A term policy with a $150,000 face value could be obtained for about $215 per year starting at age 40 and slowly rising from there.
•The value of the policy accrues quickly because it is expensive.
•Notice the vast difference between the guaranteed value and the projected value. The guaranteed value is the only accrual of worth is certain. It is based on a reasonable interest rate (4 percent) versus an optimistic one (9.54 percent).
•In this policy the "cash value" is the amount that can be borrowed against and the "surrender value" is the amount that you would receive should you cancel it and take out the accrued value.
•From ages 40 to 65, $44,775 will have been paid in premiums. The guaranteed surrender value at age 65, assuming that no money was borrowed against the cash value, is $27,225. That is $17,225 less than the premiums paid.

When you are looking into cash value policies, be sure to *compare several earnings projection charts* and pay special attention to the guaranteed projected earnings as opposed to the rosy projections the company will project to try to get you to sign on the dotted line.

CONSUMER ALERT: HISTORICALLY, THE PERCENTAGE OF RETURNS FOR CASH VALUE LIFE INSURANCE POLICIES HAS BEEN LOWER THAN WHAT WOULD HAVE BEEN EARNED HAD THE SAME MONEY BEEN INVESTED IN BANK PASSBOOK ACCOUNTS. SO, ALWAYS TAKE THE PROJECTED EARNINGS ESTIMATE WITH A HEAVY DOSE OF SKEPTICISM. IT IS ONLY THERE TO INDUCE YOU TO BUY.

Also, if you do decide to buy a cash value policy (and a term policy for that matter) be sure to *keep a close eye on the financial stability of the company*. In recent times, there have been some disturbing rumblings about the financial instability of some life insurance companies, especially those that invested heavily in junk bonds.

GIVE YOURSELF A RAISE

If you and/or your spouse are supporting a growing family, life insurance is one of life's less pleasant necessities. But that doesn't mean you should spend more money on it than is absolutely necessary. Here are some tips that we hope will assist you to save money on meeting your life insurance needs.

Shop around (Here we go again.) *There are over 2,000 life insurance companies* that sell life insurance in the United States alone. And each of these companies has its own philosophy about how to make profits. So, take the time to shop around and find the company that best offers you the combination between low prices and security that meets your personal needs.

CONSUMER ALERT: THERE IS A VERY VALUABLE TERM LIFE INSURANCE SHOPPING SERVICE AVAILABLE THAT CAN DO THE COMPARISON SHOPPING FOR YOU. IT IS CALLED *INSURANCE INFORMATION INC.* WITHIN 24 HOURS OF RECEIVING AN INQUIRY FROM YOU, THEY WILL BE ABLE TO SEND YOU A REPORT ON FIVE OF THE LOWEST-COST INSURANCE COMPANIES TO FILL YOUR NEEDS. THE REPORT WILL INCLUDE *BEST'S* RATING OF EACH COMPANY MENTIONED. THE PRICE CHARGED FOR THE SERVICE IS MODEST, AND THE COMPANY DOES NOT SELL INSURANCE ITSELF, SO THERE WILL BE NO SALES PRESSURE WHATSOEVER. IF YOU ARE INTERESTED IN TERM INSURANCE, CALL THEM TOLL-FREE AT (800) 472-5800.

Don't smoke. If there is one thing that will send the cost of premiums soaring, it is smoking within 12 months of applying for life insurance. So, don't smoke.
Consider a mail order policy. If you order your life insurance by mail, you can save significantly because you will not be paying for the agent's commission. Of course, you should investigate a mail-order company as thoroughly as a company that uses commissioned sales personnel. NICO keeps tabs on some of the better mail-order companies and can recommend the ones they believe are offering the best coverage at the best price.
Don't buy the company propaganda. Life insurance companies go to a great length to imbed their names in your mind through "jingle" advertising and the smoke and mirrors of projection charts. When making your buying decision, you should be very cold and calculating in your choice and buy based on guaranteed earnings, premiums, price, financial stability of the company and factors other than cute cartoon spokesanimals.

Have the earnings capacity of the policies evaluated. There are ways to evaluate the investment value of cash value life insurance policies. One, the **surrender cost index**, is a tool that tells you how good a deal your cash value policy is. The index, which is computed by a complex formula too complicated to go into here, tells you the projected cost of a proposed policy. In order to be of benefit, the policies evaluated must be similar in their construction. The lower the index number, the better the buy. Ask your agent to supply this for you.

Another method of evaluating life insurance is called the **Linton yield method**. It measures the difference between what you could earn by buying term insurance instead of cash value policies and investing the money you save in premiums, compared with what you can expect to earn from a cash value policy.

> **CONSUMER ALERT: NICO OFFERS A SERVICE THAT WILL GIVE YOU A LINTON RATE OF RETURN COMPARISON FOR ALL OF THE CASH POLICIES YOU ARE COMPARING. THE CHARGE PER POLICY IS MODEST. THE COMPARISON WILL BE PERFORMED BY THE PRESIDENT OF NICO, J. ROBERT HUNTER, A WELL-RESPECTED ACTUARY. IF YOU ARE INTERESTED, CONTACT NICO AT (703) 549-8050.**

Buy group insurance. If you are eligible to purchase group insurance, think seriously about doing so.

Look into buying riders. There are two different categories of riders you can purchase for your life insurance. Some, extend the coverage provided by the basic life insurance policy. Others, protect the viability of the life insurance policy itself.

FILING CLAIMS

The heart of the insurance contract for you is when you need to file a claim in order to get the benefits. This is where the money finally begins to flow in your direction instead of the other way around. Your job as a consumer, of course, is to make sure that you get all of the benefits that your insurance contract entitles you to receive.

HOW THE CLAIMS PROCESS WORKS

The following is a typical blow-by-blow description of what happens when you file a claim.

Notification of the Insurance Company

In every policy, your duties regarding company notification of a pending claim will be spelled out. For example, you may be required to notify the company within 30 days. *In order to avoid unnecessary trouble in obtaining your benefits, make sure you understand your responsibilities under the contract and that you comply with them.*

Notification can occur in several ways, which will be specified in the policy. Read this portion of the contract and take steps to make sure you understand them. (You may be able to call your agent, or there may be an adjuster's phone number. Whatever the case, you will have to file a written claim.)

Filing the Claim

In order to reap the benefits of the premiums you have sowed, you will have to file a formal document known as the claim form, in which you formally request that benefits be paid pursuant to the policy.

When you file the claim, keep the following points in mind:

Be thorough and meticulous The quality of the work you put into the claim form will be the first impression that the adjuster will have of you and your loss.

Tell the truth Tell the truth, the whole truth and nothing but the truth. Sometimes, people tend to embellish (to put it politely) the facts surrounding their claim. Others withhold vital information that might be damaging to their chances of recovery. These can be very serious mistakes. Not only is it dishonest to lie or mislead by silence, it might be a crime - the crime of insurance fraud.

Remember, you are in a business relationship Remember, the adjuster's bread is buttered by the company and not you, so keep the relationship on a courteous and friendly level but never forget it is an arms-length business transaction.

Consult your agent Don't be afraid to discuss the matter with your agent. While it is true that your agent represents the company, his or her livelihood depends on clients like you spreading good words about the agent hither and yon.

Get legal advice if necessary If you are unsure of your legal rights with regard to an insurance claim, do not hesitate to consult a lawyer, especially if a lot of money is at stake.

Read before you sign Read everything you receive from your insurance company thoroughly before you sign it. This is especially true for the **release**. A release is a document that tells the world you release the company from any and all further claims in regard to the subject of your claim. That means, if you are underpaid by the company and you realize it after the release has been signed, you are almost always out of luck.

Document your claim Be prepared to support your claim with documentation. The better you document your request for benefits with pictures, receipts and/or other evidence, the better your chances your claim will be processed smoothly and you will be paid top dollar to compensate you for your loss.

Ask questions You have a right to understand what is happening every step of the way. So, when in doubt, inquire. Remember, the only stupid question is the one that isn't asked.

Don't be afraid to go to the top If you are unsatisfied with the manner in which your adjuster is handling your claim, don't be afraid to contact his or her superior. You can complain, and then, ALWAYS write a confirming letter detailing your objections. Write the letter carefully and think it through. You may even want to get a lawyer to write it for you. (It's amazing how the "attorney at law" letterhead can sometimes budge the immovable object.)

The following is a sample letter of complaint:

JULY 22, 1992

WE ARE CHEAP INSURANCE COMPANY
ATTN: MARVYN BOSSDUDE
8282 RECALCITRANCE LANE
BALTIMORE, MARYLAND 55999

RE: CLAIM # 43456 - POLICY # HO 87564

DEAR MR. BOSSDUDE:

I HAVE BEEN A POLICY HOLDER WITH WE ARE CHEAP INSURANCE COMPANY FOR OVER FIVE YEARS. DURING THAT TIME I HAVE NEVER BEEN LATE IN PAYING MY PREMIUMS. I HAVE ALSO REFERRED SEVERAL PEOPLE TO YOUR COMPANY AND THE AGENT WHO SOLD ME MY INSURANCE, FRED SINCERE.

ON FEBRUARY 10 OF THIS YEAR, MY HOME SUFFERED A FIRE IN WHICH THE LIVING ROOM WAS DESTROYED ALONG WITH SOME VERY VALUABLE FURNITURE I HAD PURCHASED ONLY SIX MONTHS BEFORE. ON FEBRUARY 21, I FILED A CLAIM, A COPY OF WHICH IS ENCLOSED.

SINCE THAT TIME, MY LIVING ROOM HAS BEEN REBUILT AND REPAIRED. I THANK YOU FOR THAT FINE SERVICE. HOWEVER, I HAVE NOT BEEN ABLE TO OBTAIN A FAIR SETTLEMENT FROM YOUR ADJUSTER, RONALD TIGHTWAD, FOR THE LOSS OF OUR LIVING ROOM FURNITURE WHICH WAS DESTROYED IN THE FIRE. SPECIFICALLY, MR. TIGHTWAD HAS OFFERED TO PAY ONLY $10,000 FOR FURNITURE THAT COST $22,000 ONLY SIX MONTHS BEFORE. I HAVE ENCLOSED THE RECEIPTS FOR YOUR PERUSAL. HE HAS ALSO REFUSED TO PAY FOR A NEW BED WHICH SUFFERED SMOKE DAMAGE AND STILL SMELLS OF SMOKE, DESPITE TWO CLEANINGS. THE BED WAS WORTH $1000.

IN ADDITION TO BEING UNABLE TO REACH A FAIR SETTLEMENT, MR. TIGHTWAD HAS BEEN IMPOLITE. HE HAS REFUSED TO RETURN PHONE CALLS FOR DAYS AT A TIME AND HE HAS REFUSED TO ACKNOWLEDGE THE COPIES OF THE RECEIPTS WE SENT HIM. IN ADDITION, HE THREATENED US WITH INSURANCE CANCELLATION, WHICH I BELIEVE IS NOT WITHIN THE SCOPE OF HIS JOB DUTIES.

I WOULD LIKE TO DISCUSS THIS MATTER WITH YOU AT YOUR EARLIEST CONVENIENCE. I HAVE CONSIDERED CONSULTING A LAWYER BUT AM SURE THAT WE CAN ARRANGE A FAIR RESOLUTION OF THIS DISPUTE.

I CAN BE REACHED DURING THE DAY AT 555-3434. MY HOME PHONE IS 555-4567.

THANK YOU FOR YOUR COURTESY.

MARY P. TOUGHCONSUMER
4545 GET MY WAY LANE
BALTIMORE, MARYLAND

CC: RONALD TIGHTWAD
STATE DEPT. OF INSURANCE

Remember, when writing a letter of complaint to your insurance adjuster's superior:

- Always use your claim number and your policy number.
- Support your contentions with documents whenever possible.
- Outline all complaints in a clear, concise and unemotional manner. This is a business letter and the credibility of what you contend occurred will be judged by how you write it.
- Always let the person you are writing to know where you can be contacted during business hours.

If the supervisor does not give you satisfaction, and you continue to believe that you are in the right, don't be afraid to go to the very top of the company. (You should be able to get the names and addresses of the company head honchos by calling their home office. Your agent or local company representative will be able to give you the address and phone number of the home office.)

FIGHTING FOR YOUR RIGHTS

If you find yourself in a dispute with your own insurance company, you will have a choice: you can either stand up for your rights or give in and allow yourself to be fleeced. If you choose to assert yourself, the question becomes how to do it.

PURSUE INTERNAL REMEDIES

Many consumers believe that a disagreement with an insurance company can have one of two outcomes: either the consumer gives up and is walked upon, or lawyers get into the act. Happily, there is a middle ground between slinking away with your tail between your legs, and cutting off diplomatic relations.

Informal Complaints

Letters of complaint, such as the one above, can have very beneficial results. Mel Budnick, owner of Trident Insurance Agency in Los Angeles, tells the story of a friend who was having difficulty with an adjuster after a fire in his home. It seems that the adjuster got a bee in his bonnet about arson, when there simply was no evidence whatsoever that the fire was of suspicious origin. A letter to the adjuster's boss was all it took to open the company coffers and a fair settlement was achieved within a very short time of the letter of complaint.

Meet the Decision Makers

It may be important to humanize your claim by putting a face behind it: yours. Thus, if you are having trouble, seek to make an appointment in person with the decision makers.

Before your meeting, organize your facts. Thus:

Bring a Copy of Your Policy

Be prepared to show the adjuster or insurance executive the policy language that supports your position.

Bring Documents That Support Your Claim

Know the History of Your File

You should be prepared to answer any question the executive might have about your case.

Know Your Legal Rights

If the dispute threatens to turn nasty or involves a lot of money, run the case by an attorney before the meeting. You might even want to bring your lawyer to present your side of the story.

You should also avoid unnecessary emotionalism. If you rant and rave and shout, the only thing you will succeed in doing is to alienate the very people you want to decide in your favor.

You should also be willing to reasonably compromise. Don't be too rigid in your demands but be flexible in looking for a solution. Remember, three quarters or even half a loaf will be better than no loaf at all.

Once you have had your meeting, don't forget to follow up. Whether the meeting ends up in a settlement, a compromise or an agreement to disagree, always follow up with a courteous confirming letter.

PURSUE POLICY REMEDIES

At this point, if you can't reach a satisfactory conclusion to your dispute, you can either raise the white flag and accept whatever you can get (not a bad idea if you don't have the time, temperament or money to pursue your rights) or you can roll up your sleeves and get to work. If you choose the latter course, your next step is to pursue the remedies available as specified in the insurance policy itself.

The usual avenue of dispute resolution is an **arbitration**. Arbitrations are similar to trials but they are conducted by individuals called arbitrators. Arbitrations are either nonbinding, meaning you or the company can pursue the matter further in a court of law if displeased with the outcome or they are binding, which means the arbitrator's decision is the last word in the matter. Be careful to determine which.

Arbitrations can be very handy. For one thing, they could be quicker than court trials. Also, they permit each side to present its case before an impartial third party. Often, this is enough to resolve the matter. On the other hand, arbitrations can be very unfair. For example, you may have to pay for your effort to seek justice, since arbitrators usually are paid for their services by the parties in arbitration.

> **CONSUMER ALERT: IF THERE IS A LOT OF MONEY AT STAKE IN AN ARBITRATION, THINK SERIOUSLY ABOUT HIRING AN ATTORNEY TO REPRESENT YOU BECAUSE YOU CAN BET THAT THE INSURANCE COMPANY WILL BE REPRESENTED BY A LAWYER WHO HAS YEARS OF TRAINING AND EXPERIENCE IN HANDLING CASES IN COURT AND BEFORE ARBITRATORS.**

Once the arbitration is complete, you will be notified of the decision by mail. If you win, pat yourself on the back and see whether the insurance company throws in the towel. If you lose, decide whether you want to continue to pursue your rights.

FILE A LAWSUIT

If you still are unhappy, you may wish to file a lawsuit. (Most of the time, lawsuits can be filed without going through an arbitration. Ask your lawyer for advice on this issue.)

CONSUMER ALERT: IF YOU ARE IN A SIGNIFICANT DISPUTE WITH YOUR COMPANY, THERE IS A BOOK YOU MAY WANT TO READ. IT IS WRITTEN BY WILLIAM SHERNOFF, A LAWYER WHO SPECIALIZES IN SUING INSURANCE COMPANIES. THIS BOOK IS: *HOW TO MAKE INSURANCE COMPANIES PAY YOUR CLAIMS* (1990, HASTINGS HOUSE, MAMARONECK, NEW YORK). THIS PAPERBACK BOOK WILL GUIDE YOU THROUGH THE PROCESS OF FILING A CLAIM AND TEACHES YOU IN DETAIL HOW TO FIGHT BACK IF YOU ARE NOT TREATED FAIRLY.

REPORT YOUR COMPANY

Insurance companies are regulated in all 50 states and in all the provinces of Canada. This regulatory power gives consumers another avenue in their quest for truth, justice and the consumer power way.

One of the important functions of state insurance departments is to assist consumers in getting an even break from their insurance companies. Thus, if you feel like Pee Wee Herman in the ring with Mohammed Ali in his prime, you may wish to call for help from your insurance department.

State insurance departments should handle pressing problems for consumers, including:
- •Improper denial of claims
- •Unreasonable delays in settling claims
- •Illegal cancellation or termination of policies
- •Misrepresentation by company or agent
- •Misappropriation of funds paid in trust to an agent
- •Premium disputes

Be sure to hold your insurance department to these standards. When writing to the Insurance Department, be sure to send a copy of the letter to your state legislator.

CONSUMER ALERT: IF YOUR COMPANY GOES BANKRUPT OR CANNOT OTHERWISE PAY YOUR CLAIM, YOU PROBABLY STILL HAVE AT LEAST A PARTIAL REMEDY SINCE MOST STATES HAVE *GUARANTEE FUNDS* TO PAY CONSUMERS WITH VALID CLAIMS WHOSE COMPANY HAS GONE BELLY UP. CONTACT YOUR DEPARTMENT OF INSURANCE FOR DETAILS.

CONSUMER'S AGENDA

Where to begin? There is so much reform needed in the field of insurance that it is almost impossible to know where to start, or how to keep the discussion from growing into a three volume book!

As consumers, it is in your self interest to get involved politically and support reform that will make insurance more affordable, more responsive to your needs, and even though the insurance industry powers that be will deny it, more competitive and consumer-friendly.

REMOVE THE INSURANCE INDUSTRY ANTI- TRUST EXEMPTION

The insurance industry enjoys an exemption from federal anti-trust laws. How does this state of exemption affect your pocketbook? It allows the Insurance Services Office (ISO) to set "advisory rates" which most insurance companies use as a reference point in pricing their wares. ISO rates reflect what the least efficient companies need to charge in order to make a profit. Therefore, rates based on ISO advice tend to push the rates of all companies upward, regardless of each company's individual profit and loss picture. Banning ISO advisory rates would force companies to base their prices on their own economic projections and productivity levels. True competition would be introduced into the picture, strengthening the forces of the marketplace that reward efficiency and productivity. The result: lower premiums overall.

REPEAL ANTI-GROUP AND ANTI-REBATE LAWS

Every time a state lawmaker introduces bills permitting consumers to form insurance buying groups or permitting agents to rebate part of their commissions to consumers, the industry stomps them into the ground. Only California specifically and unequivocally allows these practices, and that was only accomplished by the Initiative known as Proposition 103 in 1988.

INCREASE THE EFFECTIVENESS OF STATE REGULATION

The insurance industry is supposed to be one of the most regulated industries in the United States. And it is true that each of the 50 states has its own department of insurance which has the job of regulating the prices charged by the industry, the language of the policies offered and other aspects of the insurance business.

Of course, saying that the industry is regulated is one thing, actually regulating it is usually quite another. GAO studies have concluded that the industry has far too much influence over most state regulatory agencies and legislatures.

Here are a few suggestions that we think might begin to correct the current imbalance of power in favor of the industry over the consumer in most states:

MAKE THE OFFICE OF INSURANCE COMMISSIONER AN ELECTED OFFICE

As it stands now, most insurance commissioners around the country are political appointees. This allows them to be insulated from the citizens they are serving.

ESTABLISH CONSUMER ADVOCACY ORGANIZATIONS

One of the major problems facing consumers of insurance is their voicelessness in the corridors of political power. Lacking an independent and informed organization to represent them in front of state legislative committees and administrative agencies, consumers' rights often take a backseat to moneyed interests who use their wealth and power to influence state legislatures and the permissive executive administration of state law. The playing field could become more level if citizen insurance boards were established to represent consumer concerns in rate proceedings and in front of legislatures considering insurance legislation. The boards could be financed through voluntary individual membership fees based on invitational inserts in insurance bills or state government mailings.

ESTABLISH NATIONWIDE STANDARDS FOR INSURANCE REGULATION

The effectiveness of state regulation varies depending on the comparative strength of consumers and the special-interest forces of the insurance industry. Minimum federal standards should be established concerning the level of insurance regulation each state must follow.

REQUIRE REGULATORY APPROVAL OF RATE INCREASES

In order for insurance premiums to be kept down, the companies should be required to justify their proposed rate increases BEFORE they go into effect. This should include a full opening of insurance company books and public hearings where the pros and cons of a rate increase can be publicly aired.

ESTABLISH COMPUTERIZED INFORMATION SERVICES

Each state should establish consumer information bureaus to help make it easier for consumers to comparison shop for insurance. In addition to price information, the state should make available data on how long it takes for companies to settle claims, assessment of financial health and similar information. The information should be available from a toll-free 800 number.

REVITALIZE "BAD FAITH" LAWS

Bad faith laws penalize insurance companies for dealing with their insureds or others with malice or reckless disregard of their rights, by assessing punitive damages against them. Such damages, which exceed out of pocket losses of the insured, serve as a financial incentive to insurance adjusters and executives to comply with their legal obligations to process claims fairly and in good faith. In recent years, several court rulings have limited the bad faith remedy. Legislation is essential to restore the viability of bad faith laws and to overcome these anti-consumer court decisions.

ESTABLISH VOLUNTARY MEDIATION BOARDS

Most consumer disputes with insurance companies involve relatively few dollars. This makes it harder to fight if your insurance company, "does you wrong." This imbalance can be rectified by each state establishing voluntary mediation boards or other dispute resolution mechanisms where consumers and insurance companies can resolve problems without having to pay high court filing fees and hiring high priced lawyers.

RESIST "TORT REFORM"

The insurance industry is engaged in a massive political campaign urging you to give up many of your legal rights in return for assurances that by doing so, you and others can pay lower premiums. Thus, the industry pushes "no-fault insurance" that promises more than it delivers and opposes punitive damages and strict liability in defective products cases. We urge you to remember the infamous Ford Pinto, Dalkon Shield and asbestos cases and not this anti-consumer company line. We are not opposed to administrative reforms to overcome administrative problems in the courts, but we shall resist pseudo reform which is designed to increase insurance industry profits at the expense of your legal rights.

INSIST THAT INSURANCE COMPANIES INCREASE THEIR LOSS PREVENTION ACTIVITIES

Insurance companies should be either legally required or "jaw-boned" into increasing their loss prevention activities. If the power of the industry and its agents were unleashed, we would have safer cars, safer jet liners, less pollution, better fire regulations and a safer workplace. A safer environment means that there will be fewer injuries and fewer injuries mean fewer claims. Fewer claims, in turn, will lead to lower premiums. Lower premiums, mean that you will have more money to spend elsewhere in the economy, thereby strengthening the nation. Now that's a domino theory that we can all get behind! For a beginning effort on loss prevention, write for information to Advocates for Highway and Auto Safety, 777 North Capitol St., NE, Suite 410, Washington, D.C., 20002. Or call (202) 408-1711.

GIVE YOURSELF A RAISE

Don't Waste Money on Insurance Which You Don't Need or Which is of Little Real Value

There are many insurance policies on the market today that are not worth the money, at least not according to J. Robert Hunter of NICO. Hunter warns against purchasing the following policies based on the fact that they are either noncomprehensive or noncatastrophic or both:

•*Air travel insurance* Have a good all purpose life insurance policy instead

•*Life insurance if you are single* The principal purpose of life insurance is protection of a family.

•*Life insurance on your children* Using cash value as an investment for your children's college may not be the best way to save the most amount of money since you will be spending some of the money on commissions and company profits.

•*Contact lens insurance*

•*Cancer insurance* Why buy cancer insurance when you can purchase broad general health insurance protection?

•*Health insurance on your pet*

•*Life, health sold to cover payment of a loan* (To which we add disability insurance to cover minimum payments on credit payments).

•*Indemnity hospitalization policies* These are usually not worth the cost of the premium.

•*Mortgage insurance* Annual renewable life is cheaper and your beneficiaries can use the money for any purpose they want.

•*Rental car insurance* It is overpriced, especially if you have a comprehensive policy of your own.

Chapter Nine

SERVICES POTPOURRI
CONTRACTORS, BANKING
AND AUTO REPAIR

We close our tour of the service industry with a look at three other important services which consumers deal with frequently. Of the three, home building contractors and craftspeople seem to have the ability to cause consumers the most stress. Then there are auto mechanics. Many consumers feel completely at the "wrench jockey's" mercy, especially those who don't know a crankshaft from a piston. Finally, we'll take a brief tour through the world of personal banking where a dollar saved here and a dollar saved there can add up to a hefty sum and where the mistakes you prevent can save you anguish.

HOME CONTRACTORS

Tens of billions of dollars are spent each year throughout the country on home building and remodeling. Unfortunately, too many householders don't know how to go about finding a good contractor, how to judge the work and how to make sure the job is completed on time and on budget. As a result, at least some of that money spent on the building trades is often just so much water being poured down the drain.

A RECONNAISSANCE OF THE TERRITORY

The field of building is very broad and covers a wide range of territory. There are carpenters, plumbers, electricians, painters, laborers and others. There are supervisors known as general building contractors who coordinate workers when the job is large and complex. There are building liens to learn about and performance bonds and permits. Whew, and we've just begun.

But, let's get organized. As the old saying goes, you can't know the players without a program. So, let us introduce you to the world of the building contractor.

HIRING A MEMBER OF THE BUILDING TRADE

According to the California State Contractors Licensing Board, there are 41 different types of licensed building crafts.

Here are some of the things you need to know about the many species of contractors:

They should be licensed Each state has an agency in charge of licensing building contractors, usually called the Contractors Licensing Board. Contractors licensing boards also handle consumer complaints and discipline misbehaving contractors (at least in theory) as well as engage in consumer education to a greater or lesser degree.

They should be bonded The **Contractor's License Bond** is money that has been put up by the contractor or a bonding company on behalf of the contractor which is to be used to pay for damages when the contractor is found to have acted improperly and which the contractor either will not or cannot pay.

> **CONSUMER ALERT: THE CONTRACTING LICENSING BOND IS ACTUALLY LESS THAN MEETS THE EYE! IT IS NOT A GUARANTEE OF PERFORMANCE, COMPETENCE OR FINANCIAL RESPONSIBILITY. MOREOVER, THE CONTRACTING LICENSING BONDS THAT STATES REQUIRE ARE RARELY SUFFICIENT TO PROTECT YOU AGAINST CONTRACTOR MISCONDUCT OR DEFICIENT WORK.**

They should be insured As the famous Murphy once said, "If something can go wrong, it will." That being so, for your own protection, even the best building contractor should have sufficient liability and workers compensation insurance to meet any contingency.

The General Building Contractor

If your building job requires the hiring of at least three licensed craftspersons, you are probably better off retaining the services of a person who will act as the conductor of your home improvement or building "symphony," known in the jargon as the **general building contractor**. A general contractor oversees the entire building project, including but not limited to: hiring the workers, supervising the work and otherwise being responsible for getting the job done "on time and on budget."

Subcontractors

If the general contractor is a park ranger that oversees and cares for your building project forest, than the **subcontractors** are the trees. Subcontractors are the craftspeople who work in specific areas, i.e. painting, roofing, tiling, carpentry, etc. When hired by a general contractor, the subcontractor has no direct contract with the consumer.

> **CONSUMER ALERT: LEGALLY, YOU CAN PERFORM THE SERVICES OF A GENERAL CONTRACTOR YOURSELF AND SAVE MONEY BY DOING SO. PEOPLE WHO CHOOSE TO DO SO ARE KNOWN AS *OWNER/BUILDERS*. HOWEVER THERE IS A BIG CAVEAT HERE, (WHICH IS A BIG LAWYER WORD FOR "WARNING"): DO NOT, WE REPEAT, DO NOT TRY TO BECOME AN OWNER/BUILDER UNLESS YOU KNOW WHAT YOU ARE DOING! THERE IS JUST TOO MUCH THAT CAN GO WRONG IN A BUILDING PROJECT FOR YOU TO "LEARN ON THE JOB."**

Building Permits

For most construction jobs, you will need the permission of your local government entity. This is called a **building permit**. Building permits are issued based on plans and specifications of the job and assurances contained therein that the work will be up to local building legal requirements known as **building codes**.

> **CONSUMER ALERT: IF YOUR JOB NEEDS A BUILDING PERMIT, THE CONSUMER'S RESOURCE HANDBOOK, PUBLISHED BY THE FEDERAL GOVERNMENT, RECOMMENDS THAT THE PERMIT BE TAKEN OUT IN THE CONTRACTOR'S NAME. THAT WAY, IF THE WORK DOES NOT PASS INSPECTION, YOU ARE NOT FINANCIALLY RESPONSIBLE FOR ANY CORRECTIONS THAT MUST BE MADE.**

Inspections

In order for your construction job to be officially completed, it will require the approval of a building inspector whose job it is to make sure the work was performed according to plan and up to the applicable building codes.

Mechanic's Lien

A **mechanic's lien** permits the general contractor, licensed subcontractors and certain material suppliers to "cloud" the title to the property where the work was performed until payment is made in full. This cloud on title is called a mechanic's lien. NOTE: If your general contractor does not pay subcontractors, you could be forced to pay them or face foreclosure of the mechanics lien! This is true even if you paid the general contractor in full.

Bids

Without getting too legalistic, a **bid** can be defined as an offer to perform contracting services for a specific price and terms. A **single bid** is one that is arrived at through negotiations with a contractor. **Competitive bids** occur when several contractors send out bids in competition with each other in an attempt to "win the contract" to do the job.

Cost Overruns

If a job takes more work or materials than originally planned for, then, the additional expense incurred as a result is known as a **cost overrun**.

GETTING STARTED

Ok, so you have decided that you want to build a house, add a room, replace your old plumbing, redo your kitchen or whatever. What do you do and when do you do it?

Decide What You Want Done

As the old Chinese proverb says, "The longest journey starts with the first step." In this case, the first step is deciding what you want to do.

Preplanning is important and it can be a lot of fun. You can look through design books, attend building trade fairs, read magazine and newspaper articles, consult with architects, drafters and building contractors and otherwise investigate the lay of the land.

> **CONSUMER ALERT: IF YOU ARE PLANNING A LARGE CONSTRUCTION PROJECT, ARCHITECTS CAN PROVIDE VERY IMPORTANT SERVICES FOR CONSUMERS. AMONG THEM ARE CONCEIVING THE PROJECT BASED ON YOUR DESIRES, PREPARING THE PLANS, SAVING YOU MONEY BY MAKING SURE THE BUILDING OR ROOM ADDITION IS BUILT WITH ECONOMY AND EFFICIENCY IN MIND, HELPING YOU TO SORT OUT AND UNDERSTAND ISSUES SUCH AS BUILDING MATERIALS, BUILDING CODES AND ZONING LAWS AND INSPECTING THE CONSTRUCTION TO MAKE SURE THE CONTRACTOR IS FOLLOWING THE PLANS AND SPECIFICATIONS.**

Figure Out How to Pay For It

If you can pay cash, that is always best. But if the job requires you to obtain financing, there are loans available which can help pay for the job. *A construction loan* A construction loan is short term, usually due within a year. Often, a construction loan will have provisions wherein the lending institution keeps the money on premises and pays the general contractor directly as different phases of the work are completed.

A construction loan that rolls over into a permanent loan Some lending institutions offer a construction loan that can be rolled over into a mortgage or trust deed.

A home improvement loan If your stated purpose in borrowing the money is to engage in home improvements, then the lender may wish to grant you a home improvement loan, secured by a deed of trust (often referred to as a "2nd trust deed" if you already have a mortgage or 1st trust deed on the premises). Some lenders will want to control the disbursement of funds and others will not.

> **CONSUMER ALERT: SOME LENDING INSTITUTIONS PEDDLE LOANS THAT CALL FOR PREPAYMENT PENALTIES IN THE EVENT OF EARLY PAY OFF. DO NOT FALL FOR THIS TRAP. YOU SHOULD HAVE A RIGHT TO PAY A LOAN WITHOUT HAVING TO PAY EXTRA MONEY FOR THE PRIVILEGE OF GETTING OUT OF DEBT.**

Contractor assisted financing Some contractors assist their clients with financing.

> **CONSUMER ALERT: IF YOUR CONSTRUCTION PROJECT IS TO PROMOTE ENERGY EFFICIENCY OR STRUCTURAL RENOVATION, YOU MAY QUALIFY FOR GOVERNMENT GRANT OR LOW INTEREST LOAN ASSISTANCE. FOR INFORMATION ON GOVERNMENT FUNDING ASSISTANCE, ASK YOUR LOCAL LIBRARIAN TO HELP YOU FIND THE CATALOGUE OF FEDERAL PUBLIC ASSISTANCE. ANOTHER SOURCE OF THIS INFORMATION IS THE FEDERAL ASSISTANCE PROGRAMS RETRIEVAL SYSTEMS (FAPRS) WHICH, FOR A MODEST FEE, WILL CONDUCT A SEARCH**

FOR PROGRAMS YOU MAY QUALIFY FOR. TO FIND AN ACCESS POINT NEAR YOU, CONTACT GENERAL ASSISTANCE SERVICES ADMINISTRATION AT (202) 708-5126.

Regardless of the type of loan you want, it is a good idea to shop around for financing since different lenders will have differing interest charges, loan costs and terms, all of which can materially affect the "price" of the loan.

> **CONSUMER ALERT: IF YOU ARE GOING TO FINANCE A LOAN, BE SURE TO PUT A CONTINGENCY CLAUSE IN YOUR BUILDING CONTRACT THAT YOU ARE BOUND TO PROCEED ONLY IF YOU CAN FIND A LOAN BELOW A SPECIFIC RATE OF INTEREST.**

Finding the right contractor or craftsperson

Regardless of whether your job is relatively small, such as redoing your bathroom sink, or as large as building a new house, now comes the most important part, finding the right building professional to do the job. PAY CAREFUL ATTENTION TO THIS TASK! HIRING THE WRONG CONTRACTOR CAN COST YOU MONEY, AGGRAVATION (IF NOT HEARTACHE) AND THE POTENTIAL THAT THE JOB WILL BE DONE POORLY, LATE OR NOT AT ALL.

Ok, now that we have put a little adrenaline into your system, let's calm down and look at how to go about the task at hand.

Decide on the kind of contractor you need This won't usually be too difficult. If you need a lot of work, you will probably want a general building contractor to be in charge of the work. If your job is specific, such as repiping your home, you will want a plumber. If you need a new roof, you will want a roofer, etc.

Find the names of candidates Finding the names of good contractors is a similar process to finding good doctors and lawyers. Look to the following sources:

•*Friends, loved ones and associates* If you know someone who has had work done similar to that you need performed, ask for the name of the contractor(s) who worked the job. Word of mouth by satisfied customers is the way good contractors build their businesses.

•*Your mortgage banker,*

•*Your real estate agent, and*

•*Your homeowner's insurance agent:* These people deal with construction jobs and frequently know the wheat from the chaff of the contracting community.

•*Other contractors* Perhaps your cousin is a plumber and you need a good electrician or roofer. Your cousin may have worked on jobs with good ones and may know the names of those in your area who can do a good job.

> **CONSUMER ALERT: RELYING ON ADVERTISING ON TELEVISION OR IN THE YELLOW PAGES AS A SOURCE FOR FINDING A CONTRACTOR CAN BE DANGEROUS. A STUDY BY THE NEW YORK DEPARTMENT OF CONSUMER AFFAIRS FOUND THAT HOMEOWNERS WHO HIRED CONTRACTORS BASED ON RADIO, TV OR PRINT ADS, RATHER THAN UPON KNOWLEDGEABLE RECOMMENDATIONS, REPORTED SUBSTANTIALLY MORE PROBLEMS WITH THEIR HOME IMPROVEMENTS.**

Get competitive bids It is vital to your pocketbook and the well being of the job you want performed, that you talk to and get bids from, several competent contractors.

Check out the candidates' credentials and references You are putting a precious possession into your contractor's hands - your home or other owned property. Thus, you should be as careful in checking out the contractor as you would a baby sitter. Here are some things to look into:

•*Check each contractor's license* If the contractor is not properly licensed, do not give him or her the job. Hiring unlicensed personnel may save you a little money but it can cause a lot more trouble if the job is done improperly. Phone numbers for the State Contractors Licensing Board should be in your phone book. (Most boards can also give you information on whether contractors have been disciplined for unethical behavior or have had legal action taken against them.)

•*Check the status of the contractor's bond* You should also check the status of the contractor's bond with the board and the bonding company the contractor tells you has issued the bond.

•*See if the contractor is a member of a trade association* Membership in a trade or professional association is no guarantee that he or she is good at what they do, but it may indicate a higher level of concern and professional pride, especially if the association has a code of ethics and an ombudsman service.

•*Look into each contractor's references* Your contractor should have references to give you of satisfied customers. Be sure and call several of these references, since stories abound of references which are phony. Also, ask for the addresses of jobs that the contractor has performed and see if you can get permission to view the workmanship as well as speak with the customer to see if they were satisfied.

•*Make sure each contractor has a well established reputation* The last thing you want in a contractor is a "fly-by-night" who is here today taking your money and gone tomorrow after having done a poor job or skipping out of the job altogether. One way to avoid this problem is to hire a contractor who has a well established business in your community.

CONSUMER ALERT: NEVER HIRE A CONTRACTOR WHO WORKS DOOR TO DOOR! SCAM ARTISTS WHO PRACTICE THE "ART" OF THE DREADED HOME IMPROVEMENT FRAUD FREQUENTLY WORK THIS WAY, OPENING THE CONVERSATION BY TELLING YOU THEY "HAVE A CREW IN THE AREA" AND THAT THEY "CAN GIVE YOU A DEAL ON A NEW DRIVEWAY" OR ROOF OR WHATEVER MAY LOOK LIKE IT NEEDS WORK.

•*Make sure the contractor has insurance* For your own protection, your contractor should have liability and workers compensation insurance which will protect you during the job. Ask your contractor for the certificate of insurance or other proof that his or her insurance is currently in effect.

Make the choice Once you have compared the contractors, compared the prices they are bidding, the time within which each is willing to promise performance, you should choose the contractor that you believe offers the best chance of quality performance at a reasonable price.

UNDERSTANDING THE BUILDING CONTRACT

The heart of your building or home improvement project is your contract. To paraphrase that old television show's introduction, "It controls the price, it controls the terms and it controls the rights and obligations of the parties." This being so, negotiating a good deal and making sure it gets put into writing is vital to your protection as a consumer.

It is impossible in a book of this nature to set forth every detail you will want in your contract because many of the terms will be based upon your individual needs. However, regardless of the idiosyncrasies of your deal, you will want to pay close attention to the following:

The Price

Generally, there are two ways to go when it comes to paying for contracting work: **cost-plus** and the lump sum, aka the **flat fee.**

A flat fee is just that; you pay an agreed upon fixed price and the contractor does the work. A cost-plus deal is a bit more complicated. You agree to pay the contractor's out of pocket costs "plus" an agreed upon percentage above that amount which is the builder's profit.

Which is best for you? That depends. A fixed-price contract has the benefit of predictability as to the price of the job and simplicity. However, the financial incentive will be for the builder to use lower-end materials since that will increase profits. A cost-plus deal has the advantage of allowing you more flexibility and gives you greater access to the true "cost" of the job. However, the financial incentive here is for the builder to build up the costs, which in turn, increases the dollars paid by you for the materials and "plus."

> **CONSUMER ALERT: WERNER R. HASHAGEN HAS WRITTEN A BOOK, *HOW TO GET IT BUILT FASTER FOR LESS.* WHILE IT IS WRITTEN FROM A CONTRACTOR'S POINT OF VIEW, IT DOES OFFER A LOT OF USEFUL INFORMATION ON BUILDING PROJECTS. IT CAN BE PURCHASED BY CALLING (619) 459-0122.**

> **CONSUMER ALERT: DO NOT AGREE TO A *TIME AND MATERIALS* CONTRACT. HASHAGEN STATES, "A 'T & M' MEANS YOU TELL THE GENERAL CONTRACTOR, IN EFFECT, BUILD IT AND SEND ME A BILL! NO COMPETITIVE BIDDING, NO CONSTRUCTION COST PROJECTION, NO GUARANTEED MAXIMUM COST."**

The Method of Payment

Another important part of your building contract, is the method by which payments are made. This is one occasion that you definitely do not want to pay cash ahead of time. Instead, you will want to pay over time as work on the job is completed.

A typical contract might provide the following payment schedule:

Small down payment It is best to keep this amount as small as possible. In no event, should the down payment exceed ten percent (and may not by law in some states) of the total contract cost.

Periodic payments over the length of the job You should schedule your payments to the contractor over the life of the job. In order to keep your contractor's interest in the job running high, it is a good idea to tie the payments to the completion of key aspects of the total building project. For example, the contract might call for a payment when the foundation is completed and for another payment when framing is finished, etc.

CONSUMER ALERT: MAKE SURE THAT YOUR CONTRACT CALLS FOR WHAT IS KNOWN AS A *"RETENTION"*. A RETENTION ALLOWS YOU TO KEEP A SMALL PERCENTAGE OF EACH PERIODIC PAYMENT IN ABEYANCE, WHICH YOU RETAIN UNTIL THE JOB IS COMPLETED IN A WORKMANLIKE MANNER. THIS HELPS YOU TO KEEP THE CONTRACTOR'S INTEREST IN CORRECTING ERRORS AFTER THE CONTRACT IS COMPLETE.

Final payment Final payment should be made due thirty days after completion. During this time, you should inspect the work and make sure it is up to par, so that you can request any corrections you might need before the final payment.

CONSUMER ALERT: AT THE END OF EACH JOB, YOU WILL BE ASKED TO SIGN A COMPLETION CERTIFICATE, WHICH STATES THAT THE JOB HAS BEEN COMPLETED AND THAT ALL IS WELL. DO NOT SIGN THIS DOCUMENT AND DO NOT MAKE THE FINAL PAYMENT UNTIL AND UNLESS THE JOB IS DONE PROPERLY.

Penalties The contract should contain penalties for late performance by the contractor. THIS IS VITAL, since perhaps the most common consumer complaint about contractors is the sweet time that too many take to complete their work. This being so, a financial penalty for each day that the job is late will give your contractor a financial incentive to do the work on time.

Fund control If the job is quite large, many lenders require the use of a **fund control** company, which, for a fee, makes periodic payments to the builder as the job progresses. Fund control companies normally work from vouchers you sign indicating that certain phases of the work have been completed. But some will also inspect the work if they are obliged to in your fund control agreement. If you use fund control, we recommend that you hire a company that is well versed in the building trades and that they be required to inspect the work themselves before issuing any disbursements.

Terms of performance Your contract will provide the exact agreement between you and the contractor as to his or her obligations to you as a contractor. The contract should consist of specific and precise language concerning the following issues:

• *What is to be done* Your building contract will provide exactly what is to be done in the project. If the job is large, that will be in the building plan.

• *What materials are to be used* If the quality of materials is an important issue in your job, be sure that the types and grades of materials to be utilized in the job are specifically laid out in the plans or the contract itself.

• *Time for performance* At best, being involved in a building contract is a nuisance, especially if the building is going on in your home. Thus, the date work is to commence, the time frame by which certain aspects of the work are to be completed and the finish date, are all vital to your peace of mind and should be precisely spelled out in the contract.

CONSUMER ALERT: TIME IS A VERY IMPORTANT PART OF ANY BUILDING CONTRACT. YOU NEED TO PUT AS MUCH WORDING IN YOUR CONTRACT ABOUT TIME AS YOU CAN TO PROTECT YOURSELF AND TO "STIMULATE" YOUR CONTRACTOR TO

LIVE UP TO CONTRACTUAL OBLIGATIONS REGARDING TIME OF PERFORMANCE. BE SURE TO PUT IN PENALTY CLAUSES WHICH FINANCIALLY PUNISH THE CONTRACTOR FOR LATE WORK AND ADD LANGUAGE INDICATING THAT, "TIME IS OF THE ESSENCE." (CONSULT YOUR LAWYER FOR DETAILS OF THE LAW REGARDING TIME CLAUSES IN YOUR STATE.)

•*The payment plan* As we discussed above, you will want to make sure your obligations to pay are specifically set forth and that your obligation to pay only arises after the contractor has satisfactorily performed the building or remodeling.

•*Changes in plans* It is the rare job that is completed without at least some alteration of the original plans. Perhaps you don't like the look of a sink or you decide the closet you thought was plenty big on paper is really just a hole in the wall and you want it enlarged. Whatever the case may be, you can expect to have changes and you can also expect these changes to cost you money.

When you decide to permit a deviation or alteration of the original work, MAKE SURE YOU DO SO IN WRITING! You should be just as careful about changes as you were about the original contract. Also, if the contractor agrees to make a change as work is ongoing, be sure to take the time to write up a written note or "**change order**" on the spot, so that there will be no disagreement later on as to the price of the alteration or whether you specifically authorized the different performance.

•*Warranties* If you can, it is a good idea to have the contractor give you a warranty guaranteeing his or her work. A warranty should be in writing and cover as much of the work as you can get the contractor to agree upon. Remember, that a warranty is only as good as the company which issues it, so be sure you have done your homework investigating the builder before problems arise rather than after so that you don't find yourself facing a "wrong without a remedy."

CONSUMER ALERT: AS WITH ANY BUSINESS RELATIONSHIP, YOU SHOULD MAKE SURE THAT EVERYTHING IS IN WRITING AND THAT YOU KEEP COPIES. WITH REGARD TO BUILDING PROJECTS, THE CALIFORNIA DEPARTMENT OF CONSUMER AFFAIRS SUGGESTS THAT YOU KEEP A JOB FILE CONSISTING OF THE FOLLOWING:
   •THE CONTRACT AND ANY CHANGE ORDERS
   •THE PLANS AND SPECIFICATIONS
   •ALL BILLS AND INVOICES
   •CANCELLED CHECKS
   •LIEN RELEASES FROM SUBCONTRACTORS AND MATERIAL SUPPLIERS (SEE BELOW).
   •LETTERS, NOTES AND CORRESPONDENCE WITH YOUR CONTRACTOR, (TO WHICH WE ADD, INCLUDING BIDS, ADVERTISEMENTS AND ALL OTHER WRITTEN MATERIALS YOU MIGHT HAVE CONCERNING THE CONTRACTOR AND YOUR JOB.)

CONSUMER ALERT: UNDER THE LAW OF MOST STATES YOU WILL HAVE THREE BUSINESS DAYS FROM THE SIGNING OF THE CONTRACT IN THE PRESENCE OF THE CONTRACTOR TO

CHANGE YOUR MIND. DON'T TAKE THIS FOR GRANTED. MAKE SURE YOUR CONTRACT CONTAINS PROVISIONS SETTING FORTH YOUR CANCELLATION RIGHTS AND MAKE SURE YOU HAVE THE FORMS YOU NEED TO DO SO IN CASE YOU DECIDE TO CHANGE YOUR MIND.

The Problem of Mechanic's Liens

Workers and the suppliers of materials have a legal right to enforce payment through the use of a legal bludgeon known as the **mechanic's lien**. A mechanic's lien allows person with valid lien claims to force you to pay them in order for you to preserve a clear title to the property where the work was done.

There are some things you can do to protect yourself from the nightmare of having to pay twice for the same work or supplies.

Use a funding control company One of the purposes of this method of payment is to provide a fail safe against subcontractors and others not being paid. With a funding control company reviewing disbursements and obtaining necessary releases, the risk to you of suffering a mechanic's lien is reduced (although not completely eliminated). You will have to decide if the cost of this service is worth the price.

Make sure there is sufficient bonding Bonds are issued by "sureties" who guarantee payment for losses occasioned by the failure of the contractor to perform pursuant to the contract. Especially in a large job, you will want the contractor to be able to qualify for a **labor and materials bond** and a **performance bond**.

Stay involved You must make sure you know what is happening step by step during your construction. Thus, if you have had cement poured, you will want to ask the contractor to provide proof that the concrete workers and suppliers have been paid and all necessary releases signed. Ask the contractor for copies of all payment documents so that you can keep an up to date and accurate construction file.

WHEN TROUBLE BREWS

Most construction projects have at least some minor problems. After all, construction is an intricate and demanding process being performed by human beings, who have yet to achieve a state of perfection. Happily most problems can be worked out to the satisfaction of all parties. However, you will need an organized approach:

Bring Up Problems Sooner Rather Than Later

If the contractor breaches his or her contract through poor performance, that does not mean that you have no legal obligations in the matter. In fact, you do. It is known in the legal trade as "mitigating damages" and that means that you must act in a reasonable manner to avoid injury, thereby reducing the contractor's ultimate liability. When you communicate about a problem, always do so in writing. If things turn nasty, memories may differ (to put it tactfully) about "what went down."

> **CONSUMER ALERT: IT IS A GOOD IDEA TO TAKE PICTURES OF THE OFFENDING AREA OF CONSTRUCTION. IN COURT OR ARBITRATION, A PICTURE OFTEN IS WORTH A THOUSAND WORDS.**

Change Contractors

If your contractor breaches the contract, you probably have the right to "fire the bum" and bring in new blood to finish the job. If that means there is more money that comes out of your pocket than you would have paid if the work had been done right, under the law, you probably have the right to have the original contractor pay you the difference.

There is a problem here. You are not the one who ultimately decides whether a breach has occurred. If you and the contractor disagree, that may become a matter for a court of law. And if you are found to be wrong, you may have to pay the original contractor for the full price of the job, even if you hired someone else to finish it. Thus, before you fire your contractor, we urge you to consult a lawyer to advise you of your legal rights, the potential cost.

Go to the Law

If you and your contractor cannot resolve your difficulties, you may have to file a lawsuit or going to an arbitration. In larger matters, this will probably mean you will have to hire a lawyer and seek redress (or defend yourself) in court.

Report Your Contractor

Just like a lawyer or doctor, your contractor is (or at least should be) a licensed professional, answerable to the state licensing authority. If you feel that your contractor has acted unethically, such as abandoning a job, or if you believe the work was so shoddy so as to constitute gross negligence, contact the appropriate state authority.

The frustrating thing will be that you will be dealing with a "pro-contractor" bureaucracy which may not act quickly or take decisive action to assist you. When dealing with the Board, remember the old adage, "he who (politely) squeaks, gets the grease."

FINAL HINTS

Any construction project involves a great deal of time, money, effort, devotion and perhaps, luck. It should also involve consumer power and involvement. Here are some final hints to help you make sure your construction project goes according to plan:

Be home.

The old saying, "while the cat's away, the mouse will play," holds true in many construction jobs. Be on the job site. An informed and powerful consumer inspects the materials and fixtures before they are installed and points out shoddy work if and when it is discovered. Your presence will increase the likelihood that the job will be done correctly.

Make sure everything that you and your contractor agree to is set down in writing and is made a part of your contract.

We said this earlier but it is worth repeating - put everything, and we do mean everything, in writing.

Ask your contractor about inconveniences you can expect.

Inconveniences are a given in nearly every construction project. But, you also have a life to lead. Learning as much as you can about the former allows you to plan ahead to keep the latter from descending into chaos.

Do not hire an unlicensed contractor or craftsperson.

You may pay less at the outset but you may also receive more - more shoddy work, more heartache -- and spend more money than had you hired a licensed contractor.

Do not pay cash.

You want all of the records of your project handy. Paying cash leaves no trace unless you get a receipt. Even then, why not pay by check and have two receipts?

Never be afraid to ask questions.

If you don't ask questions, you will not learn the answers to what puzzles you. A good professional will be glad to take the time to fill you in on whatever queries you might have.

Never pay for work unless it is completed to your satisfaction.

If you get your payments ahead of your contractor's performance, you may find that the work slows to a crawl or stops altogether.

Make payments in a timely manner.

Conversely, if your contractor has performed and money is owed, pay it. This is a matter of integrity.

> **CONSUMER ALERT: IN TORONTO AND UNDER ACTIVE CONSIDERATION IN SOME UNITED STATES CITIES, CONSUMERS ARE BANDING TOGETHER TO FORM *HOME REPAIR ASSOCIATIONS*. THESE FOR-PROFIT OR NON-PROFIT ASSOCIATIONS USE THE COLLECTIVE BUYING POWER OF THEIR MEMBERS TO OBTAIN HOME REPAIR SERVICES AT REASONABLE PRICES. FOR AN ANNUAL MEMBERSHIP FEE, CONSUMERS CAN CALL A CENTRAL ASSOCIATION NUMBER IN CASE OF A HOME REPAIR EMERGENCY OR JUST TO SCHEDULE ROUTINE MAINTENANCE OR REMODELING; THEY ARE GUARANTEED PROMPT SERVICE FROM QUALIFIED AND RELIABLE REPAIR PERSONS.**

GIVE YOURSELF A RAISE

There are many ways to keep a handle on the expenses of construction or home repair. Most of the following have been suggested by Werner R. Hashagen in his book HOW TO GET IT BUILT, which we use here with his kind permission:

Review deed restrictions, easements, soil conditions, etc. before you start the project.

If you have to stop work in the middle of a construction job because it is illegal or impractical to go forward, you are throwing your money right into the sewer.

Purchase materials from local suppliers when you can.

It can save you money to buy from your local community. Doing so also makes it easier to deal with problems should they arise.

Avoid changes whenever possible.

Changes during construction generally cost you money. Thus, try to stick as close to the original plans as you can.

Obtain at least three bids on almost everything.

This works for you when you pay the general contractor on a cost-plus basis. When a contractor knows there is competition for your business, you are likely to get a better price. It is the way the free market system is supposed to work.

Keep a tight control over building costs.

It is, after all, your money.

Press for the shortest possible construction time if you have a construction loan.

It will save you interest.

Decide who pays for utilities (in new construction sites) and job toilet.

If you think the contractor will and it is not in the contract, you may get stuck with a bill you did not anticipate.

Purchase materials at the wholesale price through your contractor.

If you make the purchase yourself, chances are you will have to buy retail, which costs more.

Specify in the contract that you are entitled to a "one year inspection" and repair of defective building.

If something goes wrong in the first year, you should not have to pay for the repair. Be sure that you have the right to inspect the job after the first year and have any defective aspects of the job repaired at the contractor's expense.

AUTO REPAIR

If your household is like four out of five of your American counterparts, there is at least one motor vehicle "in residence." That means that unless at least one member of the family is a wrench jockey, a significant amount of money will be spent each year on auto repairs.

That would be bad enough if every mechanic and repair shop were honest and had an abundance of integrity mixed in with the grease. Unfortunately, that isn't true. According to a decade old U.S Department of Transportation study conducted on the auto repair industry, fully 40 percent of the costs associated with auto repairs are unnecessary. Think of it, 40 percent! That translates today to over 40 billion dollars spent unnecessarily by consumers each year!

The Transportation Study listed the major reasons for these astounding losses:
- •Unneeded parts sold in package deals
- •Unneeded repairs due to inadequate or incorrect diagnosis.
- •Faulty repairs for which consumers did not get their money back.

•Unneeded repairs sold with possible fraudulent intent
•Vehicle design requiring use of overly modularized parts
•Accidents due to faulty repairs (which also leads to injury and loss of life)

Unfortunately, there has been precious little action to counter this horrible situation since the study was released. Oh, there has been some strengthening of anti-fraud laws and the insurance industry is trying to fight fraud, but it still falls upon you, the consumer, to protect yourself.

FINDING A GOOD REPAIR FACILITY

The best thing you can do for yourself as an auto repair consumer, is to find the best auto repair shop in your area. This may or may not be difficult, depending on the quality of shops in your neck of the woods.

Know the Players

All repair shops are not created out of the same mold. In fact, you have several types from which to choose.

The independent shop Owners of independent repair garages are entrepreneurs who rely on the goodwill and recommendations of satisfied customers more than advertising in order to get business. Often, this works to your benefit. In fact, a 1988 survey by the Center for Study of Services in Washington D.C. found that 88 percent of customers at the average independent shop were satisfied with the work and service they received. Of course, if you receive lousy service, there is no higher chain of command at some corporate office where you can complain.

Major chains and franchises There are many national retailers that have repair facilities (i.e. Sears, Montgomery Ward). The most obvious benefit to going to a chain is the availability to have service problems handled out of your area. A major drawback of chain auto repair, according to THE LEMON BOOK by Ralph Nader and Clarence Ditlow and the Center for Auto Safety (1990, Moyer Bell Limited, Mount Kisco, New York), is that chains are often primarily interested in the easy sales, such as tires and batteries and are less proficient at dealing with the more intricate auto repairs.

Franchises also present a problem. They are backed by national advertising and promotion but are often only as good as the individual franchisee. Thus, treat franchise repairs as you should any repair shop - with caution.

Gasoline stations Service stations (we use the term loosely, since many gas stations now offer little service) are often as reliable as the independent garage. There can also be the added benefit of having a home company to complain to if problems arise.

Dealerships New car dealerships also have repair shops. You should definitely use these facilities for work done under warranty. If you find that this work was satisfactory, you may wish to call on the dealership for out of warranty repairs. On the downside, auto dealers are frequently more expensive than independents.

Specialty shops As some physicians may specialize in specific areas of your body, such as the heart, some "car doctors" restrict their "practices" to limited areas of your car, such as the transmission. If you have a specialized problem, it might be a good idea to check out the specialists who repair that part of your car.

Get Recommendations

As with finding any skilled professional, you will want to get recommendations from those who may be able to steer you toward the best mechanics in your community. The sources of recommendations can be several:

Friends and relatives who have a good mechanic.

Automobile sales persons who are willing to give an objective referral without regard to their dealership's own repair facility

Mechanics who don't work on your kind of car: Mechanics often know the reputation of their colleagues and they can often give good recommendations.

The Better Business Bureau's and local consumer groups: You should check the Better Business Bureau to see if a repair shop you are interested in has a record of complaints. Local consumer groups can also often give valuable recommendations.

Look for Certifications

The National Institute for Automotive Service Excellence (NIASE) gives voluntary examinations which test the competence of mechanics. Lack of certification does not tell you that the mechanic is incompetent, nor the presence of a certificate that the mechanic is competent. But certification does mean that the mechanic cared enough about his profession to take the time to study and pass the exam which is based on eight different skills tests. NIASE certificates are valid for two years.

> **CONSUMER ALERT: UNLESS YOUR MECHANIC HAS A CERTIFICATE OF "MASTER AUTOMOBILE TECHNICIAN" HE OR SHE MAY NOT BE UP TO NIASE'S STANDARDS IN EVERY AREA TESTED (I.E. ENGINE REPAIR, ENGINE PERFORMANCE, SUSPENSION AND STEERING, BRAKES, AUTOMATIC TRANSMISSION/TRANSAXLE, MANUAL DRIVETRAIN AND AXLES, ELECTRICAL SYSTEMS AND HEATING AND AIR CONDITIONING.) IF YOU WANT A LIST OF THE NATIONAL INSTITUTE CERTIFIED MECHANICS, CALL (703) 713-3800 OR SEND A CHECK FOR $1.95 (PRICES MAY CHANGE) TO NIASE, 13505 DULLES TECHNOLOGY DR., HERNDON, VIRGINIA, 22071.**

Investigate For Problems

Before you trust your car and your pocketbook to any repair facility, you should check the Better Business Bureau, your local department of consumer affairs, consumer groups, and the local Chamber of Commerce for records of complaints and/or difficulties that the facility in question may have experienced in the past.

GETTING ONLY THE REPAIRS YOU NEED AND NOT ANY THAT YOU DON'T

Part of your job as a consumer who is in charge of his or her own auto repair destiny, is to make sure that you effectively communicate the problems you want looked at, in a way that will tell the mechanic that you are not a person who just fell off of the proverbial turnip truck. Here's how:

Write Down The Problems With Your Car

It is easy to go to a mechanic and forget to tell the mechanic or service manager about the squeak in your car's rear end when you are more concerned about the shake, rattle and rolling in your engine. Writing a list of woes ahead of time will help keep you from forgetting anything.

Be Specific

It is not enough to say, "My car makes a terrible noise. Fix it." You must be more specific than that. For example, does the car act up when it is cold or while driving at highway speeds? Does the problem feel to you like it is in the engine or elsewhere? Have you had a history of this kind of problem before? etc.

> **CONSUMER ALERT: IN SOME AREAS THERE ARE BUSINESSES KNOWN AS *DIAGNOSTIC CLINICS* THAT CAN CHECK OUT YOUR CAR AND TELL YOU WHAT NEEDS TO BE DONE. THEN, YOU TAKE THE CAR AND THE DIAGNOSIS TO YOUR MECHANIC. THE DOLLARS YOU SPEND ON THE DIAGNOSTIC CLINIC CAN HELP KEEP YOU FROM GETTING RIPPED OFF BY MECHANICS WHO WOULD OTHERWISE "EXAGGERATE" THE PROBLEMS YOUR CAR IS EXPERIENCING.**

If You Know What Your Problem Is, Call Around for Estimates

Making good use of your telephone can save you time and money. So, if you know the problem you want repaired, for example, if you need a new radiator, then check out the prices of the different radiator repair facilities in you area. When you do, however, be wary of extremely low estimates, which can be used to get you into the shop so the price can be increased as your car is dismantled.

Always Ask If There Is A Guarantee

Different repair facilities differ as to whether they give warranties for work. One advantage of a national chain or franchise is that they generally give warranties which are honored by the chain or franchise's other shops.

When discussing the issue of warranties, always ask about the:

Length of the warranty The warranty will usually be expressed in terms of a set time (i.e. 90 days) and/or mileage (i.e. 3000 miles), whichever comes first.

Extent of the warranty Does the warranty include both parts and labor or just parts or labor? Also, ask where the warranty will be honored and whether towing is covered if a faulty repair caused the need for you to incur a towing charge.

Get a Written Estimate

Remember, an oral estimate is not a contract to do work at the estimated price. What you want is a detailed **written work order**. Normally, a repair order will be written up by the service manager. Your signature on the form constitutes an authorization to perform the services on the car as set forth in writing in the work order. MAKE SURE THE ORDER CONTAINS THE PARTS REQUIRED AND THE ESTIMATED COST FOR LABOR.

CONSUMER ALERT: BE SURE TO WRITE THE FOLLOWING WORDS ON YOUR WORK ORDER: "IF MY CAR REQUIRES ANY ADDITIONAL PARTS AND LABOR OVER THE ESTIMATE, CONTACT ME FOR AUTHORIZATION BEFORE YOU DO ANYTHING NOT ALREADY AUTHORIZED BY THIS WORK ORDER." THE STORY OF CONSUMERS BEING ABUSED THROUGH UNAUTHORIZED REPAIRS ARE LEGION.

When You Leave Your Vehicle For Repairs, Be Accessible

Always let the shop know when and how you can be contacted. If an unanticipated problem arises and it is serious, don't give authorization over the phone but go to the dealership and speak with the service supervisor to make sure that all is on the up and up.

If You Are Contacted Regarding Additional Repairs, Be Skeptical

Sometimes a mechanic will find things wrong with your car that were not anticipated when the original estimate was made. If this happens to you, take what the mechanic tells you with a grain of salt and be sure to investigate the matter until you are satisfied that the extra work is really needed.

CONSUMER ALERT: IF REPAIR WORK IS DONE WITHOUT YOUR CONSENT, YOU DO NOT HAVE TO PAY FOR THE UNAPPROVED WORK AND YOU HAVE THE RIGHT TO HAVE YOUR BILL ADJUSTED. IF YOU ARE GIVEN TROUBLE BY THE FACILITY, WARN THEM THAT YOU ARE GOING TO CONTACT THE DEPARTMENT OF CONSUMER AFFAIRS, THE STATE LICENSING BUREAU AND/OR YOUR LAWYER, AND THEN, DO IT!

Ask to Inspect and/or Keep All Replaced Parts

The proof is in the pudding, as the old saying goes, and the evidence that repairs were needed should be in the old parts. If a garage knows you will want to see the parts, they may be less likely to take out that perfectly fine water pump when all you really needed was a new thermostat.

IF YOU ARE UNHAPPY

If work is done on your car and you are not satisfied, don't just let your spark plugs sputter, get energized. Put some fire in your tank, roll up your sleeves, dig into your consumer toolbox and get to work.

Complain to the Service Manager

If you are unhappy with the work that was done on the car, your first step is to go to the service manager. But before you go in, prepare. Gather together your paperwork (which will be detailed and not general, right?) and be prepared to prove that the problem you wanted fixed, wasn't.

If the service manager gives you satisfaction, write a thank you note. It is always heartening to any person in a service business to receive the thanks of a satisfied customer. On the other hand, if you remain displeased, write a letter to the service manager describing why you are displeased and what action you intend to take to redress your grievance.

Go to the Top

If the service manager is unwilling or unable to give you satisfaction, go to the top, be it the owner, general manager or whomever. First, send a letter and then follow up with a phone call, requesting action or a personal meeting. In dealing with the top brass, it is always a good idea to let them know what a loyal customer you have been and how pleasing you will help the business because of all of the referrals you will make to your friends.

Complain To All Who Will Listen

If you remain displeased, complain to one and/or all of the following:

Home offices If it is appropriate, go all of the way to the "home office" with your tale of woe.

Your credit card company As we stated, if you pay by credit and you are displeased, you can rope your credit card company into the fray.

The BBB One of the functions of the Better Business Bureau is to help dissatisfied customers out with their problems with businesses. They may help mediate the dispute or they may not, but in any event, they will keep your complaint on record for other consumers.

The NIASE If your mechanic was certified by the NIASE and you are dissatisfied, let the NIASE know about it. Their address is:

NIASE
13505 Dulles Technology Dr.
Herndon, Virginia, 22071

When you complain to the NIASE, send the mechanic or repair shop a copy of your letter, which lets them know that you may be jeopardizing their certificate.

State offices There may be several state offices where you should go for help. One, of course, is the Department of Consumer Affairs. But you should not stop with them. You may also want to contact the Department of Motor Vehicles (or Transportation), which may be in charge of licensing garages and repair facilities, as well as the Attorney General if you believe fraud or some other actionable activity has taken place.

Mediation services There are many mediation services operated around the country which may involve auto repair. Be careful here as some mediation services may not be evenhanded.

Sue the bums If you are still unable to get satisfaction, you have the right to take the matter to court. Small claims court is probably best. If your auto repair involves a new car, you may qualify for relief under your state's **lemon laws**.

> CONSUMER ALERT: EVEN IF YOU ARE UNHAPPY, YOU WILL PROBABLY HAVE TO PAY FOR YOUR REPAIR IN ORDER TO TAKE IT OFF OF YOUR MECHANIC'S PREMISES. THAT IS BECAUSE THERE ARE MECHANIC'S LIEN LAWS WHICH GIVE YOUR MECHANIC A LIEN ON YOUR CAR UNTIL HIS OR HER BILL IS PAID.

GIVE YOURSELF A RAISE

There are several strategies you should undertake to save money as a consumer in auto repairs. Here are several that we suggest:

Properly Maintain Your Car

The less you have to repair your car, the less money you spend. You can keep repair incidents to their minimum if you properly maintain your car.

Get Warranty Work Done During the Warranty

Most car warranties are expressed in time or mileage. Be sure you understand the details of yours so that you do not procrastinate and allow the time or mileage limit to lapse unknowingly.

Get Work Done Sooner Rather Than Later

"A stitch in time saves nine."

Do It Yourself

You don't have to be an expert mechanic to perform many basic automobile maintenance procedures or to make minor repairs. Moreover, community colleges frequently offer courses in automobile maintenance and there are several books on the market which will help you learn how to do it yourself.

Be Smart If the Repairs Arise Out of an Accident

If you have been in an accident, you are often caught between the repair facility and your insurance company. Ideally, you, and not your insurance company, should choose the body shop or mechanic to do the work. If your policy permits, get at least three estimates so that you will have a better grasp of the lay of the repair land. Also, if you are given a check for repairs, don't cash it until the repairs are completed, just in case the actual cost is more than the cost that is estimated.

> CONSUMER ALERT: WE RECOMMEND TWO BOOKS ON THE ISSUE OF AUTO REPAIRS AND AUTOMOBILE PURCHASES. THEY ARE: AUTO REPAIR SHAMS AND SCAMS, BY CHRIS HAROLD STEVENSON (1990, PRICE STERN SLOAN, PUBLISHERS, LOS ANGELES, CA.) AND THE LEMON BOOK BY RALPH NADER AND CLARENCE DITLOW.

PERSONAL BANKING

There's an old expression concerning a sure thing which states, "You can take that to the bank" or its derivative, "You can bank on that!" These adages imply a view of banks and banking as a place of solidity, security, simplicity and trust. Unfortunately, as we rush into the last decade of the Twentieth Century, to quote Sportin' Life from Porgy and Bess, "It ain't necessarily so."

Banking for the average consumer has become far more complicated than it ever was, thanks in large part, to the advent of deregulation. First, there is the question of security. The savings and loan debacle alone will cost taxpayers up to ONE TRILLION dollars (including interest) and that does not include the losses of investors. To make matters worse, the danger of financial failure is spreading into the commercial banking industry as you read these words. Then, there is the growing complexity of banking. You now have a plethora of financial choices to make as a consumer. This can save you money if you go in the right direction. But, it can also lead to confusion and rip offs. Finally, there is the question of where we as a society should go from here with regard to national banking policy.

THE CURRENT CRISIS

The current problems find their roots in the Nixon, Ford, Carter and Reagan administrations and the powerful banking lobby. The first step toward the unseen cliff came in 1974 when savings and loans were permitted to convert to stock companies, rather than remain what they were: "mutuals" owned by the depositors themselves. Worse, the primary purpose of many thrifts moved away from community development toward making the almighty buck.

The commercialization of the savings and loans alone probably would not have led to the current crisis. The next step toward the precipice came during the Carter Administration which tried to help the S & Ls deal with the terrible inflation of those years. The first measure supported by Carter was the removal of the cap on interest payments. Now, the S & Ls were free to offer the sky if they chose to in order to attract depositors. In addition, the Federal Insurance companies (FSLIC and the FDIC) that guaranteed depositors' money were required to raise their maximums from $40,000 to $100,000 per account. That gave "high rollers" the incentive to invest in high interest savings and loan deposits under the "you can't lose" theory of investing.

But all of this was merely prelude. What Jimmy Carter and the Congress could not know about was the pending outbreak of the "Reagan Revolution." Under Ronald Reagan, the savings and loans were deregulated and allowed to invest in riskier and more speculative properties.

The next blow occurred almost as soon as the oath of office had left Ronald Reagan's lips. Reagan, as part of his crusade to get government off of the backs of big business, froze the hiring of new bank auditors, under the theory (we suppose), that the fewer the regulators, the less they could regulate and the freer the owners of savings and loans could be to allow the marketplace to work its so-called magic, which in too many cases became the witchcraft of greed, unwarranted speculation and corruption.

Things got more "fun" for the wheeler dealers as time went on. In quick succession the government permitted the following in its dismantling of savings and loan regulation:

•Thrifts were permitted to loan 15 percent of their entire capital to one borrower.

•The owners of savings and loans were allowed to have only 1 percent of their own money invested into the capital of their S & Ls.

•Intangibles, such as "goodwill" could now be used to secure loans where before only solid security, such as land was permitted.

•Loans were permitted to be based on 100 percent financing.

•Loans were allowed to be made for other than home purchase or repair, which meant that S & Ls could spend "their" money as equity holders in speculative commercial real estate deals and "junk bonds."

Soon, the denizens of Wall Street were packaging investments, known as brokered deposits, of $100,000 into savings and loan accounts that paid interest that was too high to guarantee that the savings and loan would even be able to stay in business. But these sophisticated investors didn't care. They were betting on a sure thing. Either the S & L would pay or the taxpayer would.

As the economy began to falter and other mistakes finally came home to roost, the extent of the crisis began to come into focus. All of the smoke and mirrors of Reaganism could no longer obscure the truth. A financial disaster was upon the country. Throughout the land, but particularly in the Southwest, savings and loans came crashing down, creating a fiscal crater that will take decades to fill.

The news isn't that much better in the commercial banking industry. Banks large and small have failed and others will soon be following suit. The moneys required to deal with bank failures are beginning to grow by the billions. Only time will tell whether the banking system as we know it will return.

TAKING CARE OF YOURSELF TODAY

With all of that in mind, it is of paramount importance that you do your personal banking in a secure institution. You should also take steps to save as much money on fees and/or earn as much on interest as you possibly can.

Make Sure Your Institution is Safe

There are several steps you can take to make sure that your money is safe.

Only bank at federally insured institutions The full faith and credit of the United States still guarantees that you will not lose your money if each individual account comes within the maximum insurance provided (currently $100,000 for Federally insured deposits.)

Keep an eye on the stability of your savings and loan or bank If you can understand the financial statement of your bank, ask for it and analyze it. Read the business section of your local newspaper. If problems are arising with a local bank, there will usually be some coverage of the pending difficulty. Keep in touch with your accountant, investment adviser or business consultant. They often hear the tom toms warning of impending doom before the bad news breaks through the forest of smiling faces and upbeat press releases. In short, keep your eyes and ears open and if you detect trouble brewing, think seriously about changing banks.

Beware of incredible deals on interest When some banks or savings and loans find that there is more money going out the door than is coming in, they will sometimes boost the interest they pay on accounts in order to attract more capital. If you see an advertisement offering interest way above the going rate in your community, it may seem too tempting to resist. But try. Dramatic increases in interest rates may be a warning sign that a big financial fall is on the horizon.

Keep Costs Down

There is a wide variety of services that a financial institution may offer, usually on the basis of the more money you deposit, the less your services cost you. Here are some of the things to look for:

Free checking account Frequently, a checking account will be offered without a service charge per check if you maintain a minimum balance.

Free safety deposit box It is always a good idea to keep important documents such as deeds, stock, wills and the like in a safe and secure place. Many financial institutions offer safety deposit boxes free with the maintenance of a minimum balance.

Free ATM banking The newest service on the banking block is the automatic teller machine which allows you to make deposits or withdraw cash 24 hours a day, 7 days a week, 365 days a year. This can certainly be a convenience but that is not the only reason for banks and savings and loans flocking to them. ATM machines also allow banks to reduce their overhead. This being so, we consider the new trend toward charging for ATM use at the consumer's own bank to be unconscionable.

Low fees All banks charge fees. For example, if you bounce a check, you will have to pay your bank a fee. Many banks also charge fees for checking accounts, balance inquiries, and the cost of check printing. When investigating where you want to bank, inquire about fees. If they seem exorbitant, it is probably a good idea to put your money somewhere else.

Finding the Right Accounts for You

The kinds of accounts you select depend on your personal needs and the differing accounts available to you in your area. Here are some tips:

Know your own account behavior To find the right account for you, you should know your own financial needs and account usage requirements. For example, if you write relatively few checks a month, you may want an account especially designed to meet the light check writer's needs. If you have a need to dip into your money on a frequent basis, you may want a passbook savings account, which earns a low rate of interest but which allows you to dip into your funds at will. If you believe you can "hoard" your money for an extended period of time, look into depositing in a certificate of deposit (CD) which pays higher rates of interest but which charges a significant interest penalty for early withdrawal.

Try to earn as much interest as you can Whatever your needs are, try to earn as much money in interest as you can. Your bank representative should be able to show you how. This advice may be obvious, but millions of savers do not follow it.

Deposit money in accounts that accrue interest in a way that is most beneficial to you You may earn the same rate of interest in three different accounts and yet, not earn the same amount. The amount you earn will be dependent on the rate, yes, but also the manner in which interest is determined.

What you want to look at is the **annual percentage yield** (APY) of the account as opposed the **annual percentage rate** (APR). The APY applied to your deposit balance gives you the amount of interest you would earn over one year if you held your deposit balance constant for the entire year. Many bank advertisements quote interest in terms of APR, which is merely the interest rate at a point in time and does not take into account the way in which the interest is **compounded** (earns interest on interest).

The APY adjusts the APR to reflect the compounding period. If compounding occurs on a daily basis, you will earn a higher APY than if it is compounded on a quarterly basis. Thus, don't ask, "What is the interest rate?" but rather, "What is the APY of this account?"

Check out how interest is credited to your account The time that interest compounds is one thing, the way it gets **credited** may be quite another. For example, assume your account compounds interest daily but credits interest monthly. Assume further that you withdraw money on the twenty - sixth day of the month, before it has been credited to your account. You lose all the interest that you accrued during the 26 days because it had not been credited when you withdrew the money. Thus, the more often interest gets credited to your account, the less likely you are to lose money if you have to take part or all of your deposit out of the bank.

GIVE YOURSELF A RAISE

Saving money in your banking relationships and earning money from your banking relationships go hand in hand. Here are some further suggestions toward that end:

Join a Credit Union

Many people automatically turn to a commercial financial institution when deciding to save money or take out a loan. You should not do so. Instead, if you want to save interest on loans and perhaps earn higher interest on savings, join a **credit union**.

A credit union is a nonprofit cooperatively owned organization created to promote thrift among its members and to provide low cost loans. Presently, about 50 million Americans belong to credit unions.

Credit unions are regulated and insured like banks. They are also subject to failure if they are not managed correctly. Thus, be as careful in choosing a credit union as you would be any other financial institution.

Bank Responsibly

Many people spend needless dollars because they bounce checks (which will cost you two fees, one to the merchant who tried to negotiate the bounced check and one to your own banking institution), miss loan payments (thereby being subject to a late payment penalty), or otherwise allow their finances to become disorganized or chaotic. By staying on top of your financial affairs, you save money, bother, aggravation and give yourself the peace of mind of being in control.

Review your Bank Statement Every Month

People usually bounce checks because their check register is inaccurate. By balancing your account every month, you will know the exact level of your account.

Bank Where the Fees are Low

If you don't shop around and find a secure financial institution with banking fees that are low, you are throwing money down the drain.

Manage Your Money To Earn Maximum Interest

Beware of Interest Forfeit Traps

As we described earlier, the way interest is credited can make a difference in the amount you collect. You want to deposit your money in accounts that pay interest computed on a daily basis and which credit interest daily, **aka day-of-deposit, day-of-withdrawal accounts (DDDW)**.

CONSUMERS AGENDA

The financial debacle that now faces the country cries out for remedial action to prevent the disaster from getting worse and to make sure that this abdication of governmental responsibility does not continue. We offer the following suggestions as an appetizer to stimulate your desire to help effect change:

Reregulate Banks and Savings and Loans

The experiment of deregulation has been an abject failure. Let us, then, return to the "traditional values" found in reasonable regulation first established during the Great Depression, which assisted the United States tin reaching its financial "heyday" during the Fifties, Sixties and into the Seventies. Unfortunately, the government is still pushing deregulation which will lead to a deepening of the continuing disaster. Remember the old adage, they who refuse to learn the lessons of history are bound to repeat them.

Work to Establish Citizen Watchdog Groups

It should be made as easy as possible for consumers to join together into watchdog groups to keep an eye on banks, S & Ls, utilities and other such powerful financial organizations. Today it isn't easy but there is a way. Simply compel these financial institutions to carry in their regular statement or billing envelopes, a printed insert inviting their customers to join financial consumer organizations. These watchdogs would have their own lawyers, organizers, canvassers and economists and would be chartered as nonprofit advocacy and educational groups by Congress and controlled and funded by an electorate of dues-paying members. Through these groups, bank consumers would have a say in future decisions about the S & L bailout and the pending banking crisis.

This idea has been proven to work. In the area of utilities, a similar concept called the **Citizen's Utility Board** (CUB) has begun to flourish. It has already saved Illinois utility rate payers over 3 BILLION DOLLARS since 1983! Imagine the impact if there were **Financial Consumer Associations** (FCA) in operation as the savings and loans headed for their great fall. We could have saved a trillion! (FCAs could also become vigorous distributors of pro-consumer information and advisory groups representing millions of banking consumers.)

There is currently pending in Congress legislation that would establish the right of FCAs to organize. If you are to participate in and benefit from the upcoming financial reorganization of the country, FCAs are essential, otherwise the fat cats who caused the problem will be the ones to design the solution - all to their benefit you can be sure.

CONTACT YOUR MEMBER OF CONGRESS AND URGE THEIR SUPPORT OF FCAS!

FOR MORE INFORMATION ON FCAs, CONTACT PUBLIC CITIZEN'S CONGRESS WATCH, P.O. BOX 19404, WASHINGTON D.C. 20036 OR CALL THEM AT (202) 546-4996.

Part Three

MAJOR PURCHASES
YOUR HOUSE, YOUR CAR AND
THE FOOD THAT YOU EAT

To say that the American economy is huge is to engage in understatement. According to the Department of Commerce, for calendar year 1990, the total gross national product was 5 TRILLION, 465 BILLION, 1 MILLION DOLLARS. Of that total, 3 TRILLION, 657 BILLION, 3 MILLION DOLLARS was expended in personal consumption of goods and services.

This economic machine is driven in large measure by the purchases that each and every one of us makes throughout our consuming lives. For those of you who like your information specific, in 1990, consumers spent 480 BILLION, 3 MILLION DOLLARS, on durable goods (refrigerators, cars, etc.) and over 1 TRILLION, 193 BILLION, 7 MILLION (give or take a few hundred thousand) on nondurable goods (underwear, towels, etc.).

With so many products on the market, it would be impossible for us to detail the ins and outs of purchasing them all. But there are some general principles that will apply to most purchases, which are designed to help you "buy smart" and save money:

LEARN ABOUT THE PRODUCT BEFORE YOU BUY
To put it simply, do your homework. Product knowledge is one of your best protections against buying shoddy merchandise or paying more than a fair price.

ONLY DEAL WITH ETHICAL COMPANIES
Before you buy anything of substance from a company, make sure you have checked out their reputation with local consumer groups, your friends or local reputable business groups. Find out how long the company has been in business. Inquire about their policies of redressing consumer complaints. In short, do whatever it takes to make sure you are dealing with people who will be fair and ethical with you and who subscribe to that old capitalist motto, "The Customer is always right."

KEEP RECORDS OF ALL YOUR TRANSACTIONS
It is vital to your life as a consumer that you keep what is known as a "paper trail" of all of your major purchases. Receipts, letters of complaint, relevant advertisements, etc., should all be kept in a file so that you will be ready in the event a problem arises with something you have purchased.

USE CONSUMER RESOURCES

There is an abundance of consumer resources available to you which you can purchase or find in your local library, to help you make wise and knowledgeable choices about the products you buy.

Consumer Reports Magazine

Published by the highly esteemed consumer protection organization, Consumers Union, Consumer Reports Magazine is filled with invaluable information about the products you buy - from lawn mowers to appliances to telephones to cleaning supplies. Its articles not only tell you what you need to know to be a smart shopper, they "name names" - brand names. Products found to be unsafe, defective or not up to their advertised claims are exposed by the magazine in its rating system. Consumer Reports accepts no advertising dollars and thus, they are not beholden to any company or product. Consumers Union now is also publishing a "Consumer Reports for kids," called Zillions. Zillions, is designed to empower and educate youth and to help them become informed and responsible consumers (you can't start them too young as far as we are concerned). Consumer Reports also publishes an annual Buyers Guide filled with information about a variety of products and services. If you are interested in subscribing to Consumer Reports, send $20 for a one year subscription (as of the date of this writing) to:

CONSUMER REPORTS
Subscription Dept.
Box 51166
Boulder, CO 80321-1166

Zillions is published bi-monthly for a one year's subscription price of $13.95 (as of this writing). If you are interested in Zillions, write to:

ZILLIONS
Subscription Department
P.O. Box 51777
Boulder, CO 80321-1777

Consumer Reports Books

Consumer Reports also publishes books on topics of interest to consumers. Among them are the *Home Electronics Buying Guide*, *Straight Talk About Weight Control*, *Personal Consumer Buying Guide*, *How to Buy a House, Condo or Co-op* and many others. For more information on Consumer Reports Books, contact them at P.O. Box 8020, Fairfield, OH 45014-9912. Or call, (513) 860-1178.

The Better Business Bureau Buying Guide

The Better Business Bureau has published *The A to Z Buying Guide* which can help you make wise decisions regarding many products and services, ranging from air cleaners, to funeral services to bicycles to burglar alarm systems. The book should be available (perhaps by special order) from your local book store or in your library.

Now on to the areas we will discuss: the purchase of a home, automobiles and food.

Chapter Ten

PUTTING A ROOF OVER YOUR HEAD

It is probably safe to say that purchasing a house is the largest single sales transaction that you will ever enter. And no wonder. "Affordable" houses now sell for over $100,000 in many areas of the country and in some urban areas such as Los Angeles and New York, "cheap" homes are those that sell to the tune of $200,000, $300,000 or even more per year! And if you want to live well or in a "better neighborhood," you are looking at spending over a half million dollars just to put that quality roof over your head.

With so much money, not to mention the emotional commitment, at stake, it is important that every consumer take great care in going about the important task of buying a home. After all, this isn't just any purchase. It is your home we're talking about here and there are a lot of issues to think about, a lot of things to know. There is also a great deal of money that can be saved for the purchaser who is willing to take the time to do the job right. And, it's exciting, right? It's the pursuit of the American dream.

DECIDING ON THE HOME THAT IS RIGHT FOR YOU

The first step in buying a home is obvious: finding the right home for you. But behind that obvious statement there is a lot to think about. Among the things to look for when searching for a home, are the following:

LOCATION

Location may be the biggest single factor that determines the house you buy. Here are some things to look at when considering the concept of location:

Proximity to Work

Anyone working outside the home has to face that modern day gauntlet known as the commute. But, there are commutes and then there are COMMUTES. Some people spend hours a day just getting to and from work. Unfortunately, in many urban areas, affordable housing only exists in outlying areas and so a decision may have to be made as to whether to buy more house and a longer commute or less house and a shorter commute.

Nearness of Family

A growing trend in this country is for extended families to be literally that: extended and pulled apart by the forces of life that often cause parents and children, brothers and sisters, cousins and all the rest to be separated from each other by hundreds or even thousands of miles. Many want to resist this trend and want to live where they can "reach out and touch someone" in the flesh rather than over the telephone wires.

Convenience

Another factor in thinking about location has to do with convenience. Is the home close to the places that you frequent, such as shopping areas, doctors offices, volunteer centers and the like. Many of us would like to live in the country but the idea of having to drive twenty miles in the snow to buy groceries may make us decide that the city is really the place we want to be.

NEIGHBORHOOD

In addition to thinking about the place where your home will be, you also have to think about the quality of the neighborhood you will be buying into. This is important because the pluses and minuses of your neighborhood will have a lot to do with the quality of your life (or lack thereof).

Condition

If a house you are interested in is located within a neighborhood that is run down, if the people who live there don't have pride in their property, if the city maintenance department doesn't seem to have the area in their maps, then you may want to pass on the house no matter what its particular shape and condition may be.

Safety

The safety of a neighborhood is always something to consider. What is the crime rate? Are there a lot of residential burglaries in the area? Is there a gang problem? What about the streets: are they safe or are there an inordinate amount of traffic accidents in the area? Check around and find these things out. Talk to the local police department. Walk the neighborhood and meet your potential neighbors and ask them how they like the area. In short, do whatever you feel is necessary to determine if the neighborhood is a place where you will feel comfortable and safe.

Facilities

You should also look into the local facilities to see if they meet your standards. If you have children, you will want to look into the quality of the local schools whether private or public. Are there parks in the area and are they safe? Are there adequate activities for youth such as baseball leagues and Scouting? What about recreation for adults and religious institutions? Are there community improvements being planned and if so, how are they being funded? Are there movie theaters nearby and adequate cultural facilities to allow your life to be enriched?

COST

Another major consideration is the cost of buying the house. The following should be considered when looking into the issues involving the cost of the house:

Price

The most obvious issue has to do with the price of the home. Obviously, if a house or condominium is too expensive for your budget, you simply won't be able to buy it.

The question must be asked, what is a fair price? Well, that depends on a lot of factors, many of which have to do with market forces and many of which have to do with issues such as the condition of the house, its size, the quality of the neighborhood, etc.

Because price can be a very subjective matter, it is a good idea to have any house you are thinking of buying professionally appraised, just to make sure you are not being had. Usually, an appraised value for owner occupied residential property will be based on the sale of similar homes (i.e. similar size, similar amenities such as air conditioning or a swimming pool, similar condition, etc.) in the same neighborhood. (You can also check out other listed houses in the neighborhood yourself to see if similar properties are priced in the same ball park as the house you are thinking of making an offer on.) Also, if you are working with a real estate agent, ask the agent to tell you what he or she thinks of the price of the house and why.

CONSUMER ALERT: A GOOD WAY TO FIND OUT HOW MUCH HOUSE YOU CAN AFFORD TO BUY IS TO GO TO YOUR LOCAL BANK OR MORTGAGE BROKER AND ASK THEM TO GIVE YOU A ROUGH IDEA AS TO THE AMOUNT OF LOAN YOU WILL BE ABLE TO QUALIFY FOR. (THIS PROCESS IS OFTEN CALLED A *PRE-QUALIFICATION PROGRAM*).

Interest Rates

The price of the house is only the most obvious factor when looking into its real cost to you. Another important element is the amount of interest you will have to pay on the mortgage or trust deed you take out in order to purchase the property. The higher the interest, the higher your monthly payment and that means the less house you can afford. (For example, a $100,000 30-year mortgage at 9 percent interest will cost $804.62 per month, while the same loan at 10.5 percent will cost $914.74 per month.)

Taxes

Another factor in the cost of the house is the amount of property tax you will have to pay. The more valuable the house, generally the higher the tax. Before you commit yourself to a purchase, be sure you investigate the amount of taxes you will pay on the property to see if you can afford to pay them.

Insurance

A lesser factor but still a factor in determining how much your purchase will actually take out of your bank account is the cost of property insurance. A homeowner's policy will run into the hundreds of dollars a year and if you add extra coverage such as earthquake protection, the price can really begin to add up.

Maintenance and Repairs

It costs a lot of money to keep and maintain a home. If the roof needs replacement, it may cost you thousands of dollars. A new furnace, a burst water main, the lawn dying from some exotic fungus, all can happen and all take money to deal with. Thus, when figuring out whether you can afford to buy a particular house, always keep some of your projected budget set aside for such contingencies.

Mortgage Insurance

If you can only pay 10% or less down on your purchase, your mortgage lender may require you to pay for mortgage insurance as part of the deal to give you a loan. These policies will usually be priced way above market value. Unfortunately, in many cases, it is either take the insurance or pass on the loan. (We believe this practice should be illegal.) If you intend to pay a low down payment, be sure to investigate this potential cost when you look at issues of affordability.

THE HOUSE (OR CONDO OR WHATEVER)

This is the fun part, choosing the best house for you based on the price, the neighborhood and all of the other factors that go into deciding which house to buy. There are a lot of factors that go into deciding that "this is the one." Some are subjective, others objective. Let's look at a few:

The Size

Size has to do with factors such as how many bedrooms do you need (now and in the future in case you are planning on expanding your family), do you need a den or home office, are there enough bathrooms so that you don't have a serious traffic jam in the morning as everyone prepares to start the day? Is the kitchen large enough and the living room and what about the yard? Will the room accommodate your furniture?

The Amenities

Do you want a pool or hot tub? What about trees and a play area for the kids? Is central air conditioning central to your life and what about issues of energy efficiency such as insulation? And don't forget that all important issue of closet space!

The Look

Do you like the house? Does it appeal to your taste and your sense of style? If it lacks that certain something now, will you be able to remodel to suit your personal desires? In short, can you commit to a long term relationship?

What is Included

Usually, when you look at a home, it is furnished and being lived in by the seller. This can lead to a misimpression. Remember, the furniture, drapes, furnishings and other items that turn a house into a home will often not be included in the purchase. Thus, find out if things such as that beautiful chandelier, the Swedish fireplace, etc. are included in the deal. (Fixtures, such as a built in stove and dishwasher are usually part of the sale of a piece of property, but ask just in case).

The Condition

Is the house healthy and robust or is it run down and beginning to sag or affected by radon, chlordane or asbestos? You will need to take this into account, because it affects issues of price, maintenance and the amount of time, energy and money you can spend on taking care of "your place."

Okay, you have found your dream home. Now, let's talk about how you go about turning your desire into a reality.

THE PURCHASE

Buying a home should be approached with as much caution and seriousness as the occasion warrants. After all, what is at stake? Only hundreds of thousands of dollars, your happiness and your sense of well being. Other than that, it's not very important at all.

SHOULD YOU USE A REAL ESTATE BROKER?

The first question to arise in many nervous home buying hearts, is: should I use a real estate agent or broker?

Real estate agents and brokers are state licensed professionals. They are permitted to deal professionally with both the buyers and sellers of real property. Generally they get paid by commission based on the sales price when a piece of property is sold. Usually, *the buyer does not pay the commission*, the seller does. That is good news for the buyer, although the house may be priced to reflect the average 6% commission that real estate agents earn when a property is sold.

But, as is often the case, where there is good news, there is also bad news. If you use a real estate agent to help you find a house and that person is paid by splitting the commission with the listing agent, HE OR SHE MAY NOT REPRESENT YOU. You are not paying the agent, the seller is. Technically, "your" agent becomes a sub-agent of the seller. Thus, unless your state's laws permit the selling agent to represent the buyer, *that agent represents the seller*!

This is a vital issue because the fiduciary relationship (i.e. the duty of highest loyalty and trust) of the agent is owed to the person they represent. This being so, there are some common sense things to keep in mind when using a real estate agent to help you find a home.

Don't Talk Too Much

If your agent is actually the seller's fiduciary, common sense tells you to treat the process of making an offer and coming to an agreement with a healthy dose of *caveat emptor* (buyer beware). For example, if you decide to offer $125,000 for a home but are really willing to pay $150,000, it is not a good idea to tell "your" agent because he or she would probably be duty bound under the rules of a fiduciary to tell that important fact to the seller.

Demand Written Disclosures

If you are to be represented by the selling agent, make sure the fiduciary obligations to you are set forth in writing. If you get to the point where you want to "make an offer" on a property, ask "your" agent in writing for a full disclosure of all known defects, problems with the property or other material facts (such as if a freeway will be built in the neighborhood next month) and ask that such disclosure be in writing. Some states require such disclosures by law and others do not. In either case, you should demand one so that you and your agent (as well as the listing agent) are put on notice that you want to know any material fact that might materially affect your decision to buy.

Get An Independent Opinion

You may want to pay a little extra money in order to obtain an independent opinion of the property and its value and/or help with the negotiation of purchase. This is especially true if you are a first time buyer or lack sophistication and expertise in the field of real estate (in other words, most of us).

There are two places you can go to find some help: buyer-brokers and lawyers. Buyer-brokers are licensed real estate agents who you pay to represent you in the transaction. Lawyers can, of course, represent you in all aspects of the purchase. Lawyers will tend to charge you by the hour and buyer - brokers will most often charge a flat fee.

The Proper Use of a Real Estate Agent

The above warnings notwithstanding, it is probably a good idea to use a real estate agent to assist you when you are buying a home, even if they do not represent you. A good real estate agent can be of significant help to you in the following ways:

They can help you find the right house At any given time there may be hundreds or even thousands of homes up for sale in the region where you want to live. One of the problems you will face is sorting through all of those properties in order to find one that meets your size, quality and price requirements.

A licensed real estate agent can do a lot to make this process easier, allowing you to take a "rifle" approach to home shopping rather than a "shotgun" approach. That's because most agents and/or their companies subscribe to something called the **Multiple Listing Service**.

No single agent or company can have a majority of the current home listings in their files or among their clients. That's where the multiple listing service comes in. Most real estate companies subscribe to the service, which list all of the homes currently on the market as reported by subscribing real estate companies. According to the National Association of Realtors, between 80 percent and 90 percent of the homes on the market at any given time will be listed in the service. This means that your agent has access to a large majority of the available homes without leaving his or her office. The real estate agent can, in turn, help steer you exclusively to homes that meet your needs as discovered in the pages of the multiple listing service.

They can tell you the price of a home you can afford A well trained real estate agent can sit down with you, get the scoop on your financial condition and give you a ball park figure about the size of mortgage you can expect to obtain and how much house, condominium or other property that will buy you.

They can get to know your desires Unless you are buying income property, what you are looking for is a home, a place where you "belong." That being so, there will be a lot of subjectivity in your selection. A real estate agent who has talked to you, gotten to know you, walked you through several houses and has seen what you respond to (as well as what may have left you cold), will have a good idea of your personal taste.

CONSUMER ALERT: WHETHER YOU ARE BUYING OR SELLING PROPERTY, CHANCES ARE YOU WILL WANT TO USE A REAL ESTATE AGENT. HERE ARE SOME TIPS ON FINDING A GOOD ONE:

•*DO SHOP AROUND.* INTERVIEW SEVERAL FOR THE "JOB" AND SELECT THE ONE WHOSE COMBINATION OF TRAINING, EXPERIENCE, PERSONALITY AND WILLINGNESS TO HUSTLE SEEM BEST SUITED TO YOU.

•*DO NOT CHOOSE AN AGENT BECAUSE HE OR SHE IS A FRIEND OR RELATIVE.* PERHAPS MORE THAN ANY PROFESSION, REAL ESTATE AGENTS ARE OFTEN HIRED BECAUSE THEY ARE FRIENDS OR BECAUSE THEY BELONG TO THE SAME CHURCH OR SERVICE ORGANIZATION. A PREVIOUS RELATIONSHIP IS THE WRONG REASON TO SELECT AN AGENT. YOU WANT TO SELECT YOURS BECAUSE OF EXPERTISE.

•*DO CHECK ON TRAINING AND EXPERTISE.* ALL REAL ESTATE AGENTS ARE LICENSED BY THE STATE. BUT THERE IS MORE TO BEING A GOOD REAL ESTATE PROFESSIONAL THAN THE PASSING OF A TEST. WHAT IS THE AGENT'S BACKGROUND? HOW FAMILIAR ARE THEY WITH THE NEIGHBORHOOD INVOLVED IN THE SALE? WHAT IS THEIR PAST TRACK RECORD? WHAT STEPS ARE THEY WILLING TO TAKE IN ORDER TO MAKE SURE YOUR DESIRES ARE MET? HOW EASY ARE THEY TO REACH? WHAT PROFESSIONAL ORGANIZATIONS DO THEY BELONG TO? THESE AND OTHER ISSUES MUST BE DELVED INTO BEFORE YOU MAKE YOUR SELECTION.

•*OBTAIN A COPY OF THE CODE OF ETHICS FOR THE NATIONAL ASSOCIATION OF REALTORS AND HOLD YOUR AGENT TO THEM.* THE NATIONAL ASSOCIATION OF REALTORS IS THE LARGEST TRADE ASSOCIATION IN THE REAL ESTATE INDUSTRY. AMONG ITS PURPOSES IS PUBLIC EDUCATION AND THE PROMULGATION OF ETHICAL GUIDELINES FOR REAL ESTATE PROFESSIONALS. (ONLY REAL ESTATE AGENTS WHO BELONG TO A LOCAL BOARD AFFILIATED WITH THE NATIONAL ASSOCIATION CAN USE THE TERM "*REALTOR*".) WHILE EVERY GOOD AGENT IS NOT NECESSARILY A MEMBER, ALL AGENTS SHOULD CONFORM TO THE CODE OF ETHICS.

THE QUESTION OF FINANCING

One of the biggest issues you will face when you buy a piece of property is financing. In fact, your ability to obtain financing may very well be the determining factor in being able to buy the home of your dreams, or for that matter, any home at all.

The Different Types of Mortgages

A mortgage is a form of secured loan, where the security to make sure the loan is repaid is real property. At one time when housing was more affordable, the types of mortgages that you could obtain were limited. However, because of historically rising housing prices, there are now several different types of mortgages on the market. Among them are the following:

The fixed rate mortgage Old reliable. The **fixed rate mortgage** sets a specific, unchanging interest rate for the loan and the number of years you have to pay it back (typically thirty years but the number can vary). The fixed rate mortgage has two primary benefits; predictability - the amount of your house payment does not change - and affordability - in times of high interest rates your rate of interest remains the same no matter how high interest rates may go. There are downsides to the fixed rate mortgage, most having to do with your ability to qualify for the loan. For example, many fixed rate mortgages today require the purchaser to pay a 20 percent down payment. If you are buying a $200,000 home, that amounts to $40,000, not easy to save in these days of economic anemia. Also, you may need a higher income to qualify for a fixed rate mortgage.

The adjustable rate mortgage (ARM) In response to the inflation of the Seventies, a new type of mortgage was created called the **adjustable rate mortgage**. The adjustable rate mortgage starts accruing interest at a low rate and then the mortgage "adjusts" upward, eventually changing with the economic times. For example, the beginning interest rate for an ARM may be as low as 6 or 6 1/2 percent, but within a year it may rise to 8 or 9 percent. Thereafter, the rate of interest will change, being pegged to an economic indicator or the prime interest rate.

The primary benefits of an ARM are:

•You can qualify more easily for the loan. The low interest rate that is charged up front allows you to qualify for a loan that you might not be able to get if you were applying for a fixed rate mortgage.

•You usually don't need as high a down payment. Frequently ARM loans are obtainable with a lower down payment than fixed rate mortgages.

•Your mortgage rates go up over an extended period. If you expect your income to rise over the same period of time, the ARM allows you to buy sooner than you might have otherwise.

There are also down sides to an ARM that you need to know about:

•Your monthly payment may keep going up. Depending on the economy, it is possible that the adjustable interest rate in your mortgage will have a one way adjustment; up.

•You may end up with a negative amortization. As you pay off your house, you build up equity. As you pay down on your mortgage, you reduce the amount of principal you owe. In the mortgage game, this process is known as **amortization**. In some ARMs, the payment you owe is not sufficient to pay the total owed for interest being charged. In such cases, you may negatively amortize, that is, you may find the principal you owe on your mortgage going up rather than down.

•The amount of interest charged can vary widely. Depending on the economic index the lender pegs your interest to, the amount you are charged can vary widely over a relatively short period of time.

CONSUMER ALERT: IF YOU ARE GOING TO TAKE OUT AN ADJUSTABLE RATE MORTGAGE, BE SURE TO GET THE FOL- LOWING TERMS INTO YOUR CONTRACT. (IF YOU CAN'T CHECK INTO THE LOANS AVAILABLE FROM OTHER LENDERS):

1) CAPS: YOU WILL WANT A CAP (THE MAXIMUM YOU CAN BE CHARGED) ON THE AMOUNT OF INTEREST YOU CAN BE CHARGED (*A RATE CAP*) AND ON THE AMOUNT THAT YOUR MONTHLY PAYMENT CAN RISE OVER A SPECIFIC PERIOD OF

TIME (*A PAYMENT CAP*). OTHERWISE, YOU MAY BE ADJUSTED OUT OF YOUR BUDGET'S ABILITY TO PAY YOUR HOUSE PAYMENT.

2) STABLE INDEXES: MAKE SURE THE ECONOMIC INDEX THAT YOUR INTEREST IS TIED TO IS A STABLE ONE THAT WILL NOT WILDLY FLUCTUATE OVER THE YEARS.

The question naturally arises, which is better for you, a fixed term mortgage or an adjustable rate mortgage? According to Michael C. Thomsett and the Editors of Consumer Reports Books, in their book *How to Buy a House, Condo or Co-op*, (1990, Consumers Union, Mount Vernon, New York), an ARM is best if you do not plan to stay in the home you are buying for more than five years, you cannot qualify for a fixed rate mortgage, you expect your income to rise and you have properly negotiated caps on the amount of interest you can be charged and on how often and how high your monthly payment can rise. On the other hand, they believe that a fixed rate mortgage is best if you plan to remain more than five years, you want your payments to stay the same and your income is fixed or not expected to rise sufficiently to keep up with the rising payments of an adjustable rate mortgage.

Government mortgages The Federal government and State government offer different mortgage programs to help Veterans and those of moderate means obtain mortgage financing. The rates offered are usually under the prevailing market. Some of these programs include, Veterans Administration Mortgages, FHA loans and Farmers Loan Administration. For more information on these and other government programs, contact the appropriate government agency.

CONSUMER ALERT: THERE ARE VARIATIONS OF THE MORTGAGE TYPES WE HAVE DESCRIBED ABOVE. FOR EXAMPLE SOME LOANS ALLOW PAYMENTS TO INCREASE OVER A DEFINED PERIOD (THE GRADUATED PAYMENT MORTGAGE). OTHERS ALLOW FOR THE LENDER TO SHARE IN THE APPRECIATION OF THE VALUE OF THE PROPERTY (THE SHARED EQUITY MORTGAGE). BEFORE TAKING OUT A HOME LOAN, BE SURE YOU CAREFULLY CHECK OUT ALL OF THE ANGLES TO FIND THE BEST PROGRAM TO SUIT YOUR PARTICULAR NEEDS.

NEGOTIATING THE PURCHASE

You've found the house you want. It fits, it's the right size in the right neighborhood at the appropriate price range. Now comes the nerve racking part, negotiating the sale.

The "script" of a sale goes something like this: You make an **offer**. When you make an offer, it has legal significance in that an accepted offer (the **acceptance**) becomes a legally enforceable contract if it is supported by **consideration** (in the case of buying a home, your promise to pay). Thus, with the offer having so much potential importance, you should be very careful when coming up with its terms.

Among the terms you will want to put in your offer are the following:

The Price

How much you are willing to pay for the property.

The Length of Escrow and Date of Closing

Escrow is a process wherein an independent third party acts as a go-between for the parties to the sale of property. The escrow makes sure all contingencies of the contract have been met, all documents properly signed and all moneys paid. Most escrows last about 60 days, but they can be faster or slower depending on the agreement of the parties.

Other Terms of Sale

In addition to the price, there may be other terms you want to put into your sales contract. Among these are the following:

The deposit You will have to deposit some money when you make your offer. This is known as earnest money and the amount becomes a term of sale.

Down payment You will probably have to make a down payment on the property in order to qualify for a loan. The amount will be placed in the offer.

Contingency clauses A "contingency" allows you to rescind the deal under specific circumstances set forth in the contract. Contingency clauses can provide you with significant protection. You should put contingency clauses in your offer to protect you against changing market conditions. For example, you may wish to put a contingency clause concerning your ability to obtain financing, your ability to obtain favorable interest rates (i.e. the sale is contingent on your being able to obtain financing at or below a defined rate of interest) and other issues such as the property passing a home inspection. You should also make sure that the sale is contingent on the owner having a clear title to the property (which will involve a title search according to the laws of your jurisdiction).

> **CONSUMER ALERT: IT IS VERY IMPORTANT THAT YOU PUT IN THE OFFER YOUR RIGHT TO HAVE A HOME INSPECTOR OF YOUR CHOICE INSPECT THE PROPERTY AND THAT THE PUR-CHASE ONLY GO THROUGH IF THE RESULTS OF THE INSPEC-TION ARE SATISFACTORY TO YOU. YOU SHOULD ALSO PRO-VIDE FOR A PROMPT REFUND OF YOUR DOWN PAYMENT IF YOU DECIDE NOT TO PROCEED WITH THE SALE FOR REASONS OF AN UNSATISFACTORY INSPECTION.**

What is included in the sale A controversy can often arise between a buyer and a seller as to what exactly is included in the sale. For example, let's say you have fallen in love with the crystal chandelier in the entry way. In such a case, state in your offer that the chandelier is part of the sale and stays with the house when you assume ownership. Be sure you also include a list of **fixtures** (items attached to the property and intended to remain with it, i.e. the built-in stove) in the offer just to make sure you and the seller see eye to eye on what the fixtures are.

Rent prohibition Until title of the property passes to you, the seller is the technical owner of the property. As such, he or she can rent the property unless you prohibit that from happening in your contract of sale.

Termite inspection You will want to have the property inspected for termite infestation and/ or damage. (If you are getting a mortgage, the lender will require one.) Be sure that if an infestation is found that one of the terms of sale are that the seller fully repair the damage at his or her expense.

**CONSUMER ALERT: MAKING AN OFFER IS A VERY COMPLI-
CATED AND TRICKY SUBJECT. THUS, BEFORE YOU GET IN-
VOLVED, EITHER** *GET HELP FROM A LAWYER OR BUYER-BRO-
KER,* **OR BE SURE YOU UNDERSTAND THE INS AND OUTS OF
PURCHASING A HOME (THERE ARE SEVERAL FINE AND DE-
TAILED BOOKS THAT ARE HELPFUL). WE RECOMMEND TWO
BOOKS.** *HOW TO BUY A HOUSE, CONDO, OR CO-OP*; **BY MICHAEL
C. THOMSETT AND THE EDITORS OF CONSUMER REPORTS
BOOKS AND** *BUY YOUR FIRST HOME NOW*; **BY PETER G. MILLER
(1990, HARPER AND ROW PUBLISHERS, NEW YORK, NY).**

**CONSUMER ALERT: THERE ARE USUALLY FORMS YOU CAN
USE TO MAKE YOUR OFFER, OFTEN CALLED "DEPOSIT RE-
CEIPTS." BUT REMEMBER, JUST BECAUSE SOMETHING IS ON
A FORM, THAT DOESN'T MEAN YOU HAVE TO USE IT. THUS, IF
YOU CHOOSE TO USE THE FORM, FEEL FREE TO SCRATCH OUT
THOSE ITEMS YOU DO NOT WISH TO BE PART OF YOUR OFFER
AND TO ADD OTHER TERMS TO THE FORM THAT YOU WISH TO
BE PART OF YOUR OFFER.**

Disclosure of defects Many a lawsuit has been initiated because of the seller's failure to disclose a fact about the property that the buyer later discovered and considered important. The best way to avoid legal problems is to prevent controversy from arising in the first place. One good way to avoid trouble in the purchase of real property is to demand a full written disclosure of all "material facts" and make your performance contingent upon your review of the disclosure letter or form.

The following are some of the areas you may want disclosed:
•Any structural problems with the house or other structures on the property.
•Environmental hazards, such as the presence of asbestos, radon or lead based paint.
•Neighborhood problems such as noise or a high crime rate.

Once disclosure has been given, then you can decide whether to go forward or exercise your contingent right to back out of the deal. Just make sure that you have the right to back out set forth specifically in your offer and make sure it survives the negotiation to become part of the contract.

NOTE: **THIS SECTION IS NOT INTENDED TO GIVE YOU LEGAL ADVICE.
IF YOU HAVE ANY LEGAL QUESTIONS ABOUT AN OFFER AND ITS
LEGAL CONSEQUENCES, CONSULT WITH AN ATTORNEY WHO HAS A
PRACTICE IN REAL ESTATE LAW.**

THE NEGOTIATION

Once you have made your offer (which should be in writing), the seller will review the terms you have set forth. He or she can either accept the offer as you have communicated it (which will usually create a contract between you), communicate different terms to you, called a **counter offer**, or **reject** your offer outright. In either of the latter two cases, there is no contract and you are free to walk away from the deal without further legal obligation.

From there, assuming the parties are close enough to a deal to warrant continued negotiations, you and the buyer may send counter offer after counter offer back and forth until all of the substantive terms have been agreed upon. Then, once the papers have been signed in which both parties agree on the terms of sale, a contract will have been created which either party can enforce in a court of law.

> **CONSUMER ALERT: WITH VERY FEW EXCEPTIONS, A CON-TRACT FOR THE PURCHASE AND SALE OF LAND MUST BE IN WRITING TO BE ENFORCEABLE. THUS, DO NOT ENTER INTO AN ORAL CONTRACT FOR THE PURCHASE OF REAL PROP-ERTY. IF YOU DO, YOU WILL PROBABLY NOT BE ABLE TO ENFORCE THE CONTRACT AT LAW.**

THE ESCROW

After a contract of sale has been signed, the next step is for an escrow to be opened. You open an escrow by going to a licensed escrow company and giving instructions as to how the transaction is to be handled. This usually involves handing over the written land purchase contract and any deposit moneys that you may have paid to the escrow officer in charge of your transaction.

Once the escrow is opened, the escrow officer will draft escrow instructions that are consistent with the purchase agreement. These instructions will then be signed by all parties to the agreement and become the basis for the activities of the escrow company.

> **CONSUMER ALERT: BE SURE YOU READ THE ESCROW IN-STRUCTIONS CAREFULLY TO MAKE SURE THEY ARE CONSIS-TENT WITH THE PURCHASE AGREEMENT YOU HAVE ENTERED INTO. THAT'S BECAUSE ESCROW INSTRUCTIONS BECOME PART OF THE CONTRACT ITSELF AND IF THE TERMS OF ESCROW DIFFER FROM THE TERMS OF THE PURCHASE AGREE-MENT, YOU COULD RUN INTO A LEGAL PROBLEM.**

During escrow, both you and the seller will have to perform certain acts as set forth in the escrow instructions. For example, a title search will need to be performed before the transaction can close. When this has been done, the search report will be deposited in escrow. As another example, you will have to deposit all of the purchase money into escrow before the transaction can be completed and the seller will have to execute all appropriate documents, such as a grant deed.

Once all of the terms and conditions of the transaction have been accomplished, the escrow officer will "close" the escrow and the seller will get his or her money and you will get the deed to the property, which the escrow will have had recorded with the County Recorder. (Congratulations! You now own your new home!) If all of the terms are not met, the escrow officer will refuse to close the transaction, thereby compelling performance or putting the parties on notice that there is a problem with the deal that may require lawyers at forty paces.

When the escrow closes, you will get a closing statement. The statement will give a full accounting of all of the deposits and disbursements into escrow and will detail the escrow fees that have been charged and the closing costs that have been paid. For example, out of escrow may come payment of existing mortgages, the real estate agent's commission, the escrow fees, recording costs, title insurance fees, transfer taxes, payments for termite repairs, etc. Be sure you read your closing statement carefully to make sure it is correct and accurate.

CONSUMER ALERT: WHO PAYS THE ESCROW FEES AND OTHER COSTS OF ESCROW IS SUBJECT TO NEGOTIATION BETWEEN BUYER AND SELLER. BE SURE YOU DEAL WITH THE ISSUE IN YOUR CONTRACT OF PURCHASE.

Escrow is a far more complicated process than we have been able to detail here. If you want a more complete description of the ins and outs of escrow, read *All About Escrow*, by Sandy Gadow (1989, Express Publishers, El Cerrito, CA).

SPECIAL NOTES FOR CONDOMINIUM BUYERS

For a variety of reasons, the sale of condominiums and town houses are on the increase. If you are one of the growing number of persons interested in these forms of home ownership, there are a few additional things you need to know about.

YOU ARE BUYING MORE THAN YOUR INDIVIDUAL HOUSING UNIT
When you purchase a single family house, you are buying the structures as well as the land upon which the buildings have been built. When you buy into a condo, you are not only purchasing your individual unit but a proportionate ownership in the **common areas**, such as the swimming pool, the walkways, the landscaping, etc.

YOU ARE RESPONSIBLE FOR MORE THAN YOUR INDIVIDUAL UNIT
When you own a house, you are responsible for all of the costs of maintenance and repair. The same is true for maintaining and repairing your individual condominium unit. However, because you are also an owner of the common areas, you have a responsibility to maintain and repair those areas in direct proportion to your percentage of ownership in the condominium complex. This means that there will be more money out of your pocket than your mortgage payments. You will also have a monthly dues to be part of the **condominium association** (the governing body of the condominium complex). These dues will pay for common expense items such as insurance for the complex and the cost of a gardener to maintain the grounds. From time to time, you may also be hit with a **cost assessment**, to pay for items such as a new roof for the complex or swimming pool repairs.

CONSUMER ALERT: THE ASSOCIATION MAY BE ABLE TO EN-FORCE ITS RIGHT TO LEVY AN ASSESSMENT AGAINST YOU BY HAVING A LIEN PLACED ON YOUR PROPERTY IF YOU FAIL TO MAKE PAYMENT AND/OR BRINGING A LAWSUIT AGAINST YOU. THIS, IN TURN, CAN HAVE OTHER REPERCUSSIONS, SUCH AS HAVING AN ADVERSE IMPACT ON YOUR CREDIT RATING.

If you are a condominium owner, the association's rules and regulations are binding and can be enforced against you. Such rules and regulations may include a limitation on the color you paint your unit, on the times you can use the common facilities, and may require you to receive association permission before you make improvements. THUS, BEFORE YOU BUY, MAKE SURE THAT YOU READ THE ASSOCIATION RULES AND THAT YOU UNDERSTAND THEM.

> **CONSUMER ALERT: IF YOU ARE BUYING INTO A NEW CONDOMINIUM COMPLEX, MAKE SURE YOU ASK THE DEVELOPER WHETHER OTHER ADDITIONS TO THE COMPLEX ARE CONTEMPLATED. OTHERWISE, THAT BEAUTIFUL VIEW YOU ENJOY TODAY MAY BECOME A VISITORS PARKING LOT, TOMORROW.**

GIVE YOURSELF A RAISE

Looking before you leap can save you a lot of money when you are purchasing a home. Here are some thoughts that we hope will help you keep a lot of your hard-earned income in your own wallet and out of the mortgage banker's and others' whose hands may be out hoping that you will grease their palms.

CONSIDER MORTGAGE ACCELERATION

One way to save BIG bucks on interest is to pay your mortgage off earlier than called for in the mortgage agreement. For example, if your mortgage is a 30-year mortgage and you pay it off in 20 years, you will have saved 10 years worth of interest.

Mortgage acceleration is accomplished by paying more than your house payment calls for each monthly payment. The reason this works is that for most of the length of the mortgage, most of the money you are paying is going to pay interest. It is only in the latter period of the mortgage that most payments pay down on principal. By paying extra monies each month and applying it to the principal (assuming you don't have a prepayment penalty), you reduce the amount that is having interest charged against it and you reduce your total out of pocket expenses over the years. If you have any questions about how to accelerate your payments, contact your mortgage banker.

TRY TO TAKE OUT A SHORTER TERM MORTGAGE

Mortgages are now being offered for 15 years or less. This means that your payments are higher and it may be harder to qualify for the loan, but if you get past those barriers you can save tens of thousands of dollars in interest over the term of the loan. Another piece of good news: Shorter term mortgages often have slightly lower interest rates.

PERIODICALLY AUDIT THE INTEREST CHARGED ON YOUR ARM MORTGAGE

With the interest rates on ARM mortgages continually changing, it may pay to have a mortgage consulting service run an audit for you to see whether you have been overcharged. There are also kits on the market allowing you to run your own audit. The kits contain tables on interest rates over several years on several indexes.

MAKE SURE YOU GET A GOOD HOME INSPECTION

As we stated earlier, it is very important to put a contingency clause in your purchase agreement allowing you to inspect the home before being completely bound under the contract. Once that clause has been made a part of the contract, make sure you exercise your rights under it. The inspection will cost between $100 and $400, but it is worth it. Make sure the inspector inspects the exterior, the structure, the heating system, the plumbing, the insulation, the electrical wiring, the floors and any other areas that are deemed important. Then, make sure you get a written report on the condition of the property. If it is not up to par, be sure to cancel the purchase within the time permitted under the purchase agreement. Otherwise, you may be stuck paying for major repairs once you are the owner. Or you can better negotiate downward the price of the house.

There is a book well worth your while if you are having a home inspected. It is *Inspecting A House; A Guide For Buyers, Owners and Renovators*, by Alan Carson and Robert Dunlop (1986, Stoddard Publishing Co., Ltd, Toronto, Canada).

CONSIDER PURCHASING A "FIXER UPPER"

For those of you who are handy and have building skills, you can save a lot of money by purchasing a home that has seen better days and investing your own elbow grease and repair skills in renovating it. Homes that are badly in need of repair often sell for well below the market price and offer great values to those with the skills to take advantage of the opportunity.

LOOK INTO BUYING A HOME AT AUCTION

Houses are often sold at auction, whether due to foreclosure, probate, as part of the savings and loan bailout or otherwise. Great bargains can sometimes be had by purchasing homes in this manner, but you have to be careful since there will be those in attendance who earn their livings by purchasing homes at auction and then selling them for a profit. You also have to be aware that sometimes homes sold at auction sell for more than their fair market value.

If you are interested in auction purchases, be sure you research the property you are considering buying ahead of time and also be sure you learn the rules of the particular auction, such as how much money you have to pay down and how long you have before the price must be paid in full.

DON'T BUY MORTGAGE INSURANCE

Mortgage insurance is a form of decreasing term life insurance which sells for a higher premium than regular term insurance. If you want to have enough insurance to pay off the mortgage should you die, fine. But get annual renewable term and save a lot of money on premiums for better coverage than you can get with mortgage insurance. If you can avoid mortgages that compel you to take out mortgage insurance, do so.

CONSIDER "EQUITY SHARING"

If the cost of housing is too high or you don't feel you can afford to pay for the full down payment yourself, consider equity sharing as a way of becoming a real property owner.

Equity sharing involves an owner-occupant (that's you) and a co-owner-investor, pooling your resources to purchase the property. Usually, this involves sharing the down payment and sharing the ownership and the increase in value of the property. Both the owner-occupier and the co-owner-investor are named on the deed.

Equity sharing requires a contract between you and the investor that precisely sets forth your rights and obligations. With so much at stake, you may also wish to consult a lawyer. But if you are one of the many responsible consumers out there who can't quite afford to get into your own house, equity sharing may be a way to become a property owner while saving money at the same time.

The Equity Sharing Book, by Diane Bull and Elaine St. James (1990, Penguin Group, New York, NY) describes the concept in detail.

LOOK INTO WARRANTIES

When you buy a home, you may be able to receive a full or partial warranty, known as a "limited warranty." For example, many builders offer warranties when you buy one of their homes. Some real estate firms also offer partial protection if you purchase a property represented by them. Warranties can save you money if a problem arises during their term and if you then assert your rights under the warranty's terms. You can also sometimes purchase warranties. If you do, pay careful attention to the price, the deductible and to what is covered. Also, be sure you understand all of the terms so that you are not surprised when you make a claim to have a repair.

> **CONSUMER ALERT: WARRANTY INSURANCE COVERS WORK-MANSHIP AND MATERIAL FOR ONE YEAR, MAJOR SYSTEMS SUCH AS ELECTRICAL, PLUMBING, HEATING, ETC. FOR TWO YEARS AND STRUCTURAL DEFECTS FOR 10 YEARS. THE CONCEPT IS A GOOD ONE BUT THE PERFORMANCE HAS NOT MET THE PROMISE. RECENT CONGRESSIONAL TESTIMONY INDICATES THAT THERE ARE ABUSES IN THE INDUSTRY, SUCH AS ADJUSTERS THAT MAKE LOW "TAKE IT OR LEAVE IT" OFFERS OR CONSTRUE CONTRACTS SO NARROWLY THAT NOTHING SEEMS TO BE COVERED. IF YOU HAVE HAD PROBLEMS WITH HOME WARRANTY POLICIES, CONTACT RIDGEMERE INSTITUTE, WHICH IS TRYING TO PERSUADE CONGRESS TO TAKE ACTION TO CORRECT ABUSES. THEIR ADDRESS IS P.O. BOX 8247, HERMITAGE, TENN. 37076.**

MAKE SURE YOUR IMPOUND ACCOUNTS PAY YOUR TAXES AND INSURANCE

Some mortgage bankers insist that you pay into an escrow **impound account** for the amortized cost of taxes and insurance to make sure these payments are made when due. You are better off avoiding impound accounts if you can, but if you can't you should make sure your lender makes the payments when due so that you avoid penalties and/or a lien being placed on your home or your being uninsured. Also, try to have a clause requiring the account to accrue interest (this is the law in some states). After all, if you have to pay money into an account for taxes and insurance that are not yet due, the very least the lender can do is allow you to earn some interest on it.

Chapter Eleven

WHERE THE RUBBER MEETS THE ROAD

PURCHASING YOUR WHEELS

Cars: American as Mom, the flag and apple pie. It may only be mild hyperbole to say that Americans probably spend more time in cars than they do anyplace else, with the possible exception of work and bed. That being so, the decision to purchase a car is a major one in anyone's life. There is so much to consider; safety, price, style, economy, comfort, options - that consumers need to learn all they can about buying a car so that they can find the best and safest car at a price they can afford.

WHAT TO DO BEFORE
YOU HIT THE SHOWROOMS

As with any of life's important endeavors, preparation is the key to buying a new car. After all, there's a lot to think about and learn - about the cars on the market, about financing, about safety, the impact on your insurance premiums and more.

STEP 1: DECIDE HOW MUCH YOU WANT TO SPEND

The prices of automobiles vary all over the lot. Small imports can sell for as little as seven or eight thousand dollars while the alleged royalty of motor vehicles, the Rolls Royce, sells for more than the price of a three bedroom house in some areas of the country.

There are several aspects to the question, "How much do I want to spend."

Your Available Cash

If you are going to finance or lease your car, you will probably have to make a down payment, the size of which will depend on the total price of the vehicle. And even if you can find a no money down deal, you will have to pay for things such as registration and other costs of purchase.

The Amount of Money You Can Borrow To Finance Your Purchase

You should arrange your financing before you go to the showroom to make your purchase, not after. There are several reasons for this:

By getting preapproved financing, you will know how much money you have to purchase your new car (down payment plus maximum financing). This can help you save a lot of time looking and drooling over cars more expensive than you can afford.

By getting preapproved financing, you can shop around for the best financing deal. As we have discussed in the sections on credit cards and mortgages, the cost of financing can vary widely from financial institution to financial institution. By shopping around for your financing before you buy your car, you can find the lending source that offers you the best terms, which in turn can save you a lot of money.

Having your financing arranged ahead of time can give you dealing leverage in the showroom. The automobile showroom may be the closest thing in the United States to the Arab bazaar, where the original asking price may have little to do with the price you can obtain - if you play the bartering game like an expert. One powerful tool for you in this psychological game of give and take is to have a "done deal" for an auto loan, so that you can hold the financing pledge in front of your auto salesperson's nose and use it as leverage to get him or her to offer you the best possible deal. This strategy can often save you money on the dealership floor.

CONSUMER ALERT: MOST DEALERS OFFER FINANCING. BUT YOU ARE USUALLY BETTER OFF ARRANGING IT THROUGH YOUR BANK OR CREDIT UNION SINCE DEALERS RARELY HAVE TERMS COMPETITIVE WITH THOSE AVAILABLE TO YOU ON THE OPEN MARKET. (THERE ARE EXCEPTIONS TO THIS GENERAL RULE, OF COURSE, SO IF AN AUTOMOBILE COMPANY IS OFFERING A SPECIAL ON FINANCING, DON'T HESITATE TO CHECK OUT THE TERMS AND COMPARE THEM WITH THE TERMS OF AN AUTO LOAN AVAILABLE TO YOU ELSEWHERE).

The Amount of Monthly Payment You Can Afford

If you are going to finance or lease your car, you will have to make a monthly payment. Make a list of all of your monthly income and expenses. See how much extra cash you have at the end of each month (if any). Then, determine how much of that cash you can afford to spend on car payments.

The Indirect Costs

There are a lot of "indirect costs" that directly affect the health of your pocketbook when it comes to buying and owning a car. These should also be considered when looking into the make and kind of car you will buy.

The cost of registration One of the expenses that you will have to spend each year with regard to your car, is the tax levied by your State, known as a registration fee. Usually, the more expensive your car, the more you pay for registration. So, if your monthly budget runs close to or in the red, check to see what registration will cost you.

The cost of insurance The amount of your auto insurance premium will be affected by the type, year and make of the car you drive. That is because different cars cost more to repair, have differing safety records, are more or less likely to be stolen and provide a wide range of protection to occupants in an accident. Thus, it is always a good idea to call your insurance agent and check out the auto insurance premium ramifications of the car(s) you are contemplating purchasing.

The cost of fuel The better the fuel efficiency of your car, the less gas you will buy and the more money will remain in your pocket. One defense against the high cost of gasoline blues is to purchase a car that gets good gas mileage. That way, if the prices shoot up to $2.00 a gallon, you might not have to mortgage your house just to be able to afford the commute to work. As a bonus, you will be doing a good deed for the environment too.

The cost of repair and length of warranty Another ongoing expense of car ownership is maintenance and repair. If you buy a new car, you will receive a warranty (see below). In order to keep the warranty in effect, you will have to perform regular maintenance, such as changing the oil and inspecting the engine parts. This regular service obligation will cost you money. Ask how much before you buy so that you don't go into "maintenance service shock" after. You should also check to see how much repairs generally cost after the warranty period expires and the rate of repair that a car you are interested in can be expected to require. (This information can be found in the annual Consumer Reports Buying Guide Issue, available in your library or local book store.)

The cost of depreciation The moment you drive your sparkling new car off the lot, it ceases to be "new" and immediately is worth less than it was before the tires hit the pavement of the street. This reduction in value is known as "depreciation." If you buy a car that depreciates a lot, it will end up costing you more money when you sell it later or trade it in on a new model.

STEP TWO: SHOP AROUND

Here comes the fun part. Once you know the amount of money you can spend on a car, you will want to explore the different makes and models that come within your predesignated budget. There are many ways to do this:

Visit Dealer Showrooms

Oh boy, what fun! The shiny new cars, the chrome, the free coffee while you browse, the smell of "new car." But beware, there are traps for the unwary. It is easy to get swept away by the glitz and hype, by high pressure sales tactics and that very dangerous seductive urge to impulse buy. Still, going to different showrooms and talking to the sales personnel about the cars will give you a good idea of the range of the choices you have in your price range.

Research

Another way to see which cars fit your budget and which do not is to do a little research. This can be as simple as opening the Sunday paper and looking at advertisements of auto dealerships, which will usually list the prices of the cars they are selling. You can also turn to publications that will help you learn about the various cars in your price range. (One source of such information is the Annual Auto Issue of **Consumer Reports Magazine** that is published in the Spring of each year.)

CONSUMER ALERT: IF YOU ARE THE MEMBER OF A CREDIT UNION, THERE IS AN EXCELLENT PROGRAM CALLED "AUTOFACTS", CREATED BY REMAR SUTTON. SUTTON, IN ASSOCIATION WITH THE CREDIT UNION NATIONAL ASSOCIATION, MAKES THE LARGE "AUTOFACTS MANUAL" AVAILABLE TO CREDIT UNION MEMBERS, ALONG WITH A MEMBER VIDEO AND THE "AUTOFACTS" LIBRARY. THE IDEA BEHIND

THIS PROGRAM IS TO HAVE AUTO ADVISERS ON THE STAFF OF CREDIT UNIONS WHO WILL GIVE ADVICE ON HIDDEN DEALER CHARGES, FINANCE CHARGE CALCULATIONS, CREDIT LIFE, NEW-CAR WARRANTIES, LEMON LAWS AND OTHER SEASONED COUNSEL. IF YOU ARE A MEMBER OF A CREDIT UNION, WE URGE YOU TO CHECK INTO "AUTOFACTS."

When you do your research, look for the following factors in determining which cars in your price range you are interested in and which you are not:

Safety Let's say that important word again: SAFETY. Auto safety should be your number one priority! After all, styles come and go, as do trends, which car is "in" and which car is "out." But you only have one body and one family, and the protection of both should be paramount when you decide which car to buy.

CONSUMER ALERT: THE PRICE OF AUTO ACCIDENTS EACH YEAR IS STAGGERING. THERE ARE APPROXIMATELY 45,000 PEOPLE KILLED ON AMERICA'S HIGHWAYS EACH YEAR IN AUTOMOBILE ACCIDENTS, AN AMOUNT EQUIVALENT TO THE TOTAL NUMBER OF U.S. SERVICE PERSONNEL KILLED IN THE ENTIRE VIETNAM WAR! THAT DOESN'T INCLUDE THE MILLIONS OF PEOPLE INJURED. IT HAS BEEN ESTIMATED THAT AN ACCIDENT INVOLVING AN INJURY OCCURS EVERY 18 SECONDS IN THIS COUNTRY. ADD THE FINANCIAL CONSEQUENCES (ABOUT $74 BILLION ANNUALLY) TO THIS PHYSICAL CARNAGE AND YOU CAN SEE THAT AUTO SAFETY SHOULD BE THE PRIORITY IN THE CAR YOU BUY.

Happily, there is a great deal of material published each year on auto safety and the safety history of the various cars on the market. A great source is *The Car Book*, by Jack Gillis, published each year by Harper Perennial Publishers. *The Car Book* covers automobile buying from all angles, including safety, economy, maintenance, insurance and complaints. If you are going to buy a car, buy this book. (If you are going to purchase a truck or van, look into the companion volume, *The Truck, Van and 4X4 Book*).

Perhaps the easiest way for you to learn about this year's crop of cars is to call the National Highway Traffic Safety Administration's (NHTSA) **New Car Assessment Safety Hotline toll free at, 1-800-424-9393.** The service can offer you vital information on auto safety, including:

•Information on the New Car Assessment Program, Car Crash Test - a crash test report on the cars in the marketplace

•Information on safety recalls on cars and trucks

•A report on child safety seat recalls

•A report on uniform tire quality grading

•Safety recall information on other types of vehicles or special equipment.

You can also use the hotline to REPORT safety defects that you discover, thereby potentially helping to save the lives and health of other motorists, just like you.

When reviewing a car's safety features, it is not enough that they meet the modest safety standards set by the U.S. Government. (All cars on the market do.) No, you want more. Look for the following:

•*Good driver visibility* In order to keep from hitting something or someone, you need to be able to see the person or thing which may be in harm's way. A good test of visibility is whether the driver can see a small child standing close to any part of the car.

You will also want to choose a car that has equipment designed to optimize your continued visibility, such as rear window defoggers, rear-view mirrors on both sides of the car that permit you to look through them without turning your head, non-obstructing headrests and tinted, nonglare windshields.

•*A car that can be seen* Celebrity and driving have one thing in common; it is important to be seen. Thus, you will want a car that is visible to other drivers. Such a car should have raised tail lights, lights in the door when you open it and should be of a light, visible color.

•*A car with good safety equipment and crash protection* Seat belts are not enough. You want a car with AIRBAGS. Also, bumpers solid enough to withstand low speed collisions and the ever-necessary comfortable seat and shoulder belts. Ask about the ability of a car you are thinking of purchasing to withstand a crash from the side and rollover protection. Finally, you need a car that has good brakes. Look for cars with good computerized anti-lock braking systems (ABS) that help prevent a loss of control when you stop suddenly.

•*A vehicle with gauges and controls that are easily accessible* When you are driving, it is important to be able to see your gauges and operate your controls easily and without forcing you to take your concentration off the road.

•*Reliability* In addition to a safe car, you will want to buy a car that you can count on as a reliable source of transportation. But how do you separate the cars that are dependable from those that may have a tendency to spend more time in the mechanic's garage than your own?

•*Reputation* Like people, cars develop reputations. This "word of mouth" network of shared information is often a good consumer's guide to buying the best cars on the market (or other products for that matter) and toward avoiding vehicles that will give you the gas. So, when you are thinking of buying a new car, ask your friends who have purchased new cars in recent years about their choices.

•*Consumer advice* Consumers Union and others put a great deal of emphasis into researching and evaluating the cars that come on the market each year. The Annual Auto Issue specifically deals with reliability, rating each model (based on owner surveys) on whether the respondents would buy the same car again. The magazine also has a Frequency of Repair section which surveys potential trouble spots, such as air conditioning, body paint, brakes, electrical system, steering, fuel system and transmission, and rates each model as to each specific area. There is also a trouble index and a cost index dealing with repairs. (The Annual Buying Guide has a similar survey.)

Warranty An important issue in the purchase of your new car is the warranty. A good warranty can save you a lot of money if repairs are required during the time it is in effect. Most warranties are expressed in terms of time and mileage, i.e. thirty-six months or thirty-six thousand miles, whichever comes first.

Thus, the longer the warranty, the less likely you are to have to dig into your pocket for auto repair dollars. So, if one car you are interested in has a three year, thirty-six thousand mile warranty and the other has a five-year, fifty-thousand mile warranty, all other factors being equal, you may wish to choose the latter car for the extra pocketbook protection buying it provides.

The laws regarding warranties will vary from state to state. There is Federal law on the subject too; the Magnuson-Moss Act, which sets minimum standards for warranties and which you can use to achieve justice for your complaint. Under the Act, written warranties must disclose the following in clear, easy to understand language:

•*Who is protected?* Some warranties only protect the first buyers, others protect any buyer so long as the warranty is in effect.

•*What is protected?* Not every part in a car is protected by a warranty. Thus, you have a right to know which parts of the car are protected by the warranty and which are not.

•*How long is the protection?* You have a right to know the exact duration of the warranty.

CONSUMER ALERT: IN ADDITION TO WRITTEN WARRANTIES, ALSO KNOW AS *SPECIFIC WARRANTIES*, MANY STATE LAWS PROVIDE FOR *"IMPLIED" WARRANTIES*. IMPLIED WARRANTIES ARE PROVIDED BY LAW AND MAY EXCEED THE WRITTEN WARRANTY YOU RECEIVE WITH YOUR VEHICLE. THUS, IF YOU ARE HAVING SIGNIFICANT TROUBLE WITH YOUR CAR AND YOUR WRITTEN WARRANTY HAS RUN OUT, YOU MAY STILL HAVE RIGHTS UNDER STATE IMPLIED WARRANTY LAWS. ASK A LAWYER WHO DEALS WITH STATE LEMON LAWS FOR DETAILS.

CONSUMER ALERT: MANY CAR COMPANIES OFFER SERVICE CONTRACTS, A FORM OF INSURANCE TO COVER AUTO REPAIRS, AT EXTRA COST. JACK GILLIS, *IN THE CAR BOOK*, STATES THAT SERVICE CONTRACTS ARE THE MOST EXPENSIVE OPTION YOU CAN BUY AND GENERALLY, A VERY POOR VALUE. IF YOU ARE INTERESTED IN A SERVICE CONTRACT, GILLIS SUGGESTS YOU CONSIDER THE FOLLOWING BEFORE YOU BUY:
•HOW REPUTABLE IS THE COMPANY RESPONSIBLE FOR THE CONTRACT?
•EXACTLY WHAT DOES THE CONTRACT COVER AND FOR HOW LONG?
•HOW WILL THE REPAIR BILLS BE PAID?
•WHERE CAN THE CAR BE SERVICED?
•WHAT OTHER COSTS CAN BE EXPECTED?
•WHAT ISN'T COVERED BY THE CONTRACT?

CONSUMER ALERT: THERE ARE MANY "LEMON LAWS" ON THE BOOKS IN VARIOUS STATES TO PROTECT YOU IF YOU PURCHASE A CAR THAT DOES NOT OPERATE PROPERLY. STATE LAWS VARY IN EACH STATE. IF YOU HAVE ANY QUESTION ABOUT YOUR STATE'S LEMON LAW, OR IF YOU WANT INFORMATION ON WHAT TO DO IF YOU HAVE PURCHASED A LEMON, CONTACT YOUR STATE DEPARTMENT OF CONSUMER AFFAIRS. ALSO, READ *THE LEMON BOOK; AUTO RIGHTS FOR NEW AND USED CARS*, BY RALPH NADER AND CLARENCE DITLOW, WHICH SHOULD BE AVAILABLE IN YOUR LOCAL LIBRARY OR LARGER BOOK STORE.

CONSUMER ALERT: IF YOU HAVE COMPLAINTS ABOUT THE WARRANTY YOU RECEIVED, CONTACT YOUR STATE DEPARTMENT OF CONSUMER AFFAIRS OR THE FEDERAL TRADE COMMISSION, BUREAU OF CONSUMER PROTECTION, 6TH AND PENNSYLVANIA AVENUE, NW, WASHINGTON D.C. 20580.

Economy Increasingly, consumers are looking for vehicles that will be economical to own and to drive. Of course, a lot goes into the concept of "economy," some of which we have already discussed, such as the quality of the warranty, the ability of the car to withstand low speed collisions and the frequency of repairs.

Another important aspect of economy, is gas mileage. Every new car has it's mileage rated (i.e., 25 mph city, 35 mph highway). These estimates are usually "optimistic." In other words, as the commercials often say, your mileage may differ, and most probably will - on the downside. However, these EPA (Environmental Protection Agency) estimates do provide a valuable comparison between and among different car models.

CONSUMER ALERT: FUEL ECONOMY IS A VERY IMPORTANT FACTOR WHEN BUYING A CAR. THE DEPARTMENT OF TRANSPORTATION OFFERS THE FOLLOWING SUGGESTIONS ON PURCHASING FUEL EFFICIENT CARS:

•*BUY A CAR WITH A MANUAL TRANSMISSION*: IT HAS BEEN ESTIMATED THAT A FOUR SPEED MANUAL TRANSMISSION CAN ACTUALLY SAVE 6.5 MILES PER GALLON OVER A THREE SPEED AUTOMATIC.

•*BUY A CAR WITH A SMALLER ENGINE*: THE SMALLER THE ENGINE, GENERALLY, THE BETTER THE GAS MILEAGE. THUS, A FOUR CYLINDER ENGINE WILL PROBABLY DRIVE FARTHER ON A TANK OF GAS THAN A SIX CYLINDER CAR, WHICH WILL BE SUPERIOR TO AN EIGHT CYLINDER CAR, ETC.

•*CHECK OUT THE TIRES ON THE CAR*: RADIAL TIRES WILL IMPROVE YOUR MILEAGE OVER CONVENTIONAL BIAS-PLY TIRES, BY AS MUCH AS 3 TO 7 PERCENT. OVER THE LIFETIME OF THE CAR, THAT CAN ADD UP TO A LOT OF GAS SAVED.

•*AVOID AIR CONDITIONING WHEN YOU CAN*: IN CITY DRIVING, THE USE OF AIR CONDITIONING CAN ROB YOU OF ABOUT THREE MILES PER GALLON. THUS, IF YOU CAN STAND THE HEAT, KEEP THE AIR CONDITIONER OFF.

A car that drives well You will want a car that handles well, takes corners safely, has smooth changes of gears, etc. Thus, the importance of the test drive.

Pizzazz (test drive, style, etc.) We know that owning a car is a relationship. We realize that you and your car will be spending hours alone together. We understand that you and your car need to be compatible in order for the relationship to work. In short, we firmly believe that you can be an effective consumer without losing the thrill and joy of buying a new car.

This brings us to the subjective stuff, or the pizzazz. When you are in the market to spend thousands of dollars on a car, you want to like it - more, you want to LOVE it. That's where the fun part comes in - visiting showrooms, taking test drives, getting to know the contenders for your auto purchase dollars and your emotional attachment.

When you take your test drives, pay attention to the following factors:

•*Comfort* You will spend hours in your car, sometimes at one time, and it is important to your physical well being that you are comfortable. The comfort and interior design of cars vary widely. Thus, pay attention to the headroom, legroom and seat support. Will you be getting a sore back on that run to your favorite bed and breakfast in the country? How easy is it to get in and out of the car? And don't forget to sit in the back seat. You will want your passengers to be comfortable too.

•*Performance* How does the engine run? Do you have sufficient power to get out of tight spots in a hurry? Is the ride smooth and what about the sound levels? If you can, turn on the air conditioner while taking a test drive. Does it affect the level of power? And try to take a hill to see how the car responds.

•*Ease of handling* How are the brakes? What about the steering? Try to parallel park. Is it easy or hard? Check out the traction on turns and the ability of the car to maneuver through traffic.

•*Fun* Many Americans are in love with their cars. Thus, you may want to ask yourself, "Is this a car that I will enjoy driving?" If it isn't, look around for other cars in your price range. Maybe you will find one more suitable to your tastes. (Of course, if it comes down to choosing safety and economy over fun, we advise choosing the former every time.)

You will also want to deal with other factors of pizzazz, such as body styles, available colors, types and colors of upholstery. Then, you take it all together; safety, economy, reliability, pizzazz, etc. and you come up with a decision - THIS IS THE ONE! Now, the countdown really begins.

STEP 3: MAKING THE DEAL

So, you have decided which car to buy. Now, and only now, is the time to seriously talk "deal" with your local car salesperson. When engaging in negotiations, the more you know, the better you will be at getting the best deal. So, you need information, information that tells you exactly how much the dealer's cost is for the car you want to buy.

Happily, the **Consumer Reports Auto Price Service** supplies such information. For a small fee you will receive a printout on any make, model and trim line you specify. Each printout notes the standard equipment, list price and dealer cost of the basic car. The service also itemizes by invoice every factory option and options package with list prices and dealer cost. Armed with this information, you can try to get the price down to as little as two to four percent over invoice (higher for some luxury and sporty cars which may be in greater demand). The Consumer Report's Auto Price Service can be reached at: Box 8005, Novi, Michigan, 48050. As of the date this is written, the price is $11 for one car, $20 for two; $27 for three and $7 more for each additional car surveyed.

Once you are armed with the information you need, visit dealers selling cars you are interested in purchasing in your area and let them know that you a) are in a buying mode and not a looking mode (you want them to salivate); b) know the amount of the dealers invoice (bring the printout with you) and that you expect a deal only a little over cost; c) have the cash or financing all lined up so the sale will be consummated once you decide on the dealer who gets your business, and; d) you intend to make your buying decision based on which dealer is willing to give you the most reasonable price. (If the salesperson disputes your figures, ask to see a copy of the invoice. It will be in the dealership on file.) That should get the sales and management personnel to offer you the best price they have to offer.

There is more to negotiate over than price. Perhaps you want special equipment or lamb skin seat covers. Some people want a step up in the stereo system, etc. Don't be afraid to deal in these areas but prepare ahead of time by learning the cost to the dealer for extras by contacting the Consumer Reports Auto Pricing Service so that you don't get fleeced.

CONSUMER ALERT: IN ORDER TO PREVENT YOURSELF FROM BEING SWEPT AWAY BY THE MOMENT AND THEREBY SPENDING MORE THAN IS NECESSARY, REMEMBER:
1) YOU HAVE THE POWER TO WALK AWAY FROM THE DEAL AT ANY TIME.
2) DO NOT PAY A DEPOSIT ON A CAR UNTIL AND UNLESS THE MANAGER HAS SIGNED ON THE DEAL, BINDING THE CAR DEALERSHIP.
3) IF THE SALESPERSON SAYS NO TO AN OFFER YOU HAVE MADE, ASK TO SPEAK TO A HIGHER AUTHORITY.

The Better Business Bureau also recommends the following in their book *The BBB A to Z Buying Guide* (1990, Council of Better Business Bureaus Inc.)

•Don't be rushed into a quick decision by hard-ball sales tactics or "limited time offers."

•Try and save a few dollars by ordering a car from inventory rather than buying one on the dealer's lot.

•Don't let rebate offers dissuade you from comparison shopping.

•Negotiate the price of your new car first *before* you talk about the value of your trade in. (Otherwise, the dealer may give with one hand and take away with the other by getting the benefit of the bargain on the trade in.)

CONSUMER ALERT: IF YOU HAVE A CAR TO TRADE IN, YOU MAY BE BETTER OFF SELLING IT YOURSELF FOR THE CURRENT FAIR MARKET PRICE. REMEMBER, WHEN YOU TRADE YOUR CAR IN, THE DEALER WILL BE RESELLING IT, OR SELLING IT TO A USED CAR BROKER AND WILL THEREFORE PROBABLY GIVE YOU LESS MONEY THAN YOU MAY BE ABLE TO GET ON THE OPEN MARKET SO THEY CAN MAKE A PROFIT ON THE TRANSACTION.

STEP FOUR: TAKING DELIVERY

When you are ready to take delivery of your car, be sure and check it over thoroughly. Look particularly for any damage, such as small dents to the body or bumpers and make sure all of the body moldings are in place and properly installed. Also, look to see if the spare tire and jack are in place. (Many cars now offer spares that are not full sized tires. You may want to bargain for a full sized spare when you are negotiating with the sales person). Check your invoice with the window sticker to make sure everything you bargained and paid for has been delivered. Have the salesperson show you how all the fancy gadgets and knobs work so that you don't get confused on the highway. Finally, check to make sure you have your owner's manual, warranty forms, and all necessary legal documents.

BUYING A USED CAR

If money is a factor to you, or if you do not want to foot the price of a new car, you may want to buy a used car.

Buying a used car can be risky. After all, no matter how bright or shiny the car may look on the surface, the wax and clean up job may be masking an automobile which may be a mere husk of its former self. For example, it may have been in a serious accident. Or, it may have been driven hard, causing unseen problems waiting to bite you once you have put your money down. Or, it may simply be a tired car with its best years and performance left on the roads that it has driven over the years.

Even though you will save money when you buy used over new, the cost of a used car will usually run into the thousands of dollars. Thus, be careful and remember the following tips:

Examine the Car

It is important that you inspect the outside of the car very carefully.

•Look at the odometer to see how many miles the car has driven. The more miles the car has gone, the less likely it is to remain in good repair over a long period of time.

> CONSUMER ALERT: SOME NEFARIOUS DEALERS COMMIT FRAUD ON THE PUBLIC BY ROLLING BACK THE ODOMETER TO MAKE THE CAR APPEAR AS IF IT WAS ONLY DRIVEN TO CHURCH AND BACK BY THE PROVERBIAL LITTLE OLD LADY FROM DUBUQUE. ODOMETER FRAUD IS A CRIME AND SHOULD BE REPORTED IF IT HAPPENS TO YOU. IN SUCH AN UNHAPPY CIRCUMSTANCE, CALL THE NATIONAL HIGHWAY TRAFFIC SAFETY ADMINISTRATION'S HOTLINE AT 1- 800- 424-9393.

•Look for dents, rust and any evidence that parts of the car have rusted out or have been repaired with body putty.

•Check under the car for rust or breaks in the frame. It is especially important to look for signs that the frame has been welded since that may indicate weakness in the car's structure.

•Look for ripples in the fender, dents or paint that does not match, all evidence that the car may have been in an accident.

> CONSUMER ALERT: BE SURE TO SHOP FOR A USED CAR DURING THE DAY. FLUORESCENT LIGHTING, DARKNESS COMBINED WITH A HIGH GLOSS WAX JOB CAN HIDE MANY PROBLEMS.

•Stand back from the car and make sure that it is level. If one corner is lower than another, one of the springs may be weak or broken.

•Check the condition of the tires to make sure they match. Also, look at the inside surface of the tires; sometimes a badly scuffed tire may have been turned around.

•Check out the upholstery. Worn or frayed upholstery is a good indication of heavy usage.

•Check the engine to see if there is oil splattered or if the battery is cracked. Also check the oil to see if it is clean or dirty. If the car is an automatic, check the transmission fluid to see if it is clear.

•Look inside the tail pipe. Black, gummy dirt or soot in the tail pipe can mean the car will soon need expensive repairs. A white powdery deposit usually means good fuel combustion in the engine.

•Make sure all of the headlights, taillights, break lights, back up lights, etc. are in good working order as they are an essential part of any car's safety mechanisms. Also, be sure to try out the radio, air conditioner and windshield wipers.

Take a Test Drive

When you take a test drive, pay very careful attention to how the car rides and handles. Be alert to any vibrations that should not be there. Let the engine idle and listen for noises and vibrations that may indicate a poorly-tuned engine or bad valves. Pay attention to the shifting of the gears. If the transmission is automatic, does the car slide smoothly between gears or is there a jerking? If the car has a stick shift, feel for grabbing or rattling of the clutch and whether the shifting is easy or difficult. Be alert for smoke coming out of the exhaust. In short, be alert to any troubles. Because once you buy the car, unless the problem is covered by a written limited warranty, you will pay for the repairs, effectively adding to the price of the car.

Have the Car Looked At by an Expert

It is impossible to know from a surface look the precise mechanical shape of a given car. Thus, it is VITAL that you have a used car you are thinking of purchasing, checked out by an expert in auto mechanics. If the seller of the used car, be it a private individual, auto dealership or otherwise, balks at allowing you to do this, walk away from the deal no matter how sweet it may seem. In a used car, what you don't know can and will hurt you. For those of you lucky enough to be friends with a mechanic or car buff, ask that person to assist you.

Know the Reputation of the Vehicle

Different models of cars get different reputations. Happily, it is not difficult to learn the reputation of a used car you are thinking of buying. For example, the Consumer Reports Used-Car Price Service (see above) also offers a "Trouble Index," based on their "Frequency of Repair" data. (Call 1-900-446-1120 @ $1.50 per minute). Consumer Reports Books also publishes a yearly GUIDE to USED CARS, which does a very good job of pointing out potential repair problems and potential difficulties to watch out for. And, don't forget, the National Highway Traffic Safety Administration's toll free hotline for information on safety recalls (1-800-424-9393).

Know the Value of the Vehicle

Just as it is important to know what the invoice of a new car is for the dealer, it is important for you to know the fair market value of a used car to keep from falling prey to overpricing. Here's a list of helpful sources:

•Your local newspaper: Check the prices of similar makes and models of the car you are thinking of buying in the classified section of your paper.

•Go to your local library or ask your auto insurance agent to show you a copy of the National Automobile Dealers Official Used Car guide. Also, look at the Kelly Blue Book, which is published monthly, or for older cars, the Old Car/Truck Red Book, which is published quarterly.

•Check used car dealers to see if the kind of car you are thinking of buying is similarly priced to the vehicle you are thinking of buying.

> **CONSUMER ALERT: CONSUMER REPORTS ALSO HAS A USED-CAR PRICE SERVICE THAT QUOTES UP-TO-DATE PRICES OVER THE PHONE ON ALL VEHICLES BUILT SINCE 1982, FOR ANY AREA OF THE COUNTRY. THE SERVICE PROVIDES A PRICE FOR BUYING OR SELLING PRIVATELY, BUYING FROM A FRANCHISED DEALER OR TRADING IN A VEHICLE.**

> **THE CALL COSTS $1.50 A MINUTE (AS OF THE DATE OF THIS WRITING) AND ACCORDING TO CONSUMER REPORTS, THE TYPICAL CALL TAKES 5 MINUTES. YOU WILL BE CHARGED ON YOUR PHONE BILL. BEFORE CALLING, HAVE YOUR ZIP CODE, THE MODEL NAME AND YEAR OF THE VEHICLE, THE MILEAGE, MAJOR OPTIONS AND APPROXIMATE CONDITION.**

> **THE PHONE NUMBER FOR THE CONSUMER REPORTS USED-CAR PRICING SERVICE IS, 1-900-446-1120.**

Know the Warranty on the Vehicle

If you buy your used car through a commercial dealership, you have to be told whether there is a warranty or whether you are buying, "As Is." The Federal Trade Commission requires all non-private owner sellers of used cars to display a large sticker in the car window, known as the "Buyers Guide." The Buyers Guide will tell you if you have a warranty, and if so, what the warranty covers and for how long it is in effect. If you buy as is, chances are that the problems that you inherit when you buy the car will be yours to deal with - and pay for. (If a car is not specifically sold as is, there may be an implied warranty under your state's laws. Ask your Department of Consumer Affairs or your lawyer for more details.)

TO LEASE OR TO BUY, THAT IS THE QUESTION

In the "good old days," car buying life was simple. The cars were simple, often coming in one color: black, with few extras. The method of payment was simple too. There was only one way to pay for that Model A and that was to pay cash.

Today, car buying (as with nearly everything else in life), has become more complicated. Not only can you pay cash (and some people even do) or borrow the money to buy the car but you don't even have to buy your car at all. You can lease instead. In fact, leasing is now one of the major ways in which people obtain their vehicular transportation.

FACTS ABOUT LEASING

There are several facts about leasing a car that you need to understand if you are going to be able to decide whether it is in your financial interest to lease rather than buy:

You Do Not Become the Owner

When you lease, you do not become the owner of the car. Instead, ownership remains with the leasing company.

Monthly Payments are Usually Lower

When you buy a car through financing, you pay for the entire car plus the interest on the loan. When you lease, you do not pay for the entire car through the lease payments themselves (although you can probably arrange to purchase your car from the leasing company if you choose to do so.) Since you are not buying the car but renting it through your lease contract, your payments are lower.

The Total Cost of a Lease Can Be High

Just as you pay interest on a loan, you pay interest on a lease. And, while the total in principal you pay on a lease will be less, the cost of the lease can be as high as the cost of a loan.

You Don't Own The Car At The End of the Lease

At the end of the lease, you don't own the car. Thus, you do not build up equity with your payments nor do you obtain any property rights in the leased vehicle.

There May Be Penalties

Leases provide financial penalties under certain circumstances. These penalties can prove expensive so it is a good idea to be aware of them at the time you enter into your contract. Some of the typical penalties, include:

Excessive mileage Most leases permit you to drive about 15,000 miles per year under the terms of the contract. If you exceed that amount (or whatever amount is specified in the lease), there will often be a mileage penalty of between 8¢ and 12¢.

> **CONSUMER ALERT: A LEASE IS A CONTRACT, SO DON'T BE AFRAID TO NEGOTIATE. IF YOU KNOW YOU DRIVE FURTHER EACH YEAR THAN THE MILEAGE PERMITTED UNDER THE TERMS OF THE LEASE, YOU MAY WISH TO ADD A PROVISION ALLOWING YOU TO DRIVE MORE MILES PER YEAR AND PAY A SLIGHTLY EXTRA MONTHLY FEE. REMEMBER, EVEN AT 10¢ A MILE, THE COSTS OF A MILEAGE PENALTY CAN ADD UP. FOR EXAMPLE, IF YOU DRIVE 20,000 MORE THAN IS PERMITTED, THE PENALTY AT 10¢ A MILE IS $2,000.**

Pre-payment Some leases provide for a penalty if you decide to end the lease before its time.
Default If you cannot live up to the contractual terms of the lease and have to turn the car in, you will have to pay an extra fee for the privilege.
Late payment If you are late with your monthly payment, expect to pay for the check having been "lost in the mail."

Difference in value Under some leases (open ended - see below), if the appraised value of the vehicle when you turn it in is less than the amount estimated when you took out the lease, you have to pay all or part of the difference, depending on the terms of the lease itself.
Excessive wear and tear If you mistreat or neglect the auto and then turn it in with excessive wear and tear, you may pay a penalty for the lost value of the beat up car to the leasing company.

You Will Be Required To Have Auto Insurance

The lease contract will require you to take out auto insurance on the leased car. And, the amount of coverage you will be required to maintain (often 100,000/300,000 for liability, or higher) may be more than you would have otherwise elected to purchase. Thus, your insurance might cost more than it would if you purchased the car.

> CONSUMER ALERT: WHEN YOU LEASE A CAR, THERE IS A DANGER OF OWING MORE ON THE LEASE THAN THE VALUE OF THE CAR. THIS PRESENTS THE PROBLEM OF THE INSURANCE GAP. IF YOUR CAR IS DESTROYED OR STOLEN, THE INSURANCE PAYMENT MAY NOT BE SUFFICIENT TO PAY OFF YOUR LEASE CONTRACT OBLIGATION.

You Will Probably Have to Pay for Repairs

Most leases require you to maintain the vehicle and to pay for all repairs (although there are some leases that include the price of maintenance and/or repairs in the monthly payment).

There are Two Kinds of Leases

Open Ended At the end of an open ended lease, you have to pay the difference between the value of the car and the value estimated in the lease (although federal law usually limits the payment to three times the monthly payment). The monthly payments for open ended leases are often lower but the total cost of the lease often is not.
Closed Ended At the end of a closed ended lease, you are finished with payments unless you are subject to penalty payments.

BUYING VERSUS LEASING

As you can see there is a major difference between buying and leasing, both in cost and in final result. Which is best for you is an individual decision. However, the Better Business Bureau (BBB) recommends that you consider buying if:

•You plan to keep your car more than four years;
•You drive more than the allotted mileage available under your lease (i.e. 15,000 miles per year);
•You plan to move during the lease since moving can cost you extra money under lease provisions or can terminate the lease and convert it into a loan.

The BBB recommends that you consider leasing if:
•You trade in your car every two or three years;
•You do not have the cash for a down payment;
•If you want to keep your monthly payments lower;
•You do not wish or cannot qualify to borrow money.

GIVE YOURSELF A RAISE

Saving money on a car is something every car owner wants to do. Here are a few tips to help you keep your costs down.

BE SURE TO SHOP AROUND

Comparison shopping is one of the consumer's greatest weapons against the high cost of products and services.

BE SURE TO DO YOUR RESEARCH

Knowledge is power when it comes to purchasing anything and that holds especially true for automobiles. Knowing ahead of time what the dealer's invoice is, what the safety record and repair history of the model you are interested in, and the amount of money the car will depreciate over its life, are all important facts you need to know if you are going to get a good deal on a car and get a car that is a good deal for you.

DON'T GORGE ON OPTIONS

One way some dealers add profits to their coffers is to sell you options that are overpriced or unnecessary. Remember, options can drive up the price of a car fast. Thus, resist the temptation to buy extras, such as that 20 speaker stereo with laser disk (an expensive sound system can run over $1,000), and other expensive gimmicks such as a special trip computer (they can run over $1,000) or larger engines which should not be needed.

DON'T BUY SERVICE CONTRACTS

If you buy a reliable car with a decent warranty, you should not need to spend extra money for a service contract. In addition, many service contracts have fine print which contains many exclusions and which may contain vague language.

BUY LAST YEAR'S MODEL

If you wait until the end of the model year (late summer/early fall), you can often get good deals from dealers who have to sell their inventory to make room for the new models.

AVOID NEW MODELS

If you ask most honest car salespersons, they will tell you that most "bugs" in new models turn up in the first model year and are corrected in subsequent years. Thus, you can save yourself money and bother by waiting to buy a model after it has had time to prove itself.

USE THE CONSUMER REPORT SERVICES

The services offered by Consumer Reports that we have outlined in this chapter can save you a lot of money. Be sure to use them to your advantage.

SELL YOUR TRADE-IN ON THE OPEN MARKET

You will probably make more money selling your used car privately rather than trading it in. If you do trade your car in, negotiate the deal for your new car first so that the dealership does not give you money on a deal for the new car and then take it back by undervaluing your used car.

TAKE ADVANTAGE OF LEMON LAWS

If you buy a car that could be used as the basic ingredient of lemonade, then be sure to take advantage of the Lemon Laws of your state. (We recommend *The Lemon Book* for details on lemon laws. *The Lemon Book* should be available in your library or local book store.)

CONSUMER ALERT: AS AN INVOLVED CONSUMER, YOU CARE ABOUT AUTO SAFETY. WE THUS URGE YOU TO ADD YOUR VOICE TO THE CENTER FOR AUTO SAFETY, WHICH IS THE ONLY CONSUMER GROUP THAT WORKS FULL TIME TO STOP DEFECTIVE CARS AND TO IMPROVE AUTO SAFETY AND QUALITY. THE CENTER FOR AUTO SAFETY CAN ONLY DO ITS JOB IF YOU LEND YOUR SUPPORT. THE MEMBERSHIP COST IS ONLY $15 AND FOR YOUR TAX DEDUCTIBLE MEMBERSHIP, YOU ALSO RECEIVE "LEMON TIMES" NEWSLETTER, TELLING YOU ABOUT THE LATEST "LEMON CROP" AND THE CENTER'S EFFORTS TO WEED THEM OUT.

TO JOIN, SEND $15 (OR MORE) TO CENTER FOR AUTO SAFETY, 2001 S ST. NW, WASHINGTON D.C. 20009.

Chapter Twelve

PUTTING BREAD ON THE TABLE

BUYING YOUR FOOD

There are a lot of things that you can do without. But there is one product no one can live without. That "product" is food.

At one time the need to eat was met by many, if not most, Americans through the sweat of their own brow. We were a rural society and most grew and shucked the corn they had for dinner, along with the wild pig they shot and the apples or berries they picked for dessert. But things have changed from those bygone days. Today, the vast majority of people must buy their food.

Buying food has become increasingly expensive. According to the U.S. Department of Commerce, Americans spent $624.7 BILLION on food in 1990.

Unfortunately, many Americans don't really know how to shop effectively for food, that is, how to get the best food at the best price.

WHAT TO LOOK FOR IN THE FOOD YOU BUY

Buying food is not as simple as going out, grabbing a package of something to eat at your local grocery and then going home and eating it. At least it shouldn't be. As a famous author once said, you are what you eat. Thus, it is vital to you and your family's health that you take special care when buying your food.

BUY FOR NUTRITION

It is very important to your health that the food you eat is nutritious and that your diet is well balanced. But what constitutes "good nutrition?" And what about the impact of additives on the healthfulness of food? This is an area of great controversy and is impossible for us to explore in great depth in a book of this general scope and size. We can tell you, however, what the government recommends:

Buy a Variety of Foods

The United States Department of Agriculture recommends that you include a wide variety of foods in your diet, in order to get sufficient nutrients, such as protein, carbohydrates, vitamins and minerals. They divide food into five basic groups and recommend the following daily servings:

Breads and cereals The publication FOOD, put out by the Department of Agriculture recommends that you have four basic servings from the bread and cereal group. FOOD suggests that you select whole-grain products along with fortified (nutrition-added) products, with emphasis on the whole grain.

Fruits and vegetables Fruit is a good source of vitamins and fiber as well as minerals, depending on the type you eat. Eat four basic servings per day, according to FOOD, and make sure that at least one fruit is a good source of Vitamin C (oranges, tomatoes, etc.)

> **CONSUMER ALERT: ACCORDING TO THE CENTER FOR SCIENCE IN THE PUBLIC INTEREST, THE FOLLOWING FRUITS AND VEGETABLES ARE PARTICULARLY NUTRITIOUS: CANTALOUPE AND WATERMELON (FOR VITAMINS A AND C); ORANGES AND GRAPEFRUIT (FOR FIBER AND VITAMIN C); SWEET POTATO (BETA-CAROTENE, VITAMIN C AND FIBER); WHITE POTATO (EAT IT WITH THE SKIN FOR FIBER); CARROTS (BETA-CAROTENE); BROCCOLI (VITAMIN C, BETA-CAROTENE AND FOLIC ACID); AND DARK, LEAFY GREENS LIKE COLLARDS, SPINACH AND KALE (VITAMIN C, BETA-CAROTENE, CALCIUM, IRON AND FOLIC ACID).**

Milk and cheese Milk and cheese can supply protein and minerals such as calcium. However, they can be a source of cholesterol and fat. FOOD recommends 2 servings per day for adults, 3 for pregnant women and 4 for nursing mothers. Children under nine should have 2-3 servings, with children 9-12 going up to 3 and teenagers 4.

> **NOTE: THERE IS A LOT OF CONTROVERSY CONCERNING THE CONSUMPTION OF DAIRY PRODUCTS, ESPECIALLY FOR ADULTS, DUE TO THEIR HIGH CHOLESTEROL LEVELS. FOR THE RIGHT AMOUNT FOR YOU TO EAT, CONSULT YOUR DOCTOR OR CERTIFIED NUTRITIONIST.**

Meat and poultry and beans Meat, eggs, poultry, fish and beans make up the fourth category. These foods are valued because of their proteins and mineral content. FOOD recommends two basic servings daily.

Fats and sweets These foods, which include butter, margarine, alcohol, candy, oils, etc. are not recommended for nutritional value. They tend to add many calories to a meal (for example, fats and oils have twice the calories per ounce as proteins, starches or sugars) although some do supply essential fatty acids. FOOD recommends that you concentrate first on the more nutritious foods listed earlier as the basis of your daily diet. No servings are recommended for nutritional needs.

> **CONSUMER ALERT: THE GOVERNMENT PUBLISHES MANY HELPFUL PAMPHLETS AND MAGAZINES TO ASSIST YOU IN PLANNING AND PREPARING A HEALTHY, WELL-BALANCED DIET. FOR EXAMPLE, THERE IS THE MAGAZINE "PREPARING FOODS AND PLANNING MENUS," WHICH PROVIDES A VIRTUAL CORNUCOPIA OF HELPFUL INFORMATION ON HEALTHY EATING. FOR THOSE WHO ARE IN A HURRY AND BELIEVE THAT**

THEY DON'T HAVE TIME FOR HEALTHY FOOD PLANNING, THE DEPARTMENT OFFERS "SHOPPING FOR FOOD AND MAKING MEALS IN MINUTES." THEN THERE ARE THE HELPFUL PUBLICATIONS PUT OUT BY MEDICAL ASSOCIATIONS AND CONSUMER ORGANIZATIONS, NOT TO MENTION BOOKS IN THE LIBRARY OR IN YOUR LOCAL BOOK STORE. IN SHORT, TAKE THE TIME TO LEARN TO EAT CORRECTLY. IT CAN ADD YEARS AND HEALTH TO YOUR LIFE.

Read the Labels

Due to the hard work of consumer activists and pro-consumer government officials, many foods that are sold must be labeled as to their nutritional value. Nutrition labeling is not required of all food products. Only those foods which add nutrients or which claim to have a nutritional value must do so.

Nutritional labeling shows the following information:

•The serving size:

•The number of servings per container:

•The amount of calories, protein, carbohydrate, fat and sodium *per serving* (not per container):

•The RDA percentages (see below) of protein, five vitamins (A, C, thiamin, riboflavin, niacin) and two minerals (calcium and iron), provided in a serving:

•The amount of sodium (salt) in the product per serving. If the product does not specify the amount, the following language may be used:

•*Sodium free* - less than five milligrams per serving.

•*Very low sodium* - 35 milligrams or less per serving.

•*Low sodium* - 140 milligrams or less per serving.

•*Reduced sodium* - At least 75 percent reduced from usual levels.

•*Unsalted, without added salt, or no salt added* - no salt added to a food normally processed with salt.

•Fat and cholesterol labeling on foods is optional. If a food label contains claims concerning fat or cholesterol, the Food and Drug Administration allows the following terms to be used:

•*Cholesterol free* - 2 milligrams or less per serving.

•*Low- cholesterol* - 20 milligrams or less per serving.

•*Reduced-cholesterol* - 75 percent or greater reduction from the original food.

Label claims for fat are permitted by the U.S. Department of Agriculture. If label claims are made, the following definitions apply:

•*Extra lean* - no more than 5 percent fat by weight.

•*Lean, lowfat* - no more than 10 percent fat by weight.

•*Light (lite), leaner, lower fat* - 25 percent or greater reduction from the comparable product.

Products making these claims must declare the total grams of fat on the label. Terms used for ground beef differ.

•Carbohydrates. The total carbohydrate level must be listed but it need not be broken down into starch, sugar or fiber.

CONSUMER ALERT: IT IS IMPORTANT TO NOTE *THAT ALL MANUFACTURERS DO NOT LABEL THEIR PRODUCTS IDENTICALLY PER SERVING.* THIS CAN BE VERY IMPORTANT WHEN COMPARING NUTRITIONAL FOOD GUIDES. FOR EXAMPLE, ASSUME YOU READ A FOOD LABEL THAT CLAIMED TO HAVE 5 GRAMS OF FAT AND ANOTHER THAT CLAIMED TO HAVE 6 GRAMS OF FAT. YOU WOULD THINK THAT THE FIRST FOOD PRODUCT HAD LOWER FAT CONTENT, RIGHT? IF THE SERVING SIZES PER CONTAINER WERE THE SAME, YOU WOULD BE RIGHT. BUT, IF THE SERVING SIZES PER CONTAINER WERE DIFFERENT, YOU MIGHT NOT BE CORRECT. SO, IF THE SECOND PRODUCT LABEL CONSIDERED A SERVING TO BE 7 OUNCES VERSES 4 OUNCES FOR THE FIRST LABEL, THE SECOND WOULD ACTUALLY HAVE LESS FAT CONTENT IN THE FOOD. THUS, WHEN COMPARING FOOD LABELS, BE SURE TO TAKE A CLOSE LOOK AT THE SERVING SIZES SO THAT YOU CAN BE SURE YOU ARE COMPARING "APPLES WITH APPLES" INSTEAD OF "APPLES WITH ORANGES."

Here is a typical label taken off of a jar of spaghetti sauce setting forth nutritional information, including RDAs:

NUTRITIONAL INFORMATION PER SERVING

Serving Size	4 Oz.
Servings per container	3
Calories	130
Protein (grams)	2
Carbohydrate (grams)	20
Fat (grams)	5
Sodium	630 mg/serving

PERCENTAGE OF U.S. RECOMMENDED DAILY ALLOWANCES

Protein	2	Riboflavin	4
Vitamin A	20	Niacin	6
Vitamin C	25	Calcium	4
Thiamine	2	Iron	4

INGREDIENTS

Tomatoes (tomato paste, water) diced tomatoes, corn syrup, corn or cottonseed oil, mushrooms, salt, concentrated lemon juice, spices (oregano, basil and other spices), dehydrated garlic, dehydrated parsley and natural flavoring.

CONSUMER ALERT: INGREDIENT LABELS ARE REQUIRED BY LAW ON ALL PROCESSED FOODS. YOU SHOULD LEARN HOW TO READ THE LABEL. THE PRODUCTS ARE NOT LISTED ALPHABETICALLY OR BY CHANCE, THEY ARE *LISTED BY THE WEIGHT* OF EACH INGREDIENT OF THE PRODUCT - FROM THE

**MOST TO THE LEAST. THUS, IN THE LABEL ABOVE, TOMA-
TOES MAKE UP THE LARGEST SINGLE INGREDIENT, AND DE-
HYDRATED PARSLEY AND NATURAL FLAVORING, THE LEAST.**

Look for Food Dating

The purpose of dating on food labels is to help you choose the freshest products when you shop. Label dating is especially important when shopping for perishables, such as meat and milk. There are four different types of labeling for dates:

Sell by A sell by or pull by dating is used of foods such as milk. The date set forth on the product is the last day the product should be sold. Thus, a carton of milk with a date of Dec. 8 is not as fresh as one with a date of Dec. 10.

Best-if-used by This label is most often found on cereals and bakery goods. The date on the label indicates the last day that the product can be expected to be at its peak quality.

Expiration date The expiration date on a product (sometimes called a "use-by" date) is the last date the food should be used.

Pack date Foods with long shelf lives, such as canned goods, often contain pack dates which tell you the date they were packed.

It is important to pay attention to dating because the information helps you select the food which is the freshest and thus, most likely to have the best nutritional value and least likelihood of early spoilage.

Pay Attention to Government Food Ratings

The purpose of USDA Food Ratings is to help you judge the quality of the food you are buying when you cannot really tell by observation. For example, two steaks may look the same and weigh the same but not be of the same quality. Unfortunately, food grade labeling is not required by federal law. Those packers who allow their foods to be graded do so voluntarily.

The foods most often graded and labeled by the processor are beef, veal, lamb, turkeys, eggs and butter. By comparing the labels and the grades of food, you can get the best values for your money. The most famous grades can be found on beef. USDA PRIME beef is the most expensive. Most cuts graded prime will be very tender, juicy and flavorful because there will be abundant marbling - flecks of fat in the lean. USDA CHOICE have less marbling but are still considered tender and juicy. USDA GOOD beef is not considered as good-tasting as the others because it has less fat. NOTE: THESE AND THE OTHER USDA RATINGS HAVE *NOTHING TO DO WITH NUTRITIONAL VALUES*, BUT WITH ISSUES SUCH AS "QUALITY," ATTRACTIVENESS" AND SOMETIMES CLEANLI-NESS OF PROCESSING. (For more information on USDA ratings, contact the United States Department of Agriculture.)

Avoid Unhealthful Food Habits

Eating too much of the wrong foods can be unhealthful. The Department of Agriculture recommends that you consider the following:

Don't consume too many calories If you eat more calories than you burn you will gain weight. If you gain too much weight, you may be subject to maladies such as heart disease, high blood pressure and other difficulties. It can be surprising how many calories there are in many of your favorite foods. For example, a one quarter pound hamburger patty starts with about 365 calories and that's without the bun, mayonnaise, ketchup, onions and sesame seeds. Your doctor or nutritionist should be able to help you plan a diet with the right number of calories for your body weight and size.

> **CONSUMER ALERT: THERE ARE A PLETHORA OF DIETS BEING SOLD WHICH ARE MARKETED TO ASSIST YOU TO LOSE WEIGHT. IF YOU GO ON A DIET, BE CAREFUL! MANY OF THE MOST POPULAR HAVE BEEN FOUND TO BE UNHEALTHFUL. ALSO, DO NOT DIET EXCEPT UNDER THE SUPERVISION OF YOUR DOCTOR. THE AGRICULTURE DEPARTMENT GIVES THE FOLLOWING SUGGESTIONS FOR CALORIE COUNTERS:**
> **•CUT DOWN ON HIGH-FAT FOODS SUCH AS BUTTER AND FATTY MEATS AND FRIED FOODS.**
> **•CUT DOWN ON SUGARY FOODS SUCH AS CANDY AND PIE.**
> **•CUT DOWN OR ELIMINATE ALCOHOLIC BEVERAGES.**
> **•REDUCE PORTIONS OF FOOD WHILE KEEPING A GOOD BALANCED DIET.**
> **•USE WHOLE MILK PRODUCTS (CHEESES, ICE CREAM) SPARINGLY.**
> **•SELECT COOKING METHODS THAT HELP CUT CALORIES. FOR EXAMPLE, DON'T FRY, TRIM OFF FATS ON MEATS AND REMOVE SKIN FROM POULTRY.**
> **•BE SURE TO WATCH SNACKING. EVERY CALORIE COUNTS.**

Keep your fat intake down People who eat too much fat are likely to risk becoming overweight and may develop blood levels with high amounts of cholesterol. Fats come in solid and liquid form (oils) and are found in high levels in many diets.

If you want to reduce the fat in your diet, there are many ways to do it. For example, you can cut down on meat, especially fatty meats. You can also eat more fish, pastas and beans. If you are a peanut butter addict, then you should try to cut down to one jar a month or cut it out of your diet altogether. And of course, that "great" American contribution to world cuisine, fast food meals of greasy cheeseburgers and chili fries, should go too. (As with all changes in your diet, consult your physician to make sure you continue to receive sufficient nutrients to suit your individual health history.)

> **CONSUMER ALERT: MANY DON'T REALIZE THAT COOKING AND SALAD OILS ARE A "HIDDEN" SOURCE OF FAT AND CHOLESTEROL. FOR EXAMPLE, COCONUT OIL, PRESENT IN MANY BREAKFAST CEREALS AND DESERTS, IS ALMOST 100% SATURATED AND MONOSATURATED FAT. PALM OIL IS NEARLY AS BAD AS ARE MANY DAIRY FATS, SUCH AS CREAM AND BUTTER. ON THE OTHER HAND, SAFFLOWER OIL IS MOSTLY MADE UP OF POLYUNSATURATED FATS, WHICH IS HEALTHIER. SO IS SUNFLOWER OIL. CORN OIL AND SOYBEAN OIL ARE ALSO HIGH IN POLYUNSATURATED FAT. (ALL HAVE THE SAME CALORIC COUNT - NINE CALORIES PER GRAM.)**

Don't take in too much sodium Salt is found naturally in most foods. However, many of the foods we eat are not in their natural state but are processed or canned. Salt is used in many of these processes, and often adds unwanted and unneeded sodium to our diet. Then, there is the habit that too many of us have of dousing food with table salt, which is definitely not among the nominees for the most healthful daily activity award. If you want to cut down on salt, the Department of Agriculture suggests:

•Avoid foods prepared in brine such as pickles and olives.

•Remove smoked or salted meats such as luncheon meats, frankfurters and sausage. The same holds true for salted fish such as sardines or smoked salmon.

•Avoid snacks such as potato chips and snack nuts which are salted.

•Reduce your use of sauces which contain high amounts of sodium, such as many barbecue sauces and soy sauce.

• Read labels on the food you eat. Many foods which don't taste salty have a lot of sodium. For example, the additive monosodium glutamate doesn't have the word "sodium" in it for nothing.

Control your sweet tooth Sugar is an energy food with low nutrient value. In other words, sugar is high in calories and low in vitamins, minerals and other nutritious qualities. Thus, you do yourself and your body a favor by keeping the amount of sugar you eat at a moderate level.

Sugar is often not labeled as such. The following products and ingredients are made up primarily of sugar:

sucrose - glucose - dextrose - fructose - maltose - lactose - sorbitol - mannitol - honey - corn syrup - corn syrup solids - molasses - maple syrup.

Many foods contain sugar. Soft drinks, candy, canned fruits, presweetened cereals and many fruit juices, to just name a few. Thus ALWAYS REMEMBER TO READ THE LABEL. If a food label states that the product is made up of flour, sugar, starch, glucose and maple syrup, you will know that what you are buying is basically, a lump of sugar with some starch thrown in for texture.

Add fiber to your diet Fiber not only helps digestion but most fiber-containing foods are nutritious in their own right, often providing protein and/or complex carbohydrates along with the fibrous materials. Thus, instead of chowing down on those smoke flavored, deep-fried potato chips, with salt added for extra flavor, try to have some carrot sticks instead. Bulghur and whole-grain bread are good sources of fiber, and both are rich in vitamins and minerals as well. They may not excite your tastebuds as much -- at first -- but you'll learn to recognize the satisfaction of eating healthily. And who knows, you just may add to the quality and quantity of your life.

CONSUMER ALERT: CONSUMER ADVOCATES HAVE FOUGHT LONG AND HARD TO MAKE PROPER FOOD LABELING THE LAW OF THE LAND. THERE IS STILL MORE WORK TO DO. BUT IF YOU READ THE LABELS OF THE FOODS YOU BUY, YOU CAN AVOID THOSE CANNED AND PACKAGED PRODUCTS WITH TOO MUCH FAT, SUGAR, CHOLESTEROL AND SODIUM, AND IN-STEAD, PURCHASE THOSE THAT CONTAIN MORE HEALTHY FOOD AND LESS UNHEALTHY ADDITIVES.

CONSUMER ALERT: THE CENTER FOR SCIENCE IN THE PUBLIC INTEREST (CSPI) PUBLISHES A LIST OF FOODS TO AVOID. THESE PREPARED FOODS ARE ESPECIALLY HIGH IN FAT, CHOLESTEROL OR SODIUM. WATCH OUT FOR:

- HAAGEN DAZS ICE CREAM -- CONTAINS THE MOST FAT OF ANY ICE CREAM
- PROGRESSO ALFREDO SAUCE -- HIGH IN FAT
- HORMEL CHILI (NO BEANS) -- HIGH IN FAT
- STOUFFER'S PASTA CARBONARA -- HIGH IN FAT
- LOUIS RICH LUNCH BREAKS -- HIGH IN SODIUM AND AS MUCH FAT AS A 9 OUNCE STEAK
- DUNKIN' DONUTS CHOCOLATE CROISSANT -- HIGH IN SATURATED FAT
- PEPPERIDGE FARM CHOCOLATE MOUSSE -- HIGH IN FAT
- DAIRY QUEEN'S LARGE CHOCOLATE MALT -- CONTAINS A HUGE AMOUNT OF SUGAR AND IS HIGH IN FAT
- BANQUET'S EXTRA HELPING BEEF DINNER -- CONTAINS THE ENTIRE U.S. RDA OF FAT
- JACK IN THE BOX ULTIMATE CHEESE BURGER -- HIGH IN CHOLESTEROL AND FAT
- TACO BELL'S TACO SALAD WITH SHELL -- THE MOST FATTY ITEM ON THE MENU
- MRS. SMITH'S OLD FASHIONED APPLE PIE -- THE MOST FATTY APPLE PIE
- SWANSON GREAT STARTS BIG START BREAKFAST -- HIGH IN FAT AND CHOLESTEROL
- BURGER KING'S SCRAMBLED EGG PLATTER WITH SAUSAGE -- HIGH IN FAT AND SODIUM

FOR MORE INFORMATION, WRITE TO: CSPI, 1875 CONNECTICUT AVENUE, NW, SUITE 300, WASHINGTON D.C. 20009-5728. THE PHONE NUMBER IS (202) 332-9110.

CONSUMER ALERT: GUIDELINES FOR BUYING, COOKING AND EATING FISH

- THINK TWICE BEFORE YOU EAT RAW FISH. RAW FISH CAN HARBOR PARASITES OR HIGH LEVELS OF BACTERIA.
- COOK FISH THOROUGHLY. PROPERLY COOKED FISH SHOULD BE OPAQUE AND FLAKE EASILY.
- PREGNANT WOMEN OR WOMEN WHO EXPECT TO BECOME PREGNANT SHOULD AVOID EATING SALMON, SWORDFISH AND LAKE WHITEFISH. THESE FISH MAY CONTAIN POLYCHLORINATED BIPHENLYS (PCBS), WHICH CAN ACCUMULATE IN THE BODY AND POSE A RISK TO THE DEVELOPING FETUS. SWORDFISH AND TUNA ARE ALSO MAJOR DIETARY SOURCES OF MERCURY, WHICH MAY HARM A FETUS. YOUNG CHILDREN, TOO, SHOULD AVOID THOSE FISH.
- MOST HEALTHY ADULTS CAN EAT FISH WITH LESS WORRY, AS LONG AS THE CHOICES ARE VARIED. DON'T EAT SALMON, SWORDFISH OR LAKE WHITEFISH MORE THAN ONCE A WEEK.

•WHEN BUYING WHOLE FISH, LOOK FOR BRIGHT, CLEAR, BULGING EYES. CLOUDY, SUNKEN, DISCOLORED, OR SLIME-COVERED EYES OFTEN SIGNAL FISH THAT IS BEGINNING TO SPOIL. THE SKIN OF A FRESHLY CAUGHT FISH IS COVERED WITH A TRANSLUCENT MUCUS THAT LOOKS A BIT LIKE VARNISH. THE COLOR IS VIVID AND BRIGHT. AVOID FISH WHOSE SKIN HAS BEGUN TO DISCOLOR, SHOWS DEPRESSIONS, TEARS OR BLEMISHES, OR IS COVERED WITH STICKY YELLOWISH-BROWN MUCUS.

•WHEN BUYING STEAKS OR FILLETS, LOOK FOR MOIST FLESH THAT STILL HAS A TRANSLUCENT SHEEN. WATCH OUT FOR FLESH THAT'S DRIED OUT OR GAPING (THE MUSCLE FIBERS ARE BEGINNING TO PULL APART). THAT'S A SIGN OF OVER-THE-HILL FISH.

•NOTE HOW THE FISH IS DISPLAYED AND LOOK FOR CLUES THAT THE TEMPERATURE MAY BE TOO HIGH. FISH THAT ARE PILED HIGH, DISPLAYED IN OPEN CASES, OR SITTING UNDER HOT LIGHTS ARE PERFECT PLACES FOR BACTERIA TO GROW. WHOLE FISH SHOULD BE DISPLAYED UNDER ICE.

•CAREFULLY EVALUATE STORE SPECIALS AND PRICE REDUCTIONS. SPECIALS MAY BE A WAY TO MOVE OLDER FISH. MOST RETAILERS WOULD RATHER REDUCE THE PRICE THAN THROW AWAY FISH. A "SATURDAY-GET-RID-OF-IT SPECIAL" WILL BE CHEAP BUT MAY NOT MAKE THE TASTIEST MEAL.

•LOOK FOR EVIDENCE THAT FISH HAS BEEN FROZEN AND THEN THAWED. NOTE WHICH FISH HAVE "FRESH" DISPLAY SIGNS ON THEM. LOOK FOR CHUNKS OF ICE FLOATING IN THE FISH LIQUID — A CLUE THAT THE FISH HAD BEEN FROZEN. IF YOU'RE NOT SURE, ASK. ALTHOUGH MANY SHELF TAGS ARE NOT HONEST, SOME CLERKS ARE. THERE'S NOTHING WRONG WITH FROZEN FISH, BUT IF YOU UNKNOWINGLY BUY FISH THAT HAD ONCE BEEN FROZEN AND THEN YOU REFREEZE IT, ITS TEXTURE AND FLAVOR WILL SUFFER. IT'S PROBABLY BETTER TO BUY FROZEN FISH INSTEAD.

•KEEP AN EYE OUT FOR DISPLAYS OF COOKED SEAFOOD SOLD NEXT TO RAW FISH. THEY'RE A POTENTIAL HEALTH HAZARD, AND BUYING ANYTHING FROM THEM CAN BE RISKY.

•USE YOUR NOSE. FRESH FISH SMELL LIKE THE SEA, BUT THEY HAVE NO STRONG ODOR. FRESH-WATER FISH IN GOOD CONDITION SOMETIMES SMELL LIKE CUCUMBERS. STRONG ODORS USUALLY INDICATE SPOILAGE.

•ONCE YOU BUY A FISH, REFRIGERATE IT QUICKLY. AT HOME, STORE IT IN THE COLDEST PART OF YOUR REFRIGERATOR, KEEP IT IN THE ORIGINAL WRAPPER, AND USE IT FAST — WITHIN A DAY.

SOURCE: CONSUMER REPORTS

BUY FOR CLEANLINESS

When we talk about cleanliness, we are talking about nothing less than FOOD SAFETY. Each year, headlines tell a frightening and sometimes deadly tale of consumers who fall ill or even die due to salmonella poisoning from contaminated milk, botulism from dried salted whitefish or some the malady from tainted ice cream. It is shocking but true: 10,000 people die from food poisoning in the United States each year.

To put it bluntly, the food that all of us eat is not safe enough. In addition to food poisoning, contaminants from pesticides, additives, antibiotics and other chemicals are used in the growing, beautifying, storing and preparation of foodstuffs. Moreover, millions of tons of pollutants are pouring into lakes, bays and estuaries. Some of the residues of such poisons reach our tables via fish and shell fish. The struggle against filth and unsanitary conditions in meat and poultry processing plants, warehouses and retail stores needs to intensify as federal inspection programs have been weakened in the eighties and continue to be weakened in the nineties. In addition, the United States is importing more foods than ever before, much of it from countries whose inspection standards are weaker than our own inadequate safeguards.

But there are ways out for the smart food consumer. With some helpful information and the willingness to walk the extra mile to provide safe food for you and your family, you can take significant steps to protect your body from the potentially deadly effects of unhealthful or contaminated foods.

Learn Proper Storage Techniques

Even the most wholesome and healthful food can become spoiled quickly if it is not properly stored. Most food poisoning bacteria thrive in room temperatures (60 to 90 degrees Fahrenheit). But, even foods stored in a refrigerator at about 40 degrees can go bad.

When some foods spoil, you know it from the odor. Unfortunately, many times when food is bad, like poisoned well water, you may not be able to taste or smell it. Thus, it is vital to you and your family's health that you know how to safely store your food.

Cooking This may seem obvious, but cooking is one excellent way to prevent food poisoning, since high temperatures kill bacteria. However, once the food cools, bacteria can begin to grow. Thus, do not leave cooked food out at room temperature for more than 2 hours. Also, follow these tips presented by the Department of Agriculture regarding cooking:

•*Cook thoroughly*. Make sure the food you cook is cooked thoroughly and sufficiently to kill bacteria. Meat should be cooked all the way through.

•*Don't interrupt the cooking*. Cook meat and poultry completely at one time. If you don't cook the food all at one time, bacteria may begin to grow before the cooking is completed.

•*Allow frozen food enough time to cook*. Check the label or your cook book for details. Generally frozen foods need one and one half as long as unfrozen food to cook thoroughly.

•*Thoroughly reheat leftovers*. Leftovers need to be reheated thoroughly to kill bacteria that may have grown from the original preparation of the food. The Department of Agriculture suggests that you cover the leftovers when you reheat in order to ensure thorough heating and to retain moisture and flavor.

Refrigerating/freezing The colder food is kept, the safer food keeps. Thus, freezing will allow for longer safe storage than refrigeration and refrigeration longer than room temperature. The Department of Agriculture has published the following tips on keeping food cold:

•*Shopping* When you shop, remember that bacteria does not wait until you get home to begin to grow. You should pick up your perishables last and get them home quickly and into the refrigerator or freezer. That means if you are running a series of errands, do your food shopping after the run to the dry cleaners, video store and hair grooming salon.

•*Refrigerating* Once you get home, put your food right in the refrigerator. The Department of Agriculture suggests that you keep the food in the original wrapping unless it has been torn, since repeated food handling can introduce bacteria to meat and poultry.

•*Freezing* Be sure to wrap your food in freezer wrap to avoid freezer burn. (Freezer burn won't make you sick but it can make food lose its taste.) You should place new items in the back of the freezer so that older food is used first. A helpful tip for making sure you use old food before new food is to date the food you freeze on the freezer wrapper.

CONSUMER ALERT: THE DEPARTMENT OF AGRICULTURE HAS PUBLISHED THIS HANDY CHART FOR DETERMINING HOW LONG YOU CAN SAFELY STORE REFRIGERATED AND FROZEN FOOD:

PRODUCT	REFRIGERATOR (DAYS @ 40 F)	FREEZER (MONTHS @ 0 F)
FRESH MEATS		
BEEF ROASTS	3 TO 5	6 TO 12
LAMB ROASTS	3 TO 5	6 TO 9
PORK, VEAL ROASTS	3 TO 5	4 TO 8
BEEF STEAKS	3 TO 5	6 TO 12
LAMB CHOPS	3 TO 5	6 TO 9
PORK CHOPS	3 TO 5	3 TO 4
HAMBURGER	1 TO 2	3 TO 4
VARIETY MEATS (ORGANS)	1 TO 2	3 TO 4
PORK SAUSAGE	1 TO 2	1 TO 2
COOKED MEATS		
COOKED MEAT AND MEAT DISHES	3 TO 4	2 TO 3
GRAVY AND MEAT BROTH	1 TO 2	2 TO 3
PROCESSED MEATS		
(FROZEN CURED MEATS LOSE QUALITY RAPIDLY AND SHOULD BE USED AS SOON AS POSSIBLE AFTER THAWING)		
BACON	7	1
FRANKFURTERS	7*	1 TO 2
WHOLE HAM	7	1 TO 2
HALF HAM	3 TO 5	1 TO 2
HAM SLICES	3 TO 4	1 TO 2
LUNCHEON MEATS	3 TO 5*	1 TO 2
SMOKED SAUSAGE	7	1 TO 2
DRY SAUSAGE	14 TO 21	1 TO 2

FRESH POULTRY

WHOLE CHICKEN OR TURKEY	1 TO 2	12
CHICKEN PIECES	1 TO 2	9
TURKEY PIECES	1 TO 2	6
DUCK AND GOOSE (WHOLE)	1 TO 2	6
GIBLETS	1 TO 2	3 TO 4

COOKED POULTRY

COVERED WITH BROTH OR GRAVY	1 TO 2	6
PIECES NOT IN BROTH OR GRAVY	3 TO 4	1
COOKED POULTRY DISHES	3 TO 4	4 TO 6
FRIED CHICKEN	3 TO 4	4

GAME

DEER	3 TO 5	6 TO 12
RABBIT	1 TO 2	12
DUCK OR GOOSE	1 TO 2	6

*ONCE A VACUUM-SEALED PACK IS OPENED. UNOPENED VACUUM-SEALED PACKAGES CAN BE STORED IN THE REFRIGERATOR FOR 2 WEEKS.

Thawing The Agriculture Department recommends that the safest way to thaw meat and poultry is to take it out of the freezer and leave it to thaw overnight in the refrigerator. For faster thawing, put the food in a watertight plastic bag under cold water. Change the water often. The reason for this is that the cold water temperature will slow the growth of bacteria. Microwave oven thawing is safe if you follow the manufacturer's instructions. DO NOT THAW MEAT AND POULTRY ON THE KITCHEN COUNTER. Bacteria love room temperatures and will thank you for the favor by multiplying rapidly.

Keep food safe Keeping food safe is not difficult but must be attended to carefully.

•Be careful while you are shopping. Be sure that you take notice of the date labeling and use the food by the time set forth. (See above) Also, it is a good idea not to push the dates to the last possible day but try to use the food as early as you can.

•Be sure to keep food clean. That includes washing the food when appropriate (for example, wash all fruits and vegetables) and making sure that everything (your hands included) that touches the food is washed thoroughly. Also, be sure to wash counter tops and cutting boards with soap and water between each food preparation usage.

•If your refrigerator or freezer fails, *keep the doors closed*. Ordinarily, a fully stocked freezer will keep food frozen for 2 days after losing power. A half-full freezer can keep food frozen for 1 day.

If your freezer is going to be out longer than that, look for alternative freezers, such as your friends'. Many stores or churches may be willing to help or you can rent space in a commercial freezer or cold storage plant. Another trick is to put dry ice in the freezer. *Dry ice is frozen carbon dioxide and requires careful handling. Be sure you understand the dangers and the proper procedures of using dry ice before attempting to place it in your freezer!*

Know the foods that require special care Harmful organisms grow more readily in foods high in protein and moisture. Thus, meats, poultry, cream pies, eggs, mild products, gravies and cooked pasta all require special attention to proper storage and attention to handling.

CONSUMER ALERT: IT IS VERY IMPORTANT THAT YOU KNOW THE SYMPTOMS OF FOOD POISONING. HERE ARE THE SYMPTOMS OF THE MOST COMMON FOOD POISONINGS AND HOW TO PREVENT THEM.

STAPH: 2-8 HOURS AFTER EATING, YOU COULD HAVE VOMITING AND DIARRHEA LASTING A DAY OR TWO. COOKING WON'T DESTROY STAPH POISONING. SO, BE SURE TO WASH YOUR HANDS AND UTENSILS BEFORE PREPARING FOODS. DON'T LEAVE FOOD OUT FOR MORE THAN 2 HOURS. THE MOST SUSCEPTIBLE FOODS ARE MEAT, POULTRY, SALADS, CHEESE, EGG PRODUCTS, STARCHY SALADS (POTATO, PASTA, TUNA, ETC.), CUSTARDS AND OTHER CREAM-FILLED DESERTS.

SALMONELLA: 12-36 HOURS AFTER EATING, YOU COULD EXPERIENCE DIARRHEA, FEVER AND VOMITING LASTING 2-7 DAYS. SALMONELLA CAN BE PREVENTED BY KEEPING RAW FOOD AWAY FROM COOKED FOOD AND THOROUGHLY COOKING FOOD BEFORE EATING. ALSO, DON'T DRINK UNPASTEURIZED MILK. ALSO, KEEP FLIES OFF OF FOOD. BE SURE THAT FROZEN POULTRY IS COMPLETELY THAWED BEFORE COOKING.

CAMPYLOBACTER JEJUNI: IN 2-5 DAYS, YOU COULD SUFFER SEVERE DIARRHEA, CRAMPING, FEVER AND HEADACHE, LASTING 2-7 DAYS. YOU CAN AVOID THIS POISONING BY NOT DRINKING UNTREATED WATER OR UNPASTEURIZED MILK. ALSO, THOROUGHLY COOK MEAT AND MAKE SURE FOOD AND ALL THAT COMES IN CONTACT WITH IT IS CLEAN.

BOTULISM: WITHIN 12-48 HOURS, YOUR NERVOUS SYSTEM COULD BE AFFECTED. THE SYMPTOMS ARE DOUBLE VISION, DROOPY EYELIDS AND DIFFICULTY SPEAKING AND SWALLOWING. YOU MAY ALSO HAVE TROUBLE BREATHING. *BOTULISM CAN BE FATAL* IF IT IS NOT TREATED. BOTULISM IS CAUSED BY EATING FOOD THAT HAS BEEN IMPROPERLY PRESERVED OR CANNED. BOTULISM IS MOST OFTEN FOUND FROM IMPROPER HOME CANNING BUT IS RARELY FOUND IN COMMERCIALLY CANNED FOODS. IF A CAN IS BULGING OR THE FOOD FROM A CAN SMELLS BAD, DO NOT EAT IT!

IF YOU BELIEVE YOU HAVE BEEN THE VICTIM OF FOOD POISONING, YOU SHOULD REPORT THE MATTER TO YOUR LOCAL HEALTH AUTHORITIES, ESPECIALLY IF YOU ATE THE SUSPECT FOOD AT A LARGE GATHERING OR AT A RESTAURANT OR THE FOOD IS A COMMERCIAL PRODUCT.

If you are interested in learning more about how to "eat clean," we recommend that you obtain the book, *Eating Clean; Overcoming Food Hazards*, published by the Center for Responsive Law, P.O. Box 19367, Washington D.C. 20036. The book sells for $8.00 and is a collection of articles, reports and instructions on how to eat cleaner and healthier.

CONSUMER ALERT: THERE IS AN EXCELLENT BOOK ON THE MARKET THAT CAN HELP YOU PROTECT YOURSELF AND YOUR FAMILY AGAINST PESTICIDES, BACTERIA AND OTHER HIDDEN HAZARDS IN OUR FOOD. IT IS, *SAFE FOOD: EATING WISELY IN A RISKY WORLD*, BY MICHAEL F. JACOBSON, LISA Y. LEFFERTS AND ANNE WITTE GARLAND (1991, LIVING PLANET PRESS, LOS ANGELES, CALIFORNIA).

BUY FOR ECOLOGY

The way we buy our food and dispose of the products and packages that food is sold in can have a very big impact on the environment. The National Consumers League, a non-profit organization, has made the following suggestions:

Buy Recyclable

By recycling, you can help save the environment and create jobs in the recycling industry. Get your local store involved in recycling. Inform your local grocery manager that you want his or her store's assistance in recycling, by having bins available for plastic, aluminium cans and newspapers on or near the premises.

CONSUMER ALERT: KNOW THE RECYCLABILITY OF THE FOLLOWING PRODUCTS:
GLASS: GLASS IS COMPLETELY RECYCLABLE. ALUMINUM: ALUMINUM CAN BE ENDLESSLY RECYCLED. PAPER: AS PAPER RECYCLES, IT SLOWLY LOSES ITS QUALITY. HOWEVER, EVEN THOUGH PAPER WILL EVENTUALLY HAVE TO BE DISPOSED OF, RECYCLING ONE TON OF PAPER SAVES 17 TREES. (SOURCE: NATIONAL CONSUMERS LEAGUE)

For your family's health, you should also try to purchase food without chemicals, hormones or other such products added. Not only will you be aiding your body but you will be helping the environment as well. (NOTE: There is no federal law at this time defining the term "organic." In order to avoid rip offs, be sure that the "organic" food you buy is food grown without chemicals, pesticides or unnatural additives of any kind.) Markets are increasingly selling organic foods. As consumers learn the health values of organic food, the price will decrease. Someday, we hope and trust, organic foods will predominate in the food industry.

GIVE YOURSELF A RAISE

There are many ways for you to save money on the food you eat. Some of the suggestions may save you pennies and dimes. Others can save you dollars. But overall, if you buy "thriftily" you can save a significant amount of money on the food you eat and consume more nutritious food as well.

USE A LIST

The typical grocery store has over 10,000 separate items for sale, most skillfully packaged to induce you to "impulse buy." According to the Better Business Bureau, the impulse buyer tends to buy wasteful items that not only end up costing more money but may have less food value. In addition, shopping without preplanning may lead you to buy food you won't eat or food that will go to waste, or you may not buy something you really need, and will have to make an extra trip.

When working with a shopping list, remember the following:

Preplan Your Meals

By making a menu for the days to come, you can be sure to buy only those foods you need and avoid foods that will end up in the refrigerator growing mold.

Only Buy Food That Can Be Easily Stored

As we described earlier, proper food storage can be a vital part of protecting your family's health. Knowing proper storage can also save you money by reducing food spoilage and the waste that creates. So, only buy the kinds and amounts of food that you can safely store.

Plan Your List Around Advertised Specials

It is a very good money saving idea to take advantage of the advertised specials that you will find every week in the food section of your Sunday newspaper. Use the specials you find in your meal preparation and then, put the items on special on your list of food to buy.

CONSUMER ALERT: MANY CONSUMERS BELIEVE COUPONS SAVE MONEY. ON PARTICULAR PRODUCTS THEY DO BUT THERE IS A BIG PROBLEM. THEY MAY INDUCE YOU TO BUY FOOD THAT YOU WOULD NOT NORMALLY BUY AND WHICH YOU MAY NOT WANT TO EAT. WE BELIEVE THAT IT WOULD BE BETTER FOR MARKETS TO LOWER ALL OF THEIR PRICES RATHER THAN FORCE YOU TO NEGOTIATE THE COUPON JUNGLE IN ORDER TO SAVE MONEY. IN ANY EVENT, IF YOU WANT TO USE COUPONS, ONLY USE COUPONS FOR FOODS THAT ARE NORMALLY A PART OF YOUR DIET AND WHICH YOU KNOW YOU AND/OR YOUR FAMILY WILL WANT TO EAT.

Don't Shop on an Empty Stomach

That growling stomach can lead to your eyes being bigger than your pocketbook and unnecessary impulse buying.

USE UNIT PRICING

The purpose of unit pricing is to provide you with an easy way to compare the prices of the foods you are buying. The unit price label shows both the retail price of the food you are buying (the total price) and the unit price, i.e. the price per pound or ounce, etc. To compare which of several brands offers the best true price, compare the units. Thus, a one pound bag of sugar that retails for $1.60 and is 10¢ per ounce, is cheaper than a one half pound bag of sugar that sells for $1.20 and 15¢ an ounce. (Of course, if you only need a small amount of sugar, you might still want to buy the smaller bag at a higher unit price rather than a bigger bag which would only go to waste.)

Pay attention to the unit pricing you will find in your grocery store. Buy those foods that offer the best unit pricing, unless the food that sells for less will go to waste because it is being sold in a package that is too large for your needs.

CONSUMER AGENDA

In New York, consumer advocates are fighting to protect an extremely important cost-saving tool for grocery shoppers: item pricing. New York's item pricing law requires supermarkets to individually price mark most store items.

Item pricing protects consumers in a number of ways. Only item-pricing allows consumers to comparison shop throughout the store, total up prices in the shopping basket, catch scanner or cashier error and check prices at home. Shelf prices alone don't provide shoppers with this flexibility. Item pricing is particularly important for senior citizens who may have difficulty seeing shelf prices that are close to the floor or high off the ground.

Work to establish item pricing laws in your state. For more information, write to New York Public Interest Research Group (NYPIRG), 184 Washington Avenue, Albany, NY 12210. Or call NYPIRG at (518) 436-0876.

REDUCE THE AMOUNT OF MEAT YOU BUY

Meat is often the biggest single expenditure on a food bill. By reducing the amount of meat you eat, and replacing it with healthful alternative sources of protein and nutrients, you can save money. As a bonus, you will also be consuming less cholesterol and fat.

COOK LARGER PORTIONS THAN YOU NEED AND STORE THE REST

If you buy in quantity, you can save money because products in bulk often sell at a lower unit price than smaller size packages. If you buy in bulk, you may want to cook more than you need for one meal and then freeze or safely store the rest for later consumption.

READ THE LABELS

Be sure to pay attention to the labels on your food purchases. Not only will you help protect your family's health by paying attention to nutrition and reducing sodium and fat, etc., but by looking at the dating, you can buy food that will last the longest, thereby reducing the money wasted by food spoilage.

RETURN ITEMS THAT ARE BELOW PAR

If you buy food that is not as fresh as it should have been, is damaged or if it does not taste right, return or exchange it, just as you would any other product that is unsatisfactory. This means that you should also keep your receipts, so that you can prove you purchased the unsatisfactory food from the store to which you are seeking to return the product.

DON'T BUY FOOD BECAUSE YOU LIKE THE PACKAGING

Attractive packaging is one way that manufacturers induce you to buy their product. But remember, you pay for that fancy packaging and generic packaged foods are usually equivalent in nutrition. (Consumers pay as much for food packaging as farmers earn selling their food.) Thus, if a less fancy food package has the same food value as the fancy product for a lower price, go with saving money. After all, how likely are you to frame a pretty food package and hang it on the wall?

SAVE MONEY ON THE WAY YOU SELECT FOOD

The way you select food can often save you money. For example:

•If you want four steaks to barbecue, you may be able to save money by buying one or two large cuts of meat rather than four individual steaks (and then having the store butcher cut it or cutting it yourself). Also, if you have a freezer, buying meat in large quantities can save you a lot of money over the long haul.

•Buying fresh vegetables is usually much cheaper than buying frozen.

•Selecting your purchase from the bulk bins instead of prepackaged produce will also usually save you money. Not only will you get the size, quality and quantity you need, but you will also be better able to judge the quality before you put the food in your shopping cart. A note of caution: be sure that the facility is clean.

•Try bakery goods that are a day old. Frequently, perfectly good bakery goods are sold at a lower price when they are a day old in bakery outlets. Shopping at such bakery thrift stores is a good way to get quality food at a lower price.

PREVENT WASTE

Wasted food is money down the drain and into the garbage disposal. Thus, don't buy food you will not eat, don't buy food you cannot store and pay attention to keeping your food fresh and healthful.

GROW A VEGETABLE GARDEN

If you have the land available, a good way to save money and a good source of fun is to grow your own vegetable garden as a family project. The cost of seeds and water will be a lot less than the cost of buying the product at the store. Plus, you can be sure that harmful pesticides are not part of the menu. Besides, the food you grow yourself just seems to taste better. Bon appetit!

JOIN OR FORM A CO-OP

The cooperative movement is growing in America. A cooperative is the voluntary joining together of consumers who use the power of numbers to save money in the purchases they make.

Food co-ops exist all over the country in a diverse array of forms and structures. Residents of a single city block get together once a week to buy produce and distribute it out of someone's kitchen; neighbors in Vermont get together once a month to buy grains and other staples; in Massachusetts, the 3,000 members of the Boston Food Co-op work two hours a month to keep their store operating. Presently there are 3,800 co-ops, ranging in size from buying clubs that operate out of garages to chains with several warehouses. These co-ops save consumers real money on their bills.

If there is an existing co-op where you live, join. If not, become an activist and help form one. For information on Cooperatives, contact COOP AMERICA, 2100 M St. N.W. Suite 403, P.O. Box 18217, Washington D.C. 20036. The phone number is (202) 872-5307.

Part Four

SAVING MONEY ON UTILITIES

Utilities: Can't afford to live with them, can't live without them. Utilities: they make life in the modern age, with all of its comforts and conveniences, possible. Yet, ask people you know if they believe they are being well served by their electric, phone and other utility companies and the frequent response will be no. Utilities: they are supposed to be regulated, they are supposed to be operated for the benefit of the people they serve. Unfortunately, too often they use their immense power and political influence to act against the real interests of the average consumer. Utilities: they are commonly perceived to be invulnerable to consumer pressures. Yet, consumers can and do act to protect themselves, their neighbors and their communities from price-gouging, environmental desecration and power structure indifference.

Chapter Thirteen

SAVING MONEY ON YOUR UTILITY BILLS

There are several ways in which you can have an individual impact on your local utility companies. Some involve political action, which we will discuss. But even for those of you who do not have the time or inclination to become activists or become politically involved, there are many common sense things you can do to help the environment and put extra money in your pocket by saving money on the utilities you use.

SAVE ENERGY

Even though Americans have increased their energy conservation, there is still a long way to go. Here are some common sense tips to saving energy as published by Public Citizen:

Heating

There are several things you can do to make sure your heating system runs efficiently and that you, in turn, run it efficiently:

Keep your thermostat down. Your thermostat should not be set higher than 65 degrees F. when someone is at home. The thermostat should be set between 55 and 60 degrees when no one is home or the household is asleep. (NOTE: THIS ADVICE DOES NOT APPLY TO THOSE WHO MAY BE VULNERABLE OR AT RISK, SUCH AS SENIOR CITIZENS, WHO SHOULD KEEP THEIR THERMOSTATS AT 65 DEGREES OR HIGHER AT ALL TIMES TO AVOID THE DANGER OF HYPOTHERMIA.)

Most people don't know it, but for each degree your thermostat is turned down, there is roughly a 2 to 3 percent energy savings. Thus, by turning down your thermostat from 70 to 65, you can save up to 15 percent in energy costs, savings that will translate to a cleaner environment and more money in your pocket after you pay your heating bills each month.

Clean your furnace regularly. Furnaces burn fuels which leave carbon and other deposits as residue. These deposits, in turn, reduce your heater's efficiency and cause it to burn more fuel (unserviced furnaces can increase oil usage by up to 25 percent), which in turn, burns a hole in your pocket. Furnaces should be cleaned at least once a year.

Keep heating vents clear and unobstructed. Do not block heating or radiator vents with furniture or other obstructions as it may be a fire hazard and it forces your heating system to work less efficiently.

Close vents in rooms not in use. Heating rooms that are not in use is a major waste of energy and money. If there is a room in the house that is not frequented or is not in use, close the heating vents. After all, why heat empty space?

Don't heat the walls. Don't waste heat on walls which will absorb energy. If you have an external heater, such as a radiator, insert an easily made heat reflector (made by covering cardboard or poster board with aluminium foil), and place the reflector, shiny side out between the wall and the radiator. This will project previously wasted heat into the room and thus project a smaller heating bill into your mail box.

Keep cold air outside and warm air inside. A lot of energy and money is wasted because an undue amount of cold air gets in or warm air escapes. To avoid this money trap, apply the following efficiency tips:

•*Insulate* A tremendous amount of heat generated to keep homes warm is lost to the outside because of faulty or nonexistent wall and attic insulation. Avoid this needless loss by having insulation installed in your home. Many utilities will offer you special programs as an inducement to insulate, so be sure you call your local gas or other utility to see if such programs are offered in your community.

•*Protect windows* If you have storm windows, install them as cool weather approaches. If you do not have storm windows, install protective coverings over your windows. The least expensive plastic is sold as drop cloths for painting. (Beware of purchasing "kits" which offer plastic covers for windows at up to five times the cost of plastic drop cloths and offer little or no added protection.) Another way to reduce cold air leakage around windows is to stick thick tape around each window frame.

•*Wall outlets* Believe it or not, wall outlets can be a source of heat loss. This hole in your heat protection line of defense can be plugged with easy to install "wall gaskets", which are placed behind outlet covers to reduce cold air penetration. These gaskets are available at your local hardware store.

•*Plug your fireplace damper* Many people use fireplaces during the cold weather months. However, often fireplaces are not in use and then become a major source of cold air infiltration. To keep your house warmer and more efficiently heated, be sure to close the fireplace flue when it is not in use and then plug the damper with insulation. (BE SURE TO OPEN THE FLUE IF YOU LIGHT A FIRE.) Plugging your fireplace damper alone can save over $50 per year.

Hot Water

Many people don't know it, but hot water is one of the most expensive pieces of their utility pie. In fact, it can account for approximately 20 percent of heating costs. Thus, anything you do to reduce these costs can put significant dollars back into your pocket, dollars that would have gone out of your life like steam through a bathroom window.

Here are some tips on saving water heating dollars:

Take shorter showers. Many of us luxuriate in the joy of a long, hot shower. But remember, your shower is definitely not free. As a taxi meter charges more for each mile travelled, you pay more every minute you shower. Thus, save some money by shortening your time under the spray. (This will also save water, which you also pay for. Plus, in drought afflicted states, you are helping the environment.)

Reduce the temperature of your hot water heater. When you lower the temperature of your hot water heater, your heater does not have to work as hard to heat the water, which means it uses less energy, which means your utility bills are reduced. It is suggested that you lower the temperature to between 110 and 120 degrees F. (140 if you have a dishwasher.)

Wrap your water heater with insulation. Just like your home loses heat to the outside, so does your water heater. This heat and money loss can be significantly reduced if you will wrap your water heater with insulation materials. (You can also save money by wrapping your hot water pipes.) There are kits available at local hardware stores which make it easy.

Wash with cold water. Your washing machine may be using up to one half of your hot water! That's a lot of heat that may not be necessary. If you don't object to cold water washing, you can save up to $100 a year by switching your washer to the cool or cold selection and using a cold water detergent (bio-degradable, of course).

Install a flow controller into your shower and faucets. You can reduce your family's hot water consumption by 2000 gallons per person per year. For a family of four, that's 8000 saved gallons of hot water per year! That can also mean a savings of between $100 and $150 per year.

Repair leaky faucets. You know the sound: drip... drip... drip. Not only can a leaky faucet keep you awake at night but it can burn a hole in your wallet. One drop leaked per second can waste 50 gallons of hot water a week or 2,500 gallons a year. Install a 20¢ washer and save dollars.

Electricity

Saving electricity can be a source of "found money." Here are some hints to help keep your money out of the utility companies' coffers:

Turn off the lights. Turn off all lights when not in use. Electricity is the most expensive source of energy. Lights that are turned off are not using electricity and are saving you money.

Keep thermostats down in the Winter and up in the Summer. Most people air condition with electric-powered units and many heat water and rooms with electric heating. This being so, save money by controlling the level of your thermostats. In summer, do not air condition below 75 degrees. In winter, keep the thermostats no higher than 65 degrees, normally.

Keep the refrigerator/freezer closed. Every time you open your refrigerator or freezer, it loses the cold air inside and has to recool the air after you close the door. This means that you use added electric power to run the cooling unit. Thus, make a habit of using your refrigerator or freezer efficiently by limiting the number of times you open it in a day and by making sure you have closed the doors completely after use.

Buy energy efficient appliances and light bulbs. Energy-efficient lighting could save Americans $18.6 billion in electric bills each year. The new compact fluorescent is a great way to save energy in your lighting needs. It has much better color than older "cool white" fluorescent lights and is better than incandescent light bulbs.

When you buy appliances or air conditioners, look for the Energy Guide or energy efficiency Ratings (EER), which will tell you the efficiency of the appliance you are considering and which will allow you to compare it to others in the marketplace. Operating energy efficient appliances will save you money over the lifetime of the product, far more than the higher price tag that some of the super-efficient appliances carry.

There are also long-lasting efficient light bulbs on the market. These products save you in two ways: fewer light bulb purchases and lower electric bills.

USE YOUR PHONE WISELY

For better or worse, the old phone monopoly is no more. Now, you have a choice: which of many carriers do you want to use for your long distance service. Local calls, however, are still a monopoly and as a result, many consumers believe they are paying too much for local service (we definitely agree).

In any event, if you are careful and efficient in the way you use your phone, you can save a little money nearly every month. And, to paraphrase Benjamin Franklin, a little money saved is a little money earned, to which we add, a little money saved again and again, adds up to a lot of money earned.

Here are some ways to save money on your telephone bill:

Limit the features you have in your service. Phone companies are offering far more than the use of a telephone line. They now offer many services which you may or may not wish to try. Features like "call waiting," which allows you to hear a beep when you are on the phone and a call is coming in, "call forwarding," which allows you to forward your calls to a different number, and other such convenience services are available to you - at a monthly cost. It is tempting to sign up for these services and many make life more convenient. However, there is also a possibility that you will sign up for a service and then rarely or never use it. In such circumstances what was billed as a convenience breakthrough only becomes an unnecessary drain on your finances.

Avoid credit card calls. Phone companies issue credit cards to credit worthy people who want them. This convenience allows you to make a phone call on your personal bill even when you are not using your own phone.

The problem with this is that it is more expensive than direct calls from your home phone. Moreover, if you use the credit card with the assistance of an operator, that further increases the cost of the call. Thus, to save money, limit your use of credit card calls to those times when it is absolutely necessary and when you use your credit card, try to avoid involving an operator in the call.

Use 800 numbers whenever you can. Many businesses have 800 toll free numbers for the convenience of their customers. If a business you are patronizing does, use the service and save on your phone bill. *THERE IS AN 800 TELEPHONE NUMBER DIRECTORY ASSISTANCE SERVICE FOR TOLL FREE NUMBERS. IT CAN BE REACHED BY DIALING 800 555-1212.*

Limit the use of 900 numbers. There are many valid services available by phone that offer information, which is paid for by using a 900 number. There are other services which are less savory and which prey on teenagers and youth, offering unwholesome calls for a high price, sometimes $5.00 per minute!

If you decide to use a 900 number, be sure that you know the price you will pay for the call before you dial, so as to avoid an unpleasant surprise. If you want to protect your children from undesirable 900 numbers (and your phone bill from the price) you can have your local phone company block access to a 900 number from your phone. For more details, contact your telephone company.

Limit the time of phone calls outside your local calling area. It is important to know which numbers are in your local area. Your basic service charge pays for your use of local calls and thus, you can call "free" to those numbers. Those numbers outside of your local calling area will be charged, *even if they fall within the same Area Code*. These charges are based on the cost per time unit charged. The longer the toll call, the more expensive it is. Thus, if the call is not within your local calling area, limit the length of your calls. Your phone book will tell you which numbers in your area are within your local calling zone.

Call during off hours. Many long distance companies have lower rates on weekends and during the evening than they do during the business day. Take advantage of this fact and make as many long distance calls during the "off season" as you can. By so restricting yourself, you will still get to talk but you won't have to pay so much for the service.

Use your phone efficiently. Many of us make business and personal phone calls and then, as soon as we hang up, we think of other things we wanted to say. If that happens on a call across the street to your mother or a neighbor, no harm is done. But, if you find yourself making two or three toll calls to finish your business, then you may be spending money unnecessarily.

Write letters. Letter writing is a lost art in this country but it is time to revive the skill. For 29¢ (subject to increase) you can take all the time you want and communicate with friends, loved ones and business associates or enterprises and often for less money than a phone call. If the call is an important one, it is a good idea to write anyway so that you can have a record of what you communicated. Besides, if you write letters you receive letters. It's fun and often more satisfying to receive a letter, which can last a life-time and provide a history of your family's life, than a phone call, which is soon forgotten.

Long Distance Telephone Services

There was once a time when you had no choice as to which company would carry your long distance telephone calls. That has long since changed. Now, there are a plethora of companies competing for your business, which is one reason that long distance telephone services are more affordable than they used to be.

That is good for consumers, but it does require that you do a little work to make sure you get the best long distance telephone service for you. But how do you know which is the best? To some extent, that will be based on trial and error, but here are some questions to ask prospective long distance carriers when you are deciding which service to sign up for:

How convenient is the service? Some companies force you to dial a complicated sequence of numbers in order to hook up with their connection. Others may not allow service from your phone to every other phone in the country. Find out the details about these and any other convenience features, such as credit card availability and decide if any lack of convenience is worth the money you may save with a discount carrier.

What is the quality of the service? There is a difference in the quality of service among the various companies that are competing for your long distance business. For example, is the quality of the sound clear and true or are there annoying hissing and popping noises? Is the company responsive to consumer complaints? Are they easy to contact, other than when they are trying to sell you on signing up? Does the company have a 24-hour toll free customer assistance number for service problems?

What are the companies rates for all hours of the day? Companies usually charge different rates during different hours of the day. Thus, don't make a decision based on the lowest rate charged. Rather, find out what the charges are for all hours of the day and then compare that to the time when you make the most calls. In that way, you will know the charges you are most likely to be billed for and you can compare the prices during such times of the companies that are competing for your business.

How are charges computed? All long distance companies will charge you for the call depending on where the call is made from and to, and upon the time the call takes. Are the charges made on a 60 second time, a 30 second time or a 6 second time, and if you add the charges up, how much are you being charged per minute?

Are there special discount deals available? Many of us have telephone patterns, which tell a story of phone usage. For example, if you live in Rhode Island and your sister lives in California, many of your long distance calls will be to California and will probably be on the week-ends or evenings when the rates are lower. Or perhaps, you have a home office and make long distance business calls during the working day. Whatever the case may be, be sure to discuss your long distance phone habits with the customer service representatives you talk to. Ask what you can expect to pay per month and whether there are any "deals" which will lower your typical long distance charges.

Are there charges made for connecting the service? Some companies charge for connecting their long distance service to your phone number. Others offer service hook-up at no cost to you. Connection fees are a cost of the service and should be factored into your decision-making process in deciding which company to use. For example, if you save $2 every month with Phone Company A over Company B but the connection fee is $25 more, it will take two years for you to begin to profit from selecting Company A.

> **CONSUMER ALERT: PETER BARNES IS WHAT ONE WOULD CALL A CONSUMER-SIDE ENTREPRENEUR. RECENTLY, HE LAUNCHED "WORKING ASSETS LONG DISTANCE" TELEPHONE SERVICE. IF YOU SWITCH, FOR EXAMPLE, FROM AT&T OR SPRINT TO WORKING ASSETS, YOU MAKE THE SAME LONG DISTANCE CALLS AT EQUAL OR CHEAPER RATES AND YOU GET OPPORTUNITIES TO BE WHAT BARNES TERMS A "FIVE-MINUTE CITIZEN." IN ADDITION TO 1 PERCENT OF YOUR CHARGES BEING DONATED TO PROGRESSIVE CITIZEN GROUPS, EVERY MONTH YOU GET BACKGROUND INFORMATION ON CONTEMPORARY PUBLIC ISSUES, SUCH AS NATIONAL HEALTH INSURANCE OR RECYCLING LEGISLATION. SPECIAL PLANS MAKE TELEPHONE CALLS TO YOUR REPRESENTATIVES LESS EXPENSIVE TOO.**
>
> **IF ALL OF THIS INTRIGUES YOU, CALL TOLL FREE 1-800-788-8588 FOR MORE INFORMATION. BE SURE TO ASK FOR A COPY OF WORKING ASSETS' FREE BOOKLET TITLED "THE FIVE MINUTE CITIZEN."**

Once you have made your decision, don't sit on the company's laurels. Instead, make sure the company's performance meets its promises regarding service, price and the quality of its connections. Never accept less than you are entitled to as a paying customer. Remember, if you are unhappy, you always have the all important consumer power to say "no" and change companies. So, do your part to make market competition work by refusing to put up with substandard or overcharged long distance telephone services.

AVOID SHUT OFFS

If you don't pay your phone bill, your electric bill, your gas bill or your water bill, the utility company has the right to shut off your utilities until they receive payment.

Shut offs are cruel and they are expensive. If you are shut off, you will be denied the use of utility service, which will be a tremendous personal burden. To add insult to injury, you will also have to pay a financial price. In order to have service restored, you will have to pay both past due amount and a reconnection fee or other penalty, which can be quite expensive. In addition, you may be asked to post a further security deposit, further adding to the erosion of your bank balance.

Of course, the best way to avoid shut-offs is to pay your utility bills. But, for people who have lost their jobs or find themselves for some other reason unable to pay their bills, that is not always possible. Still, even if you have no money to pay, you may be able to avoid a shut off. However, in such cases, however, you must take steps BEFORE YOU ARE SHUT OFF, not after. Here are a few things you can do to avoid threatened shut offs.

See If You Qualify For An Exemption From Shut Off

In many areas of the country, there are laws which prevent a utility from turning off service, if certain conditions apply. The most prominent exception is the cold weather rule. Basically, the cold weather rule prohibits regulated gas or electric utility companies from shutting off service during cold weather months if the utility is your primary source of heat and you are unable (not unwilling) to pay your bill. The exact workings of the rule will vary from locale to locale and you should contact your local utility company or consumer protection organization for the exact rules in your area.

Make Sure the Utility Has Obeyed the Law Regarding Shut Offs

Utility companies are not just allowed to shut off your service. They must comply with strict regulations regarding shut offs. Thus, if you are threatened with a cessation of service and if the utility company will only work against you instead of with you, contact the utility and the regulatory board and learn the procedural requirements regarding shut off. Then, if a single "i" has not been dotted, or "t" crossed, fight the shut off with the utility company's own regulations.

See If the Utility Company Will Agree to a Repayment Plan

Many states have laws requiring some utilities to work out payment plans when shut offs are threatened. If your utility falls under such laws and shut off is threatened, work out a plan with the utility to avoid shut off. Then, keep your payments up.

Ask the Utility Company to Apply Your Security Deposit to Your Bill

If you paid a security deposit when you signed up for the utility's service, ask them to apply your deposit to the arrears. That money may be enough to prevent the shut off.

If You Disagree With the Amount of the Bill, Complain Before Shut Off

Do not allow your utility service to be lost because of a disagreement over the bill. If you believe you have been overcharged, pay the amount you agree you owe and dispute the balance in writing, according to the procedures utilized for billing disputes. Under such circumstances, your service should be maintained until the dispute is resolved.

Ask the Utility to Set Up a Budget For Payment

Many consumers are able to pay their utility bills for most of the year but then are hit hard in the Winter with heating bills (or in the Summer by air conditioning bills) that are simply too expensive to pay. To avoid such peaks and valleys, ask your utility to allow you to spread out your Winter (or Summer) bills throughout the year. year

The federal government also offers energy assistance programs for low-income customers through the Department of Health and Human Services.

Contact your local community action agency or town hall to see if your qualify for the Weatherization Assistance Program or the Low-Income Home Energy Assistance Program.

Chapter Fourteen

CONSUMERS' AGENDA

Most consumers believe that utilities are the proverbial 800-pound gorilla in the old joke, "Where does an 800 pound gorilla sit on a bus? Answer: Anywhere he wants." In other words, consumers believe that they are essentially powerless in the face of utility money and political power, that all they can do is pay their bills and complain a little to their elected representatives if the rates get too high.

But that is not true. Consumers who band together and fight for their rights can make a big difference in their own lives and that of their communities. Here is a sampling of what you can do to tell the 800-pound gorilla where to get off.

JOIN OR PRESS FOR A CITIZENS UTILITY BOARD (CUB)

CUBs are organized advocacy groups whose purpose is to give consumers like you a voice in the regulatory proceedings which are "supposed" to but often do not control monopoly utilities very well. The purpose of a CUB is simple: to make sure you and your neighbors, the consumers, get a fair shake from regulators, utilities and lawmakers. In addition, CUBs also educate consumers on a wide variety of issues, from matters of regulation to practical ways to keep their utility bills low. This voluntary "joining together" of individual utility customers who use their money in the form of dues and their talent in the form of services and the political power of their numbers, is a very effective weapon in the consumer self-defense arsenal against the power and political clout of the utility companies.

At the outset of the CUB movement, utility companies were required as a *quid pro quo* for their legal monopoly status, by laws in three states (Illinois, Wisconsin and Oregon) and one city (San Diego), to place inserts in their utility bills announcing the existence of the CUB and containing a coupon for consumer membership. This mass communication on behalf of consumers was more than the power elite that controls the monopoly utility industry could take and so they took the matter to court. Unfortunately, the conservative United States Supreme Court struck down this type of insert rule, thereby making it more difficult for CUBs to let consumers know of their existence. Soon thereafter, the Illinois CUB secured legislation permitting it to insert CUB information in all State government mailings being sent to 50,000 or more citizens.

The hope of the utility companies, of course, was that the CUB movement would shrivel up and die as a result of the Supreme Court's ruling. After all, consumer empowerment, as represented by CUBs, creates a more equal playing field. The big shots don't like equal playing fields. They don't like you having a powerful voice in the halls of government and in the offices of regulators. They don't like you having the ability to effectively present the consumer's side of things in an organized and expert fashion. They don't like being forced to justify their actions and proposals. They don't like their greed being thwarted.

Happily, the best laid plans of rats and utility companies have gone awry. The CUB movement has not only survived, it has grown. But it needs your participation if it is to thrive and to grow beyond the three states and one city where CUBS now exist. (CUBs are also on the drawing boards in New York, Massachusetts, Missouri, Kansas and Florida. They need to be created in all 50 states.)

Here is a sample of what a CUB can do for you. It is a proposed Consumers Bill of Rights, created by the Illinois Citizen Utility Board:

CONSUMERS' UTILITY BILL OF RIGHTS

THE STATE OF (INSERT YOUR STATE) MUST GUARANTEE THAT SAFE, RELIABLE AND AFFORDABLE GAS, ELECTRIC AND TELEPHONE SERVICE IS AVAILABLE TO ALL CITIZENS:

•CONSUMERS MUST BE PROVIDED WITH THE CHEAPEST POWER AVAILABLE IN COMING YEARS. UTILITIES MUST PROVIDE ENERGY AT LEAST-COST.

•TO REDUCE ENERGY COSTS, UTILITIES MUST BE REQUIRED TO ENCOURAGE CONSERVATION AND PURCHASE POWER FROM OTHER UTILITIES WHO HAVE AN EXCESS.

•RATEPAYERS WILL NOT PAY FOR UTILITY COMPANY MISTAKES.

•CONSUMERS WILL NOT PAY FOR MORE POWER THAN THEY NEED.

• CONSUMERS WILL PAY FOR NEW POWER PLANTS ONLY AFTER THEY ARE PRODUCING POWER, NOT BEFORE.

•IF A POWER PLANT IS DELAYED BECAUSE OF A UTILITY'S MISTAKE, THE UTILITY, NOT RATEPAYERS, WILL PAY.

•UTILITIES WILL NOT BE ALLOWED TO BRANCH OUT INTO OTHER BUSINESSES IF CONSUMERS' INTERESTS MAY SUFFER.

•UTILITIES MUST BE PERIODICALLY AUDITED TO IMPROVE EFFICIENCY AND LOWER COSTS.

• MONEY NOW BEING TAKEN FROM CONSUMERS FOR THE FUTURE SHUT DOWN OF NUCLEAR POWER PLANTS SHOULD BE PLACED IN A TRUST FUND AND USED ONLY FOR THAT PURPOSE.

•ALL REGULATORY DECISIONS MUST BE DECIDED OUT IN THE OPEN. NO OFF THE RECORD CONFERENCES BETWEEN REGULATORS AND UTILITIES.

•A "CONSUMER INTERVENTION FUND" WILL BE ESTABLISHED TO FUND CONSUMER INPUT INTO REGULATORY RATE CASES.

•CONSUMERS WILL BE ABLE TO JOIN A CUB THROUGH A "CHECK OFF" ON THEIR UTILITY BILLS, AND THEIR DUES WILL BE FORWARDED TO THE CUB BY THE UTILITY.

This is the kind of consumer empowerment that can make a real difference in your lives and which can keep extra money in your bank account. We urge you to join a CUB if one is up and running in your State. If one is not, become a citizen activist and join your local consumer's movement to bring a CUB into being where you live. For more information on CUBs, contact one of the CUBs listed below, and send for the book, *Citizens' Utility Boards Because Utilities Bear Watching*, by Beth Givens, published by the Center for Public Interest Law at the University of San Diego School of Law, Alcala Park, San Diego, California 92110.

Here are the addresses and phone' numbers of existing CUBs:

ILLINOIS: Citizens Utility Board of Illinois
                     208 S. LaSalle, Rm 584
                     Chicago, IL 60604
                     (312) 263-4282

OREGON: Citizens Utility Board of Oregon
                     P.O. Box 6345
                     Portland, OR. 97228
                     (503) 227-1984

WISCONSIN: Citizens' Utility Board of Wisconsin
                     P.O. Box 1438
                     Madison, WI 53701
                     (608) 251-3322

CALIFORNIA: Utility Consumers Action Network
                     4901 Morena Blvd., Suite 128
                     San Diego, CA 92117
                     (619) 696-6966

If you want to help the New York CUB form, contact:

New York Public Research Group
184 Washington Ave.
Albany, NY 12210
(518) 436-0876

If you want general information on CUBs, contact the Illinois CUB.

FIGHT UNWARRANTED RATE INCREASES

Never underestimate the voracious appetite of utilities who have a seemingly never-ending hunger for rate increases. The only way to prevent unwarranted rate increases is to stand up and say, "No!" If a rate increase is planned, you will receive a formal notice with your utility bill. When this happens, and if you disagree with the request, get involved! Here are some things you can do to keep dollars in your pocket instead of going into the utility company's treasurechest:

Pressure the politicians. Politicians of all political stripes have one thing in common: they want to keep their elected and appointed offices. This being so, you have leverage over them - if you will use it. That means organizing (or joining) your fellow citizens into an effective lobbying campaign. Telephone your elected officials, call radio talk shows, write letters to the editor of your newspaper, get your friends to do likewise, in order to persuade your elected officials to fight the rate hike.

Let the regulators know how you feel. Most utility companies, whether privately, publicly or cooperatively owned, are regulated in what they can charge you for the service they provide. Thus, they can't "just raise their prices." Instead, regulated utilities must get formal permission from the State Public Utility Commission or other regulatory agency.

When regulators consider the utility company rate increase request, there will be an opportunity for the public to take a stand. When this time comes, speak up! This communication can take several forms:

•*Demonstrations* It is your Constitutional right as an American to seek redress from government. Thus, peaceful marches and demonstrations that are well attended can express how the people respond to the proposed rate hikes. Successful demonstrations will also attract media attention, which will get the anti-rate hike drive publicity, which will make for more citizen participation and larger demonstrations, which will attract media attention, which will garner more publicity, which will - well, you get the picture. Well-attended, persistent and timely demonstrations can make a difference in how the regulatory "powers that be" decide the request for a rate increase.

•*Attend hearings* When rate regulation hearings are held, pack it with anti- rate-increasers. If you show you care, that you oppose money being taken out of your pocket that is not warranted or justified by the circumstances, your presence at the hearing will send a loud and clear message.

•*Testify* Usually, individual consumers will testify about the impact of utility increases on their lives and/or on the quality of service received from the utility company. When testifying, use personal experiences to illustrate your points. For example, perhaps you can prove through your bills that you have reduced usage but thanks to the proposed rate increase, you will face higher payments. Or, your expenses are already so high that additional outlays will be a true hardship.

If you testify, the attorneys for the utility companies will have the right to ask you questions. Don't be surprised if they ask you about job creation and other such red herrings. Remember, the issue is whether an increase is warranted based on the circumstances of the case, not whether the utility contends that jobs may be created or some other hypothetical pie in the sky. (In fact, point out that high utility rates scare away new industry.) Don't make the mistake of answering hypothetical questions that you don't know about.

•*Support consumer groups* Individuals can increase their clout by joining and financially supporting consumer advocacy groups such as CUBs and Public Interest Research Groups (PIRGs). These organizations can use the membership dues and contributions of members and citizens to hire attorneys, experts and support organization lobbyists to work on your behalf. These groups will have the technical expertise to provide a good and powerful defense against an unjustified rate hike. When you join and support such groups with your money and time, you are going a long way to help yourself and your neighbors keep at least a modicum of equity in the utility system.

FIGHT NUCLEAR POWER

Just when you thought it was safe to move on to other consumer and environmental agendas, the nuclear power industry is once again rearing its risky head - as if we have forgotten the lessons of Three Mile Island and the disaster of Chernobyl.

There isn't the space here to discuss in detail the vital necessity of fighting nuclear power. But let's just go lightly over a few of the reasons that add up to "NO NUCLEAR POWER!"

The Danger

The proponents of nuclear power are incredibly short-term thinkers. "Nuclear power is safe," they will say. There is no denying that there have been accidents and that radioactivity from nuclear power plants has been released into the air, water and land. The full impact on the people who have been radiated cannot be known.

The long term consequences Radiation from the wastes of nuclear power plants will last - and will be lethal to human and other life forms - for tens of thousands of years! This being so, even if the radioactive material can be safely handled for 40 years until the year 2032, there still won't be a dent made in the potential for harm.

The Disaster Scenario Of more immediate concern than the long-term potential for harm that nuclear power poses, is the potential for a present disaster. Nuclear power is simply not safe in the short term. Three Mile Island was just one tip of the iceberg. Around the nation, there are many old and deteriorating nuclear power plants that are disasters waiting to happen. In San Lois Opisbo, California, there is a nuclear power plant on line only miles away from an earthquake fault zone. If a severe accident occurred, a disaster of unprecedented proportion in U.S. history could occur. The added risks posed by negligence, sabotage, design deficiencies that affect plants, storage units and transport vehicles could produce unacceptable exposures to millions of innocent people and thousands of square miles of territory. Moreover, workable evacuation capabilities for cities, especially during a nuclear meltdown, are non-existent. Too many near-misses have been documented to warrant radioactive mortgaging of our country's future.

The Cost

Nuclear power was sold to the public as a cheap and clean source of virtually endless electric power. As we now know, nuclear power is certainly not clean. But it isn't cheap either. The Seabrook, New Hampshire plant produces the most expensive electricity in the nation, not counting the enormous costs of decommissioning the plant in three or four decades and storing its radioactive wastes for many millennia. It takes at least $5 billion to build a new nuclear plant. Maybe that's why no electric company has ordered a new nuclear plant since the mid-seventies.

They Are Unnecessary

We don't need to build new nuclear power plants. The demands on our electrical generating facilities can be met in other safer ways. For example, in the Sacramento Municipal District of California, Pacific Gas and Electric and the Southern California Edison Company have stated that their customers' energy requirements can be met with increased efficiency and renewable resources.

PROMOTE ALTERNATE ENERGY

We have within our grasp sources of energy that have the potential to make the 21st Century truly glorious and pollution-free. The various forms of solar energy (including wind power) are increasingly practical sources of risk-free, clean and economical energy waiting to be expanded and made a major part of the country's energy future.

SUPPORT COOPERATIVES

Cooperatives can supply electricity, heating oil and other energy supplies at a lower cost to consumers than profit-making companies. Since consumer cooperatives are owned by the users of the power supply themselves, they are also less likely to support unnecessary, expensive and polluting energy projects. Thus, work in your area to form cooperatives or join ones already in existence. Not only will your net worth benefit, but your community and the environment will as well.

There are about 40 fuel buying cooperative groups throughout the country. Here are two groups to contact for more information about fuel buying cooperatives:

Buyers Up
P.O. Box 53005
Washington, DC 20009
(202) 328-3800

New York PIRG Fuel Buyers Group
9 Murray Street
New York, NY 10007
(212) 349-6460

Part Five

THE VITAL ART
OF SELF DEFENSE
PROTECTING YOURSELF
IN THE MARKETPLACE

In the rough and tumble of the marketplace, it is the wise consumer who learns the vital skills of consuming self defense. Some of these necessary skills can be described as organizational, that is, the proper saving and keeping of written records of your transactions as a consumer. We call this process "creating a paper trail." This is an important concept, for without a complete record of the transactions and purchases you have made as a consumer of goods and services, you may be unable to assert yourself to correct mistakes and prevent rip-offs. And that can cost you something else made of paper: money and a lot of it.

We will also be dealing with other important tools for consumer fairness. One is the art of effective complaining. Complaining can save you a lot of money, often at the cost of very little aggravation. Finally, when all else fails, we will discuss direct action you can take, from picketing to suing in one of the last bastions of equality in the judicial system - Small Claims Court.

Chapter Fifteen

BLAZING A PAPER TRAIL

What is a paper trail? It is the *evidence of the history of your business affairs* as set forth in receipts, sales brochures, contracts and other documentation. Remember, despite all of the advertisements and "friendly" salespersons vying for your dollar, it is still a *caveat emptor* world and you have to treat your business affairs as just that - business.

Business types put great store in words and numbers. They use them to keep records. They apply words and numbers to the interpretation and decision making with regard to their customers. In fact, it is often their mastery of the paper work of transactions that allows business to "have its way."

These facts of life being what they are, the best way for you to exercise power in the marketplace and maximize your chance of consumer satisfaction is to master the paperwork. Words and numbers must become you primary weapon in the continuing struggle to achieve fairness and equity in the marketplace. Because if you reach the point where you have to "do battle" with a store, lawyer or insurance company, you need to have the proper words and numbers at your disposal and be able to use them to your advantage.

GETTING ORGANIZED

The first step you should take as a strong consumer is to marshal your "word troops." The only way you will be effective in this task is to get organized. Here are a few suggestions.

SET UP YOUR FILES
Most of us are far too casual about the way we keep our business records. We toss receipts in drawers, only to lose them when we want to return our purchase. We use sales brochures as book marks. We toss warranties in our "junk drawer" where they never again see the light of day. This casual attitude can be the downfall of consumer power.

The first step toward an effective consumer defense network is to establish an organized set of files in which to keep the records of your business affairs.

Establish a Place To Keep Your Records
You should keep all of your business records in one place. That way, in time of need you won't have to organize a search party just to find the receipt for that pair of slacks with the missing zipper.

Once you have a place to store your documents, you will want to purchase the business supplies to store them in (keeping the receipt, of course). It doesn't take much. Here's what to buy:

- An "accordion style" file folder
- Manila file folders
- Identification tabs.

Now, you're ready to begin your file.

Set Up A Separate File For Each Area of Your Consuming Life

For example, you will want a file labeled "Charge Cards," one labeled "Bank Records," one labeled "Tax Records" and so on. This is important from an organizational standpoint so that you will be able to find a receipt or other record quickly in the event you have need.

It is also important to have an area in your filing for trouble-shooting or problems. This file would be used in the event you find yourself in a dispute. When in a dispute, having a separate file containing all of the documents (receipts, letters, sales brochures, summaries of telephone conversations, etc.) that are involved in the controversy will allow you to work with the file easily and efficiently so that the conflict will have minimal impact on the time you would rather spend with your family or out on the golf course.

ESTABLISH A WORKING SYSTEM OF RECORD KEEPING

If you want to keep an accurate record of your life as a consumer, you must get into the habit of good record keeping. Here are some ideas:

Keep Your Filing Up To Date

Your filing system is to serve you rather than control you; you must keep it up to date. It is tempting to take your receipts and records and either throw them out or toss them in a big box for future reference. That can only lead to record keeping gridlock. It is a law of nature that the one receipt you need is the one you threw away or is the one that is at the bottom of a huge pile of paperwork in your "receipt box" or "bill drawer." The only way to overcome this is to file your documents as you receive them or, at the very least, once a week. In that way, you will always be able to find what you need, when you need it.

Always Get Everything in Writing

The importance of having written records cannot be overemphasized for those who want to exercise power in the marketplace. For example, assume you have purchased a coffee pot. You will receive certain documents when you buy it: a receipt, which you should file in your receipt file, a warranty, which you should file in your warranty file, etc.

Such normal purchases usually pose no paperwork problems. However, that is not always the case with every consumer transaction. For example, let's say you hire a lawyer. He or she may tell you that they estimate the total cost of the representation will be $1,000. *You will want that representation in writing.* Or, assume you have purchased a washing machine from an appliance store based on the promise of the sales representative that if there is a problem with the appliance, the store will exchange it for a new one, no questions asked. You will want that promise in writing too.

There are normally two ways to get promises in writing; have the merchant or service provider put them in writing or do it yourself.

Obtaining written promises If you want a sales person or service provider to put a representation in writing, it is not difficult to do - just ask. For example, if you are shopping for a car, you can have the salesman put the price and relevant terms on his or her card or on a sheet of the auto dealer's stationary. KEEP THIS FOR FUTURE REFERENCE if you do business with that dealer or as a useful bargaining chip with another dealer.

Put it in writing yourself On other occasions, you may wish to set an oral promise in concrete yourself with that powerful consumer weapon, THE CONFIRMING LETTER. A confirming letter is a device that lawyers and business types use all of the time to reduce oral conversations into written form. What the confirming letter does, in short, is summarize an oral conversation so that later, "differing memories" cannot be used to "wiggle out" of promises made. Here is an example of a confirming letter you can use as a form:

OCTOBER 3, 1992

ALFRED MILLIONSELLER
BIG BUCKS INSURANCE COMPANY
8888 BIG BUCKS DRIVE
PROFIT CITY, ARKANSAS, 88908

RE: THE COVERAGE I HAVE PURCHASED

DEAR MR. MILLIONSELLER:

THE PURPOSE OF THIS LETTER IS TO CONFIRM OUR CONVERSATION
OF SEPTEMBER 30, 1992, IN WHICH YOU STATED THE FOLLOWING:
1) YOU WERE AUTHORIZED BY BIG BUCKS INSURANCE TO BIND THE COMPANY
TO INSURE MY 1938 STUTZ BEARCAT AUTO.
2) THE PREMIUM FOR THE COVERAGE WILL BE $625 EVERY SIX MONTHS
3) THAT UPON DELIVERY OF A CHECK IN THE AMOUNT OF $625, WHICH I
ENCLOSE, THAT I AM COVERED IN THE FOLLOWING AMOUNTS:
- $50,000/$100,000 LIABILITY
- $50,000 PROPERTY DAMAGE
- COMPREHENSIVE AND COLLISION COVERAGE WITH A $250 DEDUCTIBLE

4) I SHALL RECEIVE MY FORMAL POLICY WITHIN 30 DAYS.

IF I HAVE NOT SET FORTH YOUR REPRESENTATIONS ACCURATELY, PLEASE
ADVISE ME IN WRITING IMMEDIATELY.

THANK YOU FOR YOUR COOPERATION. I LOOK FORWARD TO DOING BUSINESS
WITH YOU AND BIG BUCKS INSURANCE COMPANY.

SINCERELY,
JOAN P. SMARTCONSUMER

The purpose of a confirming letter is to "set in concrete" representations and promises that you deem important and which might otherwise be hard to prove if a dispute happens to arise. In other words, a confirming letter overcomes the "it's my word against yours" ploy.

THE PAPER TRAIL IS A MONEY SAVER

We know that accurate record keeping may seem like a lot of work when there are baby diapers to change, Little League games to attend along with the other joys and chores of daily living, but it is important and will not take up much time at all if you keep on top of it. Moreover, the paper trail can save you money in the following ways:

You Will Have a Grasp of Your Own Business Affairs

In a way, your personal finances are like a business; you have income, expenses, and a bottom line that tells you whether you and your family are in "the red" or "the black." Good record keeping is essential to knowing where you are and what needs to be done to put you where you want to be. For example, if you don't know the extent of you personal credit card debt, you may underestimate it and charge items you would not have had you known the true state of your financial affairs. Good record keeping can, thus, help you avoid overextending yourself. Likewise, good record keeping can tell you if the garbage disposal that breaks is still under warranty, if the check book is balanced and whether or not your insurance premiums will be due soon. In other words, organization is as important to your personal financial well being as it is to the largest corporation.

You Are More Likely to Catch Mistakes

Merchants, sales personnel, lawyers, doctors and others you deal with in the consumer marketplace are all human. And being human, they will, on occasion, make mistakes. It is in your financial interest to catch these mistakes and the best way to ensure that you will is to stay organized.

It Will Be Easier To Take Action

If you are organized at the start, it will be much easier for you to begin to take action to protect yourself if you find a mistake or if you find yourself in a dispute. The reason: everything you need to effectively present your side of the story will be at your fingertips in black and white, ready to prove your side of the story.

It Will Supply Evidence If You Go To Court

If you end up in Small Claims Court or another type of lawsuit, the written documentation will provide the written evidence you may need to win your case.

It Can Help With Your Taxes

If you itemize your deductions in filing your income taxes, having records to prove your deductions is very important.

Chapter Sixteen

TAKING CARE
OF BUSINESS

"The customer is always right." When was the last time you heard your local merchant chant that consumer friendly mantra? If you are like many consumers, it has been a long time. But it shouldn't be. Quality service, well manufactured products and satisfied customers should be the basis of entrepreneurial and corporate profit. And they can be again, if the consumers of the world demand it. Let this demand begin with you.

THE ART OF EFFECTIVE COMPLAINING

So far in this book, we have been emphasizing preventive consuming, that is, using the powers and strengths you have as a client, patient and/or customer to get the best deal at the best price while avoiding problems that cost you time, money and aggravation. We believe that such activism at and before the point of sale is the best way to prevent difficulties from arising at all. However, as Burns wrote, the best plans of mice and men often go awry.

REALIZING YOU HAVE A PROBLEM
As with any difficulty in life, the first step toward solving it is to acknowledge that the problem exists. For many consumers, acknowledging that they are dissatisfied is difficult. There are several reasons why consumers often fail to acknowledge that they have been had, many of which were identified by Arthur Best, in his book *When Consumers Complain* (1981, Columbia University Press, New York, NY).

Difficulty of Determining Facts
Sometimes consumers are unhappy with a product or service but don't know the reason for the difficulty. For example, you have a new coat dry-cleaned and it fades. Is it the fault of the dry cleaner or the manufacturer? It may be difficult to tell.

Difficulty of Determining Rights
Another reason some consumers get into trouble is that they don't know their rights under the law. For example, in the law, there is something called an **implied warranty of merchantability**. This legal doctrine says (using real people's language instead of legalese) that a product must be fit for the purpose to which it was reasonably intended. Thus, a lawn

mower must cut grass, a glass must hold liquid, etc. This implied warranty gives people a legal right against the sellers of products that fail the implied warranty if they cannot otherwise get satisfaction. Yet, if you don't know about the right, it cannot be exercised.

Consumers Have Low Expectations

This one can put a real damper on consumer empowerment. If you don't expect a lot you will not demand a lot. If a merchant knows that you do not demand a lot you will probably receive little, thereby fulfilling your own expectations.

Consumers Don't Like To Admit They Have Been Victimized

No one likes to think that they have been had or have received less than they bargained for. It isn't good for the old ego. But, refusing to look a bad deal in the face does not make it go away.

Consumers Can Be Lethargic

Even under ideal circumstances, life is - well, busy. Just getting up, going to work, raising a family, preparing meals and doing all of the other activities of a full and productive life can leave us exhausted and unable to even contemplate anything other than what's on the tube tonight. As understandable as this is, it can lead to poor service and high prices.

For example, how many of us visit our local gas station and pay 10¢ more per gallon than the station's competitor down the block, just because it saves us a little inconvenience?

EFFECTIVE COMPLAINING

Sometimes, in the course of consuming events, it becomes necessary to "take up arms against a sea of troubles and by complaining, end them." Effective complaining is a vital part of any consumer's self defense arsenal. Complaining sounds "negative," but it isn't. It is positive; for you, since your problem will likely be solved, for the merchant or service provider, since unrecognized problems can be identified through customer complaints and corrected, and for future consumers, who will have one fewer problem to face.

For the customer complaint to "work correctly" it should be approached in the appropriate manner:

Be Courteously Assertive

Some people believe that the best way to receive satisfaction is to treat the complaint taker as "the enemy." These people come charging into a complaint situation as if they were at war, assuming the worst and acting belligerently. This is not the right approach, especially at the early stages of a dispute process. No. The key is to be courteously assertive, that is, to be courteous and friendly in a businesslike manner while still strongly asserting your complaint. Here's what we mean:

WRONG: "Hey you! I want to tell you what a piece of garbage lawn mower you sold me!"

This approach is nasty and needlessly combative. It is not likely to bring out a cooperative and problem solving attitude in the person hearing your complaint.

WRONG: "Uh, excuse me, but ah, er, I think I might have a bit of a problem with a lawn mower I bought here. Of course, it may be my yard but I don't think it cuts very well."

This approach is too weak. If the seller of the lawn mower is a quality merchant, you might get by with it, but an aggressive type might try to mow you over and make you keep the defective lawn mower.

RIGHT: "Excuse me, but I have a complaint. I purchased this lawn mower here last Saturday and I am not satisfied with it. It does not cut the grass well except after repeated mowings. I would like an exchange."

This is a courteous and business like approach to a problem that will not put the merchant on the defensive but tells him or her that you expect to have your complaint handled properly.

Avoid Emotionalism

Remember that a complaint is a business transaction and should be approached in that manner. Over-emotionalism is only likely to get in the way of an effective resolution of the problem.

WRONG: "I can't believe you guys sold me such a cheap piece of junk as this lawn mower! What, are you guys crooks or something? I'm calling my lawyer!"

This emotional, combativeness is unlikely to win friends or influence people. And while being "liked" is not one of your objectives when complaining, you do want to create an atmosphere where the merchant will want to solve your problem.

RIGHT: "There is a problem with this lawn mower. It doesn't cut the grass well. This store has a great reputation and I'm sure you will want to take care of this matter."

By keeping the issue on higher ground and assuming the integrity of the people you are dealing with, you are more likely to achieve your desired results than by creating an atmosphere of hostility and anger.

Be Specific

If you are to have your complaint redressed, you will need to be as specific as you can be about the purchase and the reason you are dissatisfied.

WRONG: "This lawn mower stinks. I want my money back."

Merchants should be given more information about the problem, not only to help them deal with your problem but to possibly prevent other consumers from running into similar difficulties.

RIGHT: "I purchased this lawn mower last week here. Here is the receipt. I have noticed that the mower requires two or three passes over the lawn in order for it to cut all of the grass."

CONSUMER ALERT: THIS IS ONE OF THE PLACES YOUR CRE-ATED PAPER TRAIL CAN BE OF GOOD USE. ALWAYS BRING IN RECEIPTS, WARRANTY PAPERS AND OTHER DOCUMENTA-TION THAT SUPPORTS YOUR CLAIM WHEN YOU COMPLAIN.

Be Open Minded

When you complain, you are about the business of problem solving, not affixing blame. Thus, be sure to listen to the merchant's side of the story. You may learn you have made a mistake.

WRONG: *Merchant*: "Ah, I see the problem . . ."
           Consumer: "Don't give me any guff or excuses. You sold
           me shoddy goods!"

This approach does nothing to solve the problem and keeps the consumer from learning the cause of the difficulty. It never pays to be close minded or rude. It can hurt you by causing you to remain ignorant about an easily correctable mistake and it could cause the merchant to refuse to cooperate with you.

RIGHT: *Merchant*: "Ah, I see the problem."
           Consumer: "Yes? What is it?"
           Merchant: "Your mower has an adjustable blade. See this
           switch? Turn it down and you will get a closer cut for your
           grass."

This consumer found that there was no problem after all.

STAND UP FOR YOUR RIGHTS

If we take the time to complain assertively, specifically and courteously, more often than not, our dissatisfaction will be rectified. But, there may be times when you will not get satisfaction. At such times you can either quit and accept an injustice or move on to the next stage of the proceedings:

Go to the Top

If at first you don't succeed, go to the top. That may mean, speaking with the manager of the store. If that doesn't work, move on to the area supervisor and so forth. It may even mean contacting the CEO or other head honcho.

When you are going "over the head" of a sales clerk, insurance adjuster or any other person you are not receiving the service and satisfaction you expect from, pay attention to the following tips:

Put everything in writing. There may be a natural tendency of upper management to "back up" their front line people. If you are to overcome this, you have to present as compelling and thorough a case as you can. Usually under such circumstances, it is a very good idea to do your "talking" in writing. Here is a sample complaint letter:

NOVEMBER 14, 1992

PETER HEADHONCHO
CEO BLADE CUTTER LAWN MOWERS, INC.
4444 SAGEBRUSH LANE
BLUE GRASS FIELDS, KENTUCKY, 44444

RE: MY DISSATISFACTION WITH YOUR MOWER MODEL "BLADE BLASTER"

DEAR MR. HEADHONCHO:

ON OCTOBER 3, 1992, I PURCHASED YOUR BLADE BLASTER MODEL
LAWN MOWER FROM POORSERVICE MOWERS OF GRASS STAIN, IOWA. (I
HAVE ENCLOSED A COPY OF THE RECEIPT FOR THAT PURCHASE.)
POORSERVICE ADVERTISES ITSELF AS AN "AUTHORIZED BLADECUTTER
LAWN MOWER DEALER," WHICH IS ONE REASON I MADE THE PURCHASE
FROM THAT COMPANY.

I AM SORRY TO REPORT THAT I AM VERY DISSATISFIED WITH BOTH
THE PRODUCT I PURCHASED AND THE SERVICE I HAVE RECEIVED.
SPECIFICALLY, I HAVE THE FOLLOWING COMPLAINTS:

　1) THE LAWN MOWER IS VERY DIFFICULT TO START, OFTEN
　TAKING UP TO FIVE MINUTES FOR THE MOTOR TO TURN OVER.

　2) THE QUALITY OF MOWING IS POOR. I OFTEN HAVE TO RUN
　OVER AREAS OF MY LAWN TWO OR THREE TIMES TO GET A DECENT
　CUT.

　3) WHEN I BROUGHT THIS TO THE ATTENTION OF POORSERVICE, I
　WAS TREATED RUDELY AND REFUSED AN EXCHANGE. I SPOKE FIRST
　WITH SALESWOMAN MARY INDIGNANT AND THEN WITH THE MANAGER
　OF THE STORE, HARRY RUDEMAN.

I AM REQUESTING THAT YOU RETURN MY MONEY AND PICK UP THE
LAWN MOWER. IN THE ALTERNATIVE, I WILL ACCEPT A NEW LAWN MOWER
IN EXCHANGE ON THE CONDITION THAT IF THIS ONE PROVES TO BE
UNACCEPTABLE THAT I WILL RECEIVE A COMPLETE REFUND. I ALSO ASK

YOU TO INVESTIGATE THE BUSINESS PRACTICES OF POORSERVICE LAWN
MOWERS, WHO ARE NOT GOOD REPRESENTATIVES OF YOUR COMPANY
NAME.

I CAN BE REACHED DURING THE DAY AT (700) 555-4444 AND MY HOME
PHONE NUMBER IS (700) 555-9999. MY ADDRESS IS 1 ASSERTIVE
LANE, GRASS STAIN, IOWA, 44444.

THANK YOU FOR YOUR PROMPT ATTENTION TO THIS MATTER. MAY I HEAR
FROM YOU BEFORE NOVEMBER 30?

VERY TRULY YOURS,

HELEN GOODCONSUMER

ENC.

CC POORSERVICE LAWN MOWERS

A good letter of complaint contains several aspects:
   •It is specific as to time and place.
   •It tells the story without undue emotionalism in a simple and straightforward
manner.
   •It names names and dates and contains as much supporting documentation as is
available to you (which should be in your paper trail file).
   •It asks for a specific remedy.
   •It sets forth a time by which you expect action to be taken.

**CONSUMER ALERT: IF YOU WRITE A LETTER OF COMPLAINT
ABOUT ANOTHER PERSON OR BUSINESS, SEND THAT PERSON
OR BUSINESS A COPY OF YOUR LETTER. NOT ONLY IS THAT
THE COURTEOUS THING TO DO, BUT YOU MAY FIND THAT THE
MERE RECEIPT OF YOUR LETTER OF COMPLAINT TO "HIGHER
AUTHORITIES" IS ENOUGH TO BREAK THE LOGJAM.**

Don't exaggerate. If your cause is just, you will not want to hurt your own credibility with
the powers that be by overstating your case or engaging in falsehoods of any kind. If you
are perceived as an honest consumer who is airing a legitimate complaint, you will be treated
as such. However, if you are perceived as a dishonest griper seeking to take advantage of
the company, you will probably be told to take a hike.
Be prepared. Once you have written your letter of complaint, be prepared to deal with the
issue with the company representative who contacts you. In this regard, you will want to have
done your homework regarding issues such as your legal rights (you may want to consult with

an attorney), your intentions if you do not receive satisfaction (complaining to the Better Business Bureau, filing a lawsuit, etc.) and/or your willingness to take the next step up the line of command, all the way to the Chairman of the Board, if that is what it takes.

Express appreciation for good service. If, as you hope will be the case, your letter(s) of complaint gets the job done, send one other letter, a thank you letter complimenting the person or persons who helped rectify the errors that were originally made against you. Not only will that encourage competence and quality service in the company, but you will make the person who helped you feel good. You may even assist his or her career. And if there is one thing this country needs, it is consumer-friendly executives.

If you are unable to receive a satisfactory resolution of your dispute from within the company, you can either quit or move on to the next step in your fight for truth, justice and the consumer way. If you choose to fight, here's your next step.

Complain to the "Powers That Be" Outside the Company

If you cannot get satisfaction on the inside, the time will have come to go looking for assistance on the outside. This can include governmental agencies such as your State Department of Consumer Affairs, the Better Business Bureau (some Bureaus are attentive, others serve as mere window dressing), and licensing boards that may have jurisdiction.

When complaining to the authorities or others, use the same tools you employed when working on the inside; the specific and clearly typed letter of complaint backed up by as much documentation as you have in your possession. You may also be sent forms to fill out. When you do so, be careful and meticulous with what you say and type if you can. Remember, part of what you say will be judged by how you say it and how what you say looks. Thus, if you can't type, print carefully and legibly.

> **CONSUMER ALERT: WITH SO MANY DIFFERENT PRODUCTS AND SERVICES ON THE MARKET, YOU MAY HAVE SOME CON-FUSION AS TO WHOM YOU CAN CONTACT TO RIDE TO YOUR RESCUE WHEN THE CONSUMER COMPLAINT CHIPS ARE DOWN. HAPPILY, THERE IS A TERRIFIC BOOK ON THE MARKET THAT SHOULD BE ABLE TO TELL YOU. IT IS CALLED *THE GREAT AMERICAN GRIPE BOOK; OVER 1000 GOVERNMENT OFFICES YOU CAN CONTACT TO COMPLAIN, RIGHT A WRONG, GET SATIS-FACTION*, BY MATTHEW LESKO WITH ANDREW NAPRAWA (1990, INFORMATION U.S.A., INC. KENSINGTON, MD).**

Take It to Small Claims Court

Happily, there is a court where you can go for redress of grievances which is quick and cheap, and where you won't need a lawyer. It is called Small Claims Court, or as a popular television series dubs it, The People's Court. Judge Wapner, here we come!

Small claims matters are civil cases in which the amount of money in dispute is relatively low; usually $5,000 or less. (The "jurisdictional limit" i.e. the highest amount you can litigate over in Small Claims Court, differs from court to court. To find out your court's upper limit, call the court.) The litigants represent themselves - each telling a judge their side of the story. The case moves quickly (remember, usually no lawyers allowed!), with as many as thirty or so cases being heard a day in a busy Small Claims Court.

Generally, here's how the process works (specific procedures may differ in your jurisdiction).

•If you believe you have been "wronged" as a consumer (or in any other way that would involve a civil law suit, for that matter) and you cannot get satisfaction through informal means, you can decide to sue. If you sue, you are known as the **plaintiff**.

•Once you have decided to sue, you go down to your local small claims court and ask the court clerk for the forms necessary for you to file a case (usually called a Summons and Complaint). The forms are simple. Just fill them out in full.

•Once you have filled out the forms, you hand them back to the court clerk, along with a small filing fee. The clerk checks to make sure you have filled out the forms correctly and then sets a **trial date**. Copies of the forms containing the complaint and trial date and summons are handed back to you.

•You then take the papers to the local **Marshal's** office or other designated process server. YOU MUST SERVE THE PERSON OR COMPANY BEING SUED (called the **defendant**) WITH PROCESS or you will not be able to proceed to trial. If you are in doubt, ask the clerk who to see about serving process. The process serving will also cost a small fee. There will also be simple forms to fill out telling the process server who to serve. SERVICE MUST USUALLY TAKE PLACE WITHIN A DEFINED TIME LIMIT. THE FORM SHOULD TELL YOU WHAT THAT LIMIT IS.

•Once the defendant has been served, you will receive the proof of service form. This is a written declaration under penalty of perjury which names the person served, the date and the time of day. BE SURE TO BRING THIS WITH YOU TO COURT. Otherwise, if the defendant is a "no show," you will not be able to proceed with the case.

IF YOU ARE THE DEFENDANT and are served with such a lawsuit, you too must visit the friendly (or as is sometimes the case, the not so friendly) court clerk. The clerk will give you some different forms to fill out, denying that you owe any money. You can also counter-sue the plaintiff if the amount you believe you are owed is not over the jurisdictional amount of the court. A copy of your answer must be sent to the Plaintiff.

•When the day for trial arrives, be sure to be on time, because if you are not, the court will probably proceed without you if you are the defendant or dismiss the case if you are the plaintiff.

•At trial, the plaintiff's story is heard first, followed by the defendant. The judge may or may not ask questions. Here are some hints to help you do a good job:

Prepare before you go to trial. Write down everything you think is important and take your notes with you to court so you don't forget to tell the judge important facts.

Take notes about what the other party is saying while they are talking. Underline the points you wish to dispute when it is your turn to talk again so you don't forget them.

Be polite. Don't interrupt the other person (you'll get your turn) or the judge. Remember, you are in a court of law, so be sure to act with the proper respect and decorum.

Bring proof. Documents can be submitted as evidence and witnesses can usually be called. So, bring as much evidence as you can to prove that your side of the dispute has justice on its side.

•The judge will render a decision after both sides have been heard. The decision may be told to you there and then or it may come in the mail.

•If you LOSE and you are the defendant, you can ask to be allowed to pay monthly payments. Usually, this is permitted. You can also file an **appeal**. An appeal has a higher court judge rehear the case. The court clerk will have the forms. If you lose and you are the plaintiff, you are generally out of luck.

•If you WIN, you are now entitled to receive the money awarded you (assuming the defendant does not appeal. If the case is appealed and you win again, then you can collect the judgment.). If the defendant was a business or insurance company, you will probably receive a check. If it was a person, you may be forced by the court to take monthly payments. You are also entitled to your out of pocket costs, (service of process fees, etc.).

CONSUMER ALERT: IF THE DEFENDANT DOES NOT PAY YOU ACCORDING TO THE JUDGMENT, YOU MAY HAVE TO TAKE ACTION TO "ENFORCE THE JUDGMENT" SUCH AS FILING A WRIT OF EXECUTION. THIS CAN GET COMPLICATED AND YOU MAY WANT TO HIRE A LAWYER TO HELP YOU. ALSO, SOME COLLECTION AGENCIES WILL ACCEPT YOUR BUSINESS AND TRY TO COLLECT THE JUDGMENT FOR A PERCENTAGE OF THE TAKE. IF YOU GO TO A COLLECTION AGENCY, BE SURE TO TAKE A CERTIFIED COPY OF THE JUDGMENT WITH YOU.

If you have any questions about the small claims court process, most State Bar Associations publish consumer guides to the small claims court process in their states. Also, there are books on the market which describe the do's and don'ts of small claims court in greater detail than we are able to here. If in doubt, head to your library or local book store and take a look at one of these valuable self-help guides.

CONSUMER ALERT: EVEN IF THE AMOUNT OF MONEY IN DISPUTE IS MORE THAN THE JURISDICTIONAL LIMIT OF THE COURT, YOU STILL MAY WISH TO TAKE THE MATTER TO SMALL CLAIMS COURT. HERE'S AN EXAMPLE OF WHAT WE MEAN. LET'S SAY YOUR LOCAL SMALL CLAIMS COURT'S JURISDICTIONAL LIMIT IS $2,500 AND YOU HAVE A DISPUTE WORTH $2,700. YOUR LAWYER TELLS YOU THE CASE WILL COST $500 IN LEGAL FEES TO PURSUE. YOU MAY BE BETTER OFF SUING FOR THE $2,500 AND WAIVING THE REMAINING $200, RATHER THAN PAYING THE LAWYER $500 AND HOPING YOU WIN $2,700.

Bring a Lawsuit in Civil Court

If the amount in dispute is over the Small Claims Court jurisdictional limit, you may want to file a lawsuit. Civil suits come in many shapes and forms but all have one thing in common, they are serious business. So, look carefully before you leap into the fray.

There is a lot more involved in a civil case and you will want to ask your lawyer a lot of questions about the cost and the exact step by step process that is involved before you decide to proceed. Among the questions to be asked are the following:

•What do you estimate the total fee to be?

•How much will be spent in costs?

•What do you estimate my chances to be? Why?

•What are the weaknesses of my case? (There are almost always weaknesses. Beware the lawyer who guarantees you success!)

•How long will the lawsuit take?

•How much Discovery will be needed? (Discovery allows both sides to learn about the facts of each other's case. The tools of Discovery are generally depositions, interrogatories and document inspections.)

•Is there a way to try to settle the case before filing court papers?

•Is there a time limit I have to worry about? (For example, all civil cases must be brought within a defined time, called the Statute of Limitations, or the case is lost forever. There may be other time limits or procedural hurdles to overcome. Be sure to ask.)

> **CONSUMER ALERT: YOU CAN REPRESENT YOURSELF IN A CIVIL LAWSUIT BUT IT IS NOT GENERALLY A GOOD IDEA. NOT ONLY WILL YOU HAVE TO GAIN AN UNDERSTANDING OF THE LAW BUT COURT PROCEDURES, AS WELL.**

BUYER BEWARE

There is a thriving industry in this country that you need to know about. We want you to avoid becoming a consumer of this industry, for we are about to discuss the wild and awful world of consumer fraud.

Consumer fraud comes in an infinite variety of shapes and sizes. Maybe it's the salesman who comes to your door offering a great deal on a resurfaced driveway "because work crews are in the area." Or, maybe it is the phone solicitor who tells you that you are the lucky winner of a free vacation to the Bahamas and that all that is needed is for you to put a $200 registration fee on your credit card. Whatever the case may be, all of us should be from Missouri, that is, if we are being pitched, tell the solicitor to "show me."

SENIOR SCAMS

Some of the biggest scams are run against senior citizens. According to law enforcement experts, the reasons for this are severalfold:

•Older people often find it harder to identify the perpetrators of crimes and thus criminals tend to focus their attention upon senior citizens.

•Older people often do not react quickly to impropriety.

•Older people tend to stay in a con longer because they tend to be more trusting, especially if the person taking advantage of them appears trustworthy.

•Older people may be reluctant to report being victimized because they may fear they will be thought of as senile or "over the hill."

The criminals who take advantage of seniors are artists - word artists, actors who could put the likes of Robert De Niro and Sir Laurence Olivier to shame. Unfortunately, the purpose behind their performances is not to entertain but to steal. Here is a sampling of some of the "games" these villains play.

The Bank Examiner Scheme

This racket has a phony "bank examiner" or other purported law enforcement officer contact the victim in search of assistance in solving a crime being perpetrated at the victim's bank. The "officer" will be carrying phony credentials and he or she may even know the victim's bank account number. "We suspect that an employee at your bank is stealing money," the fraudulent law enforcement officer will tell the victim, "but, we need your help in proving it."

Most seniors are very civic-minded and want to cooperate with law enforcement, and so many agree to help. The victim is then told to go to their bank and withdraw a specified amount of money, which the phony law enforcement officer states will be redeposited in the victim's account "to make sure the paper work is done correctly." The victim does as asked and hands the money to the phony law enforcement officer. He or she is usually given an "official receipt" and thanks the victim. The examiner may even appear to redeposit the money but needless to say, most if not all of the money ends up in the crook's pocket and not back in the victim's bank account.

Medical Quackery

Seniors are very concerned about health care. Crooks know this and thus target older people as the victims of health fraud, known in the vernacular as "quackery."

Quackery is the promotion of a medical remedy that has not been proven to work. The quack promises miracle cures and overnight results when such things do not exist. It is one of crime's most vile activities because it preys on people's fears of illness and death. At best, quackery takes your money. At worst, it can take your life.

The following are some of the most common cons perpetrated by the quack on the lookout for an easy mark and a quick buck:

Arthritis Life can be difficult and painful for a person afflicted with this painful disease. Its symptoms may be relieved and the affliction may go into remission but, as yet, science has found no cure for arthritis. The quack would have you believe otherwise.

Cancer Quacks hype "miracle machines" or "new miracle herbs" that they claim will cure cancer. Quacks will also try to turn patients against their doctors and urge sufferers to leave their doctor's care and even leave the country to take treatment that is "being suppressed by the medical establishment." If you or a relative has cancer, beware the hype of the quack.

Impotence Male sexual dysfunction can be very troubling and emotionally disturbing. Often, the cause of the trouble is psychological, although some physical problems can also cause impotence, such as diabetes. And, while impotence often can be cured, it can't be taken care of with "2000-year-old miracle powders that are not a drug or a hormone" as one bold advertisement once quacked or by any other mail order treatment.

When it comes to your health, always "look before you leap." If you are interested in any health care product or service, call your trusted primary care physician and ask for his or her opinion. Another person to consult is your pharmacist. If he or she cannot confirm the efficacy of a treatment, it may be a scam.

Work At Home

Many seniors live on a limited budget and are in the market for ways to earn a few extra dollars. Some crooks know this and will place ads offering high pay for work that can be done at home, such as stuffing envelopes. Of course, there's a small catch. In order for the work to begin to flow your way, you have to pay a fee. You pay the fee and you get no work or at best, you receive a suggestion that you place an advertisement of your own to have people contact you who want someone to stuff envelopes.

FINANCIAL INVESTMENT SCAMS

There are so many forms of business scams that they are too numerous to detail here. According to the Economic Crime Project of the National District Attorney's Association, tens of thousands of people are cheated every year by con artists who promise the business moon and deliver virtually nothing. For example, there is the story of an investor who paid $5,490 for vending machines. The seller promised to place the vending machines in busy locations and guaranteed an income of $42,000 per year. The reality was that the machines were scattered over 138 miles, making them impossible to service, and produced few sales and losses instead of profits.

If you want to enter a business opportunity, make sure it is legitimate. Hire a business lawyer and/or a certified accountant to assist you. Be sure you thoroughly investigate the opportunity in order to make sure it lives up to its seller's rap. And pay attention to the Economic Crime Project's Warning Signs of Fraud:

•Undue pressure to sign a contract quickly and a demand to pay a large sum of money before sales claims can be investigated or legal advice obtained:

•Promises of extraordinarily high or guaranteed profits:

•A required initial fee which greatly exceeds the fair market value of any products, kits or training:

•A large fee payable before you receive anything in return:

•Evasive answers by the salesperson or an unwillingness to give disclosure documents required by law: Remember, when you invest your money, there is no guarantee. But if you invest in a crooked shell game, there is: that you will lose your money. So, buyer beware!

PYRAMID SCHEMES

Every few years or so a new wave of pyramid schemes seems to sweep the nation. And every time the pyramids appear, thousands of people answer their Siren call and rush to join, usually losing and inducing their friends to lose their money.

Pyramid's are illegal and for good reason - they are a scam pure and simple. Here's how a pyramid typically works: The mastermind offers "distributorships", "shares" or other such falsely named memberships in the pyramid for a given amount of money, let's say, $1,000. For their money, each member is allowed to sell six further distributorships for $1,000. Of that sum, the mastermind keeps half and the member keeps half. Each of the sub-distributorships are allowed to sell six memberships and on down the line.

Early members can do very well, assuming an "honest" pyramid. But later entrants into the game lose their shirts because eventually, the laws of mathematics catch up with scheme and the scam implodes, leaving the later participants poorer and possibly, wiser.

HOME IMPROVEMENT FRAUDS

Each year many people are bilked out of their hard-earned money through home improvement frauds. Typically, a sales person will approach door to door, soliciting home improvement work, or advertising may appear offering special discounts to senior citizens or other specially targeted groups.

The victim is pressured into signing a contract where a substantial down payment will be required before work can begin. Sometimes the "contractor" simply keeps the money and never begins the work. At other times, the work appears to have been accomplished but is done in such a slipshod way that it is virtually worthless. Unfortunately, the victim is not aware of the poor quality of the job and pays the balance of the contract in full.

TELEMARKETING FRAUD

Phone fraud is a multi-million dollar business that involves selling phony or misrepresented products or services to you over the phone. Unfortunately, it is very difficult to tell the legitimate business callers from the crooks. Luckily, the Alliance Against Fraud and Telemarketing has published "9 Tip-offs That A Caller Could Be a Crook", from which the following warnings are adapted:

High Pressure Sales Tactics

If you find yourself pressured or warned that "you'll be sorry you missed this opportunity," or some other such fear inducing claim or warning, hang up. The caller may or may not be a crook but why reward rudeness with a sale?

Insistence On an Immediate Decision

According to the Alliance, "Swindlers often insist that you should (or must) make your decision *right now*. And they always give a reason."

The Offer Sounds Too Good to Be True

According to the Alliance, it isn't always that easy to spot the "too good to be true" deals because the con man will often mix truth with lies in order to get you to suspend your disbelief. That's why you should always research what you buy before you put your money down or, as is usually the case in phone solicitation, your plastic down.

A Request For Your Credit Card Number For Any Purpose Other Than to Make a Purchase

Sometimes swindlers will ask for your credit card number(s) for purposes of "identification" or "verification" or some other such illegitimate purpose, such as a showing of "good faith" so that you can be awarded a prize. Never give out your credit card numbers for this purpose.

An Offer to Send Someone to Your House to Pick Up Your Money

If they are that much in a hurry to get your funds, there is probably a reason, such as they intend to head out of town on the next stage.

A Statement That You Are Being Given Something Free, Followed By a Requirement That You Pay For Something

One of the ways to separate the honest phone businesses from the crooks is to see whether they ask you to pay for something that is being offered to you for free. The cost may be masked as a shipping or handling charge or some other seemingly legitimate charge. But free is free and if it really isn't it could be a rip off.

An Investment That is Claimed to Be "Without Risk"

There is no such thing as a risk-free investment, with the possible exception of an obligation owed to you by the Government of the United States.

A Reluctance to Provide Written Information or References

If a phone solicitor is reluctant to send you written materials or provide verifiable references, beware.

A Suggestion That You Should Make a Purchase Based on "Trust."

Trust us, making a purchase on the basis of "trust" from a phone solicitor is an invitation to your own financial fleecing.

> CONSUMER ALERT: ACCORDING TO THE ALLIANCE AGAINST FRAUD IN TELEMARKETING, THE FOLLOWING ARE THE TOP TEN SCAMS PERPETRATED OVER THE PHONE:
> - PRIZE OFFERS - VITAMINS, WATER PURIFIERS
> - PENNY STOCKS
> - BUSINESS-TO-BUSINESS - TONER PAPER, PAPER PIRATE
> - MAGAZINE SUBSCRIPTIONS
> - CREDIT REPAIR
> - PRECIOUS METALS, COINS, GEMS
> - TRAVEL SCAMS
> - EMPLOYMENT SCHEMES, WORK AT HOME
> - BUSINESS OPPORTUNITIES, FRANCHISES, LIMITED PARTNERSHIPS
> - ART

GIVE YOURSELF A RAISE

There's more to defensive consumerism than avoiding fraud. There are legitimate selling techniques that you should be aware of and may want to avoid or at least fully understand before you buy. These include the following:

NEGATIVE-ACCEPTANCE CONTRACTS

Unlike other negative check-off systems which are based on voting referendums, the commercial negative-acceptance contract must be clearly and definitely understood before you become part of such a business transaction. The typical negative acceptance contract is utilized by book clubs and other such businesses. Credit card companies also sometimes offer this type of selling technique when offering to sign you up for free for a service. In small print will be words stating something like this: "Unless I notify you (the "I" being the consumer) that I choose not to continue my membership after my three month introductory period, I authorize you to continue my membership for another 12 months for a $49 annual fee."

Now you can see the way negative-acceptance contracts can cost you money you do not intend to spend. Instead of taking action to buy something, you have to take action not to buy. For example, let's say you are part of a book club which uses negative acceptance methods. The company will send you an order form every month, with a book or other product of the month highlighted on the order form. In order to refuse the order of the month, you have to send in the order form stating your refusal. Doing nothing constitutes an automatic order. It's easy to forget to send in the form and thus those involved in negative acceptance contracts often end up buying items they did not really want.

IMPULSE BUYING

One of the retailer's best friends is the impulse buyer. Oh you know who you are; you go into a store looking to buy some underwear and see a beautiful garment on a manikin which you "just have to have!" Then, running on pure emotion and adrenaline, you put your money down and make the purchase. Months later, you realize that you have never worn the garment and wonder why you ever liked it.

The fact is, advertisers and retailers put a lot of time and effort into creating clever displays that tap into your buying reflex. But what is good for them is not necessarily good for you.

FALLING PREY TO THE SALESPERSONS "ART"

Salespersons are in the business of selling. That is obvious. But what is less obvious, because it is designed that way, are the techniques sales professionals use to "close the sale," that is, to get you to buy.

We are not opposed to salespersons. In fact, we believe that a good sales professional can be of tremendous benefit to you as a consumer, by giving you valuable information, by assisting you in comparing products or services with competitors' and by working to get you a good price. However, the final decision to purchase should be the *fulfillment of your consuming agenda* - not the fact that the salesperson was good at convincing you to buy.

How do sales professionals "close the sale?" There are many techniques and a whole industry has been created to close more sales, including seminars, books, video tapes, audio tapes and in-company training. Here are just a few of the techniques that may be employed on you that we have heard about:

Getting You To Say "Yes"

One sales theory is that the more you are saying "yes," during the sales pitch, the more likely you will be to say "yes" when the sales professional "asks for the sale." Realize that throughout the interaction you have with a salesperson, he or she is in a continual state of sizing you up and searching you out to see what it is that will get you to sign on the dotted line. This is accomplished through asking you questions. For example, if you are buying a refrigerator, you may be asked:

> Salesperson: "Does your old refrigerator have an ice maker."
> You: "Yes."
> Salesperson: "Is that a feature you want in your new refrigerator?"
> You: "Yes."
> Salesperson: "Is color an important consideration for you?"
> You: "Yes."
> Salesperson: "Is there a special color you have in mind?"
> You: "Harvest gold."
> Salesperson: "So, the refrigerator that you buy will have to be harvest gold, right?"
> You: "Yes."

And so it would go until the salesperson knew the features you were looking for in a refrigerator. Then, when it looked like you were ready for the close, he or she might say something like this:

> Salesperson: "So, you are in the market for a side by side, harvest gold refrigerator, with an ice maker and extra storage space that is economic with electricity, and sells for under $900, right?"
>
> You: "Yes, that's right."
>
> Salesperson: "Great! I have just the model for you. It has all of the features you are looking for and we are delivering in your area on Tuesday. Is that a good day for you?
>
> You: "Yes, I'm not planning on being anywhere on Tuesday."
>
> Salesperson: "Terrific. Would you like me to reserve one in your name in our warehouse?
>
> You: "Yes."
>
> Salesperson: "Good. Let's write up the paperwork."

You may have wanted to shop around before you made your selection but by getting you into a "yes" mode, this salesperson might have gotten you to buy before you were ready.

The antidote for the "yes" tack is to say "no" when you are asked for the sale. For example, after the salesperson has gotten the information needed to point you toward a product you might be interested in, and he says, "Would you like me to reserve one in your name in the warehouse?" you might say, "No. I'm not ready to buy just yet. But I would like you to write down the information you gave me and give me any brochures you have on the refrigerator so that I can compare your product with others on the market." In other words, don't say yes to the purchase until you are ready to say yes to the purchase.

Changing the Subject

Salespersons are trained to overcome your objections to the sale. After all, they are in the business of selling, and objections thwart that goal. One of the techniques used to weaken your objections is to restate what you are concerned about in a much more benign way than you do. For example:

> Salesperson: "So, is there any reason why you shouldn't drive this Humdinger home today?"
>
> You: "Well, I'm not sure that Humdingers will hold on to their resale value."
>
> Salesperson: "If I understand you correctly, you want to be sure the product has enough quality to last, because that's what resale is all about, right?"
>
> You: "Sure, I guess so."
>
> Salesperson: "Well, we have a 5-year warranty; that proves we believe in the quality of our automobile, wouldn't you say?"
>
> You: "Yea, I guess so." (Note how you are being put in the position of saying yes again.)
>
> Salesperson: "Any quality car has good resale, right?"
>
> You: "Yes, that's true."

See how the salesperson changes the definition of the discussion? You were talking about resale and he or she switched the discussion to a different issue, the warranty. Why? Because the warranty was a strong selling point and the resale value of the car might not have been. Thus, your objection might never have actually been addressed.

Putting You on the Defensive

Sales professionals are often taught to keep you, their "prospects" (for prospective sale) on the defensive. Sometimes they can be obnoxious about it and turn you off so that you storm out of the store or sales presentation. At other times, the "turn around" is far more subtle, such as this scenario:

> Salesperson: "Really? I must say, I am surprised. I thought you were really interested in the self-cleaning feature of this oven? May I ask why you feel this is not the time to buy?"
> You: "Well, I'm still in the looking stage."
> Salesperson: "But if you found the right product, you'd buy, right?"
> You: "Well, not right now."
> Salesperson: "Is there are reason? Maybe I can help."
> You: "I'm not sure I can afford it."
> Salesperson: "You'd be surprised. Did you know that you can have this range delivered and installed for only $35 a month?
> You: "Really?"
> Salesperson: "I can have it in for you on Tuesday. Shall I reserve you one in the warehouse?"
> You: "Yea, why not?"

No one likes to be put on the defensive, as if you have to justify not buying. Don't play this game with salespersons. They are using time-tested techniques to get behind your defensive line. If you are not ready to buy, don't.

> **CONSUMER ALERT: IT IS ALMOST ALWAYS A GOOD IDEA TO MAKE YOUR BUYING DECISIONS AWAY FROM THE GLITZ AND GLAMOUR OF A SALES FLOOR, WHICH IS DESIGNED TO GET YOU TO WANT TO BUY, AND THE SALESPERSON, WHO IS TRAINED TO INDUCE YOU TO BUY. MAKE THE BUYING DECISION IN THE QUIET AND SAFETY OF YOUR OWN HOME OR OVER A QUIET DINNER. IN THAT WAY, THE REASONS TO BUY OR NOT BUY WILL BE YOUR OWN AND NOT THE AGENDA OF THE MANUFACTURER OR SALESPERSON.**

Thinking For You

Many of us try to avoid making a buying decision in the heat of the moment by telling a salesperson that we want to "think about it." This is good. Thinking before you buy is exactly what you want to do. Many sales professionals will do their best to keep you from getting away in this fashion. One way they may do this is to help you "direct your thinking." Here's how an enterprising salesperson might go about it:

> Salesperson: "So, can I have the tailor come down and mark the suit for you?"
> You: "No, I want to think about it for a few days."
> Salesperson: "Thinking about any purchase is important. But did you know that the best time to think is when you have all of the facts at hand. That makes sense, doesn't it?"

You: "Yes, I guess so."

Salesperson: "So, let's go through this together. Do you like the way the suit hangs on you?"

You: "Yes."

Salesperson: "I do too. It really looks good on you. You've already said you like the pattern and the material."

You: "Yes, I do."

Salesperson: "Is there a problem with the date I offered to have the alterations done, because if there is, I think I can put a word in with the tailor to get this for you faster."

You: "Well, I am going to a wedding on Saturday."

Salesperson: "Then if you like the suit, which you said you do, and I can get you into the suit for the wedding, then it seems to me that this is way to go, wouldn't you say?"

You: "Yea, why not?"

By all means, ask your salespersons questions and get all of the information he or she can impart to you about the product or service being sold, but *do your thinking alone*. You should decide whether to buy, not the salesperson.

Appealing to Your Emotions

Many salespersons know that the decision to buy is often an emotional one. Thus, they will begin the discussion with logic and attempt to close the sale on an emotional note, giving you, in essence, a justification for buying as well as a reason. For example:

Salesperson: "So, we know that this car has all of the features you are looking for, good gas mileage, a good warranty, the service history of the model is exemplary. So, would you like to drive one home?"

You: "I don't know. I'm not sure how practical it is to buy a new car right now."

Salesperson: "Well, air bags are practical, safety is practical and so is good mileage, but there is something I want you to think about."

You: "Which is."

Salesperson: "Don't you think you deserve a new car? You told me how you fight traffic an hour a day. Don't you think you are worth facing that traffic in comfort?

You: "Yes, I do."

Salesperson: "So, not only do you have reasons for buying this model, you have the best reason of all for buying this car. You are worth it!"

You: "Let's do it."

The salesman gets you to feel emotional which makes it less likely that you will walk off the lot. Your defense, when you realize you are in an emotional state which can lead to a "buying frenzy" is to get away to neutral ground so that your buying decision can be made when you are in a more rational state of mind. Not that emotion can't be part of your decision making, it just should not predominate and should not lead you to buy before your time.

There are many other sales techniques that are employed to get a buying decision from you and many different ones may be used in any one "sales pitch." The main thing to remember is that the when, if, and whether to buy should come from you and not a sales professional's dazzling sales techniques.

Paying Full Price For Discretionary Items

Lean economic times are difficult for everybody. But there is a benefit to those consumers who have the patience and wherewithal to take advantage of them. In tough times, retailers often run sales to sell slow moving merchandise. Sometimes, these sales are lalapaluzies, which will save you a lot of money if you take advantage of the opportunity.

Rough times or not, there is often no need to pay the full retail price for discretionary purchases. For example, if you know you are going to be buying a new refrigerator in the next several months, start looking through the newspapers for sales. After all, why pay full price if you don't need to? The same holds true for most merchandise, ranging from cars to stereos to shoes to hardware.

> **CONSUMER ALERT: IF YOU WANT TO BUY FOR LESS THAN RETAIL, YOUR FRIENDLY SALESPERSON MAY BE ABLE TO HELP. WHEN YOU SHOP, ASK WHEN THE NEXT SALE IS GOING TO BE. IF THEY KNOW, THEY WILL GENERALLY TELL YOU. IF THEY DON'T KNOW, YOU MAY WANT TO ASK THEM TO CALL YOU WHEN THEY FIND OUT. ALSO, IF A SALESPERSON DOES GIVE YOU GOOD SERVICE AND THEY ARE ON COMMISSION, BE SURE TO ASK WHEN YOUR SALESPERSON WILL BE WORKING TO MAKE SURE HE OR SHE GETS CREDIT FOR THE SALE.**

Finding bargains may not be as hard as you may think. In addition to newspaper and other forms of advertising, there are other ways to find sales or businesses that sell less than retail:

Wholesale outlets There are usually many wholesale outlets in most major cities and some in out of the way places. Some of these stores sell discontinued or slightly damaged merchandise at substantial savings.

Auctions Sometimes excellent bargains can be had at auctions. However, if you are going to attend an auction, be sure you know the true value of the items being sold and be sure you control your urge to keep bidding beyond the point where the price is a bargain.

Second-hand stores A lot of people turn their noses up at second-hand and thrift stores, but some very good bargains can be had in these establishments, especially for items such as furniture that can be spruced up into very nice pieces and sometimes, clothes, bicycles and appliances.

Out of business sales If a store is going out of business they may literally slash prices to the bone. The key in such cases is to get to the sale early and not late, otherwise you will have to settle for looking at the crumbs.

Post-season sales Some merchandise and services are seasonal, such as clothing, some sports equipment and travel. For example, if you ski, the best time to buy equipment may be in the late Spring when the ski season is over. Likewise, there are often "in season" and "out of season" for many resorts, with the best prices available off season.

Join a co-op or purchasing club There can be strength in numbers and if you join a co-op or buyers club, the power of numbers can save you a lot of money in the food you eat, the merchandise you buy and even for services such as insurance (where "group" rates are less expensive than individual rates).

> CONSUMER ALERT: THERE IS A BOOK ON THE MARKET THAT MAY BE ABLE TO SAVE YOU MONEY ON MANY OF THE THINGS YOU BUY. IT IS CALLED THE *WHOLESALE-BY-MAIL CATALOG*, (HARPER-PERENNIAL) WRITTEN BY "THE PRINT PROJECT." IT LISTS MANY CATALOG COMPANIES AND GIVES VALUABLE INFORMATION ON HOW TO BUY BY MAIL.

Discount stores Stores that sell in volume and at discount can often save you a great deal of money. Often, the merchandise offered is brand-name or brand-name-quality. If you want to save money, compare the prices offered at discount stores.

DON'T FALL FOR SALES GIMMICKS

There are several sales gimmicks (some which are of marginal legality), which can cost you money. Avoid these and the money you save will be your own.

Bait and switch As the name implies, a bait and switch scheme gets you into the store based on an advertisement of a tremendous bargain. Once in the store, you are talked out of the item on sale and "switched" to some other piece of merchandise which ends up causing you to spend more money than you have planned.

Loss leaders Loss leaders are specially marked down items which are designed to get you into a store with the hope that you will take home enough other merchandise to more than make up for the low price on the item that got you to go to the store in the first place. The cure for the loss leader: only buy the item which has been marked down, assuming it is a quality product and it is something you really want to buy.

Deceptive packaging Some items are packaged to look like more than they really are. So always look behind the veneer to make sure you are getting your true money's worth.

The phony list price Some unscrupulous retailers will say their list prices are higher than they really are to make you think that the price they are selling the item for is a bargain when it really isn't. A little consumer education can catch this maneuver. Just check out the price of the merchandise you are interested in other outlets. Then, you will be able to tell if a list price is really a list price and whether a bargain still smells as sweet.

Epilogue

The only way that a market based economy can serve the people is when consumers are knowledgeable, inquiring, critical and assertive in their business affairs. The purpose of this book is to help you become just such a consumer.

Several benefits will come from increasing your consumer confidence and abilities. The economy will benefit. When manufacturers and service providers realize that they have to earn your business based on quality and value, they will offer better products and service, rather than glitz and deception. The evidence can be seen in the history of the auto industry over the last twenty years. The Japanese worked at providing cars that Americans preferred to buy while American companies sat on their laurels and allowed their products to diminish in quality. As a result, consumers "voted with their wallets" and the Japanese manufacturers captured a large portion of the American market. Now, the American manufacturers are trying to battle back. How? By building better cars. Why the new emphasis on quality? Because you, the consumer, told them you would not buy shoddy products.

You and your family will also benefit. Times are tough and may grow tougher. Families need to be careful about every dollar they spend. By shopping smartly, you will buy better and safer products, which will mean you won't have to replace them or repair them as often. Smart shopping also means you can obtain better prices and better terms for most services or products you purchase. The less you spend, the more money you will have for other purchases or for saving and investing.

We close now, with some examples of products or services which are a waste of your money to purchase. We call these, "DON'T BUYS."

Credit cards with high interest rates

Banks are gouging consumers with interest rates in the 18 percent range. Look for cards that charge 12 to 14 percent.

Credit card insurance

The price is high and the benefits are low.

Credit reporting agency membership clubs

You can get one free copy of your report each year. In addition, you will be able to purchase your report for $10, often less than the price of one year's membership. (TRW is changing their rules and may soon offer one free report a year.)

Lawyers who don't practice in your area of need

Retaining a lawyer who is not expert in your area of legal need is foolish and can lead to disaster.

Plastic surgery from a physician who is not board certified in an appropriate medical field

Any physician can legally perform plastic surgery. Not all, however, are sufficiently trained or have enough experience to do it well.

A doctor who will not "accept the assignment" from Medicare

Unless the doctor is a physician you really need, you will probably be paying more money out of your pocket than you need to if the doctor refuses to accept the assignment.

Buying prescription drugs directly from your doctor

Usually, the "fail safe" services performed by a pharmacist are an essential safeguard to your health.

An "indemnity" hospital plan

Low benefits make these plans a poor deal.

A loan with a prepayment penalty

Generally, this is a rip off.

Home improvement services sold door to door

There's a whole lot of fraud going on.

Oral modifications to a written contract

As Samuel Goldwyn once said, "An oral contract isn't worth the paper it's written on."

Automobile service contracts

If the warranty isn't good enough to protect you, don't buy the service contract and don't buy the car.

Banks that charge for ATM transactions

ATMs are designed to save the bank money by allowing them to hire fewer employees. You should not be charged because you help them save money.

Real estate agents who will not negotiate the commission

Some agents will negotiate their commission in order to receive your listing.

A house without having it professionally inspected

The heartache and money you may save makes this bit of preventive consumerism worth the price.

A car with a poor occupant injury history

An especially unsafe car is never worth the price.

Gas saving devices that don't work

There are many devices on the market that falsely claim to save gasoline. For reports on such devices, contact the National Technical Information Service, Springfield, VA, 22161. (703) 487-4650

Food merely because you have a discount coupon

Only buy food you are likely to eat.

Long distance phone service that is over-priced

You can compare prices offered by long distance carriers. You might consider joining the Telecommunications Research and Action Center (TRAC), a nonprofit consumer advocacy and educational organization. They can provide you timely information on the varying services and prices of long distance carriers. (Send $25 to TRAC, P.O. Box 12038, Washington D.C. 20005. Phone is (202) 462-2520.)

Energy inefficient appliances

Bad for your pocketbook, bad for the environment.

THE FRUGAL SHOPPER
Ralph Nader & Wesley J. Smith

The Frugal Shopper will help you solve your consumer dilemmas.

How can I deal with auto rip offs?

How can I find a good lawyer?

What can I do to make sure I get the best medical care?

What kind of credit card is right for me?

Which automobile insurance policy will suit my needs?

How can I make sure that a home contractor is reliable?

Where can I get information about the financial stability of my bank?

What should I do if I am having problems with my utility bills?

How can I make a complaint about my doctor?

How can I improve my diet?

This book provides clear advice that will give you the confidence to assert yourself as a consumer and to assure that you obtain high quality services and products at the best prices. It will show you what it takes to be a smart and frugal shopper.

Ralph Nader is a consumer advocate and the co-author of *Winning the Insurance Game* with Wesley J. Smith.

Wesley J. Smith is a lawyer and the author of *The Lawyer Book, The Doctor Book* and *The Senior Citizens Handbook,* and co-author of *Winning the Insurance Game*.

The Frugal Shopper   **$10.00**

To order additional copies of *The Frugal Shopper*, send a check or money order to:

  The Frugal Shopper, P.O. Box 19367, Washington, DC 20036.
  Make checks payable to The Frugal Shopper.